HEAVY METAL

Studies in Popular Music

Series Editors: Alyn Shipton, lecturer in jazz history at the Royal Academy of Music, London, and at City University, London; and Christopher Partridge, Professor of Religious Studies, Lancaster University

From jazz to reggae, bhangra to heavy metal, electronica to qawwali, and from production to consumption, *Studies in Popular Music* is a multi-disciplinary series which aims to contribute to a comprehensive understanding of popular music. It will provide analyses of theoretical perspectives, a broad range of case studies, and discussion of key issues.

Published

Open Up the Doors: Music in the Modern Church
Mark Evans

Technomad: Global Raving Countercultures
Graham St John

*Dub in Babylon: Understanding the Evolution and Significance of
Dub Reggae in Jamaica and Britain from King Tubby to Post-Punk*
Christopher Partridge

Send in the Clones: A Cultural Study of Tribute Bands
Georgina Gregory

The Lost Women of Rock Music: Female Musicians of the Punk Era
(second edition)
Helen Reddington

Global Tribe: Technology, Spirituality and Psytrance
Graham St John

Nick Cave: A Study of Love, Death and Apocalypse
Roland Boer

HEAVY METAL

CONTROVERSIES AND COUNTERCULTURES

EDITED BY

TITUS HJELM, KEITH KAHN-HARRIS AND MARK LEVINE

SHEFFIELD UK   BRISTOL CT

Published by Equinox Publishing Ltd.

UK: Kelham House, 3 Lancaster Street, Sheffield, S3 8AF
USA: ISD, 70 Enterprise Drive, Bristol, CT 06010

www.equinoxpub.com

First published 2013

British Library Cataloguing-in-Publication Data
A catalogue record for this book is available from the British Library.

Library of Congress Cataloging-in-Publication Data
Heavy metal : controversies and countercultures / edited by Titus Hjelm, Keith Kahn-Harris and Mark LeVine.
    pages cm. -- (Studies in popular music)
 Includes bibliographical references and index.
 ISBN 978-1-84553-940-5 (hb) -- ISBN 978-1-84553-941-2 (pb)
 1. Heavy metal (Music)--Social aspects. 2. Heavy metal (Music)--History and criticism. I. Hjelm, Titus, editor. II. Kahn-Harris, Keith, 1971- editor. III. LeVine, Mark, 1966- editor.
 ML3918.R63H43 2013
 306.4'8426--dc23
                        2012044704

ISBN: 978 1 84553 940 5 (hardback)
ISBN: 978 1 84553 941 2 (paperback)

Typeset by CA Typesetting Ltd, www.publisherservices.co.uk
Printed and bound in the UK by Lightning Source UK Ltd., Milton Keynes and Lightning Source Inc., La Vergne, TN

Contents

List of contributors

Nicola Allett is a Research Associate at the Department of Social Science, Loughborough University. She is currently working on the Leverhulme Trust funded project 'Media of Remembering: Photography and Phonography in Everyday Remembering', which investigates how photography and music act as vehicles of memory in everyday contexts. Her research interests are in collective identifications and music in everyday life.

Lee Barron is a senior lecturer in the Division of Media at Northumbria University. His main research and teaching interests are in the areas of cultural theories and popular culture. His writings have appeared in journals such as: *The Journal of Popular Culture, Nebula, Fashion Theory, Chapter and Verse, International Review of the Aesthetics and Sociology of Music*, and *Disability & Society*. He has also published in a number of books including: *Speak To Me: The Legacy of Pink Floyd's Dark Side Of The Moon; Music; Terror Tracks: Music, Sound and Horror Cinema; Popular Music and Film* and T*he Sage Dictionary of Research Issues*. His forthcoming work includes a study of the British science fiction series *Torchwood*.

Andy R. Brown is Senior Lecturer in Media Communications at Bath Spa University, UK. His teaching/research interests include popular music, music journalism, music industries, media and youth consumption, with a specific focus on heavy metal music culture. He has published research on metal in *Postsubcultural Studies* (2003), *Youth Cultures* (2007), *Mapping the Magazine* (2008), *Heavy Fundametalisms: Music, Metal and Politics* (2009), *The Metal Void* (2010) and recently co-edited a special issue of the *Journal for Cultural Research* on 'Metal Studies?: Cultural Research in the Heavy Metal Scene' (July 2011).

Kevin Fellezs holds a joint appointment in the Music department and the Institute for Research in African-American Studies (IRAAS) at Columbia University. His book, *Birds of Fire: Jazz, Rock, Funk and the Creation of Fusion* (Duke University Press, 2011), is a study of the musical genre mixtures young musicians enacted in the late 1960s and throughout the 1970s that proved controversial at the time and remains a contentious issue within jazz criticism today.

Gérôme Guibert is Associate Professor of Sociology at the University Paris III (La Sorbonne Nouvelle). His main areas of expertise are economic sociology and popular music. He is the author of several books, including *La Production de la Culture: Le Cas des Musiques Amplifiées en France* (Irma, 2006) and has co-directed the issue of the French peer review *VOLUME!* about metal scenes (Mélanie Séteun, 2007).

Benjamin Hedge Olson is a fourth-year doctoral student in the Department of American Studies at the University of Hawai'i, Manoa. He is currently finishing his dissertation on the heavy metal scene on Oahu, in which he conducted nearly three years of ethnographic research. His research interests include new religions, occultism, ritual studies, masculinity, and metal culture.

Titus Hjelm is Lecturer in Finnish Society and Culture at UCL. His main areas of expertise are sociology of religion, social problems, social theory, media and popular culture. His recent publications include *Religion and Social Problems* (Routledge, 2011) and *Studying Religion and Society: Sociological Self-Portraits* (ed. with Phil Zuckerman, Routledge, 2012). In addition, he has published several books in Finnish and articles in journals such as *Social Compass* and *Journal of Contemporary Religion*. He is also a member of the internationally acclaimed metal band Thunderstone.

Keith Kahn-Harris is an Honorary Research Fellow and Sessional Lecturer at Birkbeck College, London. He is the author of *Extreme Metal: Music and Culture on the Edge* (Berg, 2006) and writes the blog Metal Jew (www.metaljew.org).

Brad Klypchak teaches courses in Liberal Studies at Texas A&M University-Commerce. A popular culture scholar, he earned his PhD in American Culture Studies from Bowling Green State University. While Dr Klypchak has taught and done research in film, theatre, sport, performance, and mass media studies, his particular emphasis has been on heavy metal music. His book, *Performed Identity: Heavy Metal Musicians 1984–1991*, reflects this interest.

Hélène Laurin is a PhD candidate (ABD) in Communication Studies at McGill University in Montreal. Her research interests cover the shaping of discourses about popular music and cultural memory. Her Master's thesis was about gender representations in air guitar performances in competition and she is currently working on her PhD dissertation, which deals with Mötley Crüe's autobiographical project.

Alexandra Levine is a graduate of Bowling Green State University. She majored in Popular Culture with a minor in Theatre.

Mark LeVine is Professor of modern Middle Eastern history, culture and Islamic Studies at University of California Irvine and Distinguished Visiting Professor at the Center for Middle Eastern Studies at Lund University, Sweden. He is author and editor of several books, including *Heavy Metal Islam: Rock, Resistance, and the Struggle for the Soul of Islam* (Random House/Three Rivers Press, 2008), *Impossible Peace: Israel/Palestine Since 1989* (Zed Books, 2009) and the forthcoming *The Five Year Old Who Toppled a Pharaoh* (UC Press, 2012).

Marcus Moberg is post-doctoral researcher at the Department of Comparative Religion at Åbo Akademi University in Turku, Finland. His main areas of expertise are religion, media and culture and the sociology of religion. He has published widely on Christian metal music, including his doctoral thesis 'Faster for the Master! Exploring Issues of Religious Expression and Alternative Christian Identity within the Finnish Christian Metal Music Scene' (Åbo Akademi University Press, 2009).

Rosemary Overell is completing her PhD, titled 'Feeling Brutal/Feeling at Home: Grindcore Music and Affective Belonging in Melbourne and Osaka', at the University of Melbourne. Her research focuses on affective belonging and masculinities in extreme metal music.

Michelle Phillipov is Lecturer in Journalism, Media and Communications at the University of Tasmania. Her research interests include extreme metal, media controversy and food media. She is the author of *Death Metal and Music Criticism: Analysis at the Limits* (Lexington Books, 2012).

Niall Scott is Senior Lecturer in Ethics at the University of Central Lancashire, School of Education and Social Science. Together with Rob Fisher and ID.net, he put together the first global conference on heavy metal. In addition to having spoken internationally on heavy metal, philosophy and politics he has written and published on heavy metal, political philosophy and bioethics.

Jedediah Sklower is a member of the editorial team of the French journal of popular music studies, *VOLUME!* He published *Free jazz, la catastrophe féconde* (L'Harmattan, 2006) and will be editing two issues of *VOLUME!* with

Antoine Hennion on 'listening to popular music'. He works in movie production, is a professional translator and does freelance research on the cultural
and political history of twentieth-century music.

Jeremy Wallach is a cultural anthropologist, ethnomusicologist, and associate professor in the Department of Popular Culture at Bowling Green State
University in Ohio, USA. He is the author of *Modern Noise, Fluid Genres: Popular
Music in Indonesia, 1997–2001* (2008) and co-editor of *Metal Rules the Globe:
Heavy Metal around the World* (2011). He has written on an array of topics,
including music and technology, music in Southeast Asia, world beat, punk,
and metal and is currently at work on an edited collection of popular culture
research.

Introduction: Heavy metal as controversy and counterculture†

Titus Hjelm*, Keith Kahn-Harris** and Mark LeVine***

*University College London, UK
**Birkbeck College, London, UK
***University of California, USA

Heavy metal is now over 40 years old. It emerged at the tail end of the 1960s in the work of bands including Iron Butterfly, Vanilla Fudge, Jimi Hendrix, Deep Purple, Led Zeppelin, and—most importantly—Black Sabbath. In the 1970s and early 1980s, heavy metal crystallized as a genre as bands such as Judas Priest and Iron Maiden removed most of the blues influence on the genre, codifying a set of basic metal characteristics that endure to this day: distorted guitars, aggressive vocals, denim, leather and spikes.

Although sometimes thought of as monolithic, heavy metal has always consisted of divergent styles. In the 1980s, the nascent differences within metal engendered new and widely divergent genres. On the one hand, 'lite' metal bands such as Poison and Def Leppard led metal to embrace pop and rock, with enormous success. On the other hand, thrash metal bands such as Metallica and Slayer inspired a series of 'extreme' metal genres including death, black, and doom metal, and grindcore. In the 1990s and 2000s, metal has followed increasingly diverse musical pathways, developing new sub-genres and hybrids that range from the commercially successful 'nu' metal of the mid to late-1990s, in which metal was fused with hip hop, to the experimental and avant-garde tendencies of 'post' metal bands such as Isis, Neurosis and Celeste.

In broad terms, wherever it is found and however it is played, metal tends to be dominated by a distinctive commitment to 'transgressive' themes and musicality. This collection looks at some of the consequences of heavy metal's transgressions. As we shall outline in this introduction, metal's transgression has caused it to be a frequently controversial music. Metal has variously

† This book was previously published in a special issue of *Popular Music History* 6.1-2 (2011).

embraced, rejected, played with and tried to ignore this controversy. At times, the controversy dies down and the previously transgressive becomes relatively harmless—as in the transformation of Ozzy Osbourne from public enemy to loveable dad. Still, metal remains irrevocably marked by its controversial, transgressive tendencies. Indeed, the various moral panics that metal has been subjected to are not only constitutive, at least in part, of metal scenes, but are encoded in metal's transgression itself. As with hip hop's 'ghetto' roots, metal's history of extreme sonic, lyrical and visual messages continue to give it credibility with new generations of fans today.

Although, as this introduction and many of the chapters making up this book demonstrate, controversy and what we call 'counterculture' are often inseparable, we have divided this book into two parts based on whether the focus is more on the dynamics of controversy or the creation of metal cultures. Here we offer some synthesizing and theoretical thoughts on the chapters that follow.

Heavy metal as controversy

The controversial *image* of heavy metal is something that metal musicians, fans, and researchers often agree upon. The word 'image' is important, because when examined through the theoretical framework discussed below (and the principles of which appear in various forms in many of the chapters here), controversies over heavy metal are seen as social reactions to *perceived* deviance, usually triggered by boundary-challenging events. The most common concept used in studying controversy is 'moral panic'. Although in many ways similar to moral panic theory (see Brown in this volume; Critcher 2003), the 'theory' of controversy presented here takes its cue primarily from the constructionist approach to the study of social problems (see Schneider 1985 for a dated but useful overview).

Controversies can be defined as the *activities of individuals or groups making public claims about conditions that are perceived as a threat to certain cherished values and/or material and status interests* (cf. Spector and Kitsuse 2001: 75; Fuller and Myers 1941: 320; Goode and Ben-Yehuda 1994: 124–27). This definition has four elements. First, controversies are *materialistic* in the sense that ideas as such do not create controversy; it is people that create controversies (Beckford 1985: 1). Second, controversies have a definitive *public* element. Parents' frustration over their offspring's new Dimmu Borgir record does not constitute a controversy. When this frustration becomes part of public discourse, through letters to the editor in national newspapers, interviews and stories in the media, politicians and religious leaders taking up their cause, and (more recently) blogging about the perceived threat posed by Dimmu Borgir's music, parental frustration takes on a new and more powerful dimension.

Third, controversies are *discursive-symbolic*, because raising public awareness is a process of claims-making (Spector and Kitsuse 2001: 76) and these claims are primarily discursive—that is, involving the intersection of claims to truth and circuits of power and knowledge. Yet they are discursive in a highly symbolic manner in that they are articulated first and foremost through aesthetic production, circulation and consumption. On the other hand, such aesthetic-discursive production can generate cultural discourses, which in response then penetrate into the larger public and political spheres. For example, images of concerned (Christian) parents burning heavy metal records in the USA in the 1980s convey a powerful symbolic message—a claim—that these particular cultural products are inappropriate, even evil. Similarly, contemporary crackdowns on the metal community in Iran, for example, have targeted heavy metal on a symbolic level by confiscating 'Satanic' paraphernalia such as t-shirts, and forcing metalheads to cut their long hair—a central symbol of the metal culture (LeVine 2008, ch. 5).

Finally, controversies are *subjective* in the sense that it is the *perception* of a condition that provides the framework for claims-making rather than concrete evidence or facts. Perceptions of inappropriateness, deviance, and threat can be independent of the actual conditions, but they can also be influenced by particular 'trigger moments' (see below) which create concern. Thus, controversy is seen as the product of a claims-making process, one in which various elements of the hegemonic culture respond to the aesthetic-political claims of the music by raising awareness of the 'problem' or 'threat' to the wider public, media and political leaders, specifically in a manner that objectifies and reifies it far beyond the original boundaries and meanings of the practices that originally generated the controversy.

Controversy is an integral part of heavy metal culture—almost to the point where it is in the 'nature' of heavy metal to be controversial. This view, however, needs to be qualified by putting heavy metal into a historical context. It could be argued that in the 1980s—the heyday of metal's popularity—it was the *content* of heavy metal (primarily lyrics) *in itself* that was perceived as offensive and dangerous, to youth in particular. The culmination of this concern was the congressional committee hearing in 1985, instigated by Tipper Gore, the wife of Senator Al Gore and spokeswoman of the Parents' Music Resource Center (PMRC). The hearing, which received wide coverage in the national news media, targeted heavy metal as one of the threatening genres (Walser 1993: 138–45; McDonald 1988; Wright 2000: 373–74; see many of the chapters below). Because of the sheer popularity of the genre, the controversy became a battle over wider values in society and about the boundaries of 'appropriate' (youth) popular culture (cf. Springhall 1998). While at the time the PMRC managed to gain favourable media attention for its views, the movement against metal withered alongside the mainstream popularity of its nemesis.

In contrast, very few death or black metal bands (for example) have made headlines despite their explicitly Satanic and/or pornographic imagery or lyrics *per se*. The breaking down of most of the remaining public sexual taboos since the 1980s, along with the 'celebritification' of ageing metal stars such as Black Sabbath's Ozzy Osbourne, Mötley Crüe's Tommy Lee and Poison's Bret Michaels have made it much harder to excite the broader public about the dangers of heavy metal, making it in turn much harder for claims about the content of metal to become a full controversy in post-1980s Western culture (see Brown's chapter below). Instead, it is in situations where the genre is dislocated from its perceived place in culture when controversies arise. In other words, in order for heavy metal to become a topic of public discussion there must be some *external* reason, or 'trigger moment', that produces a serious cultural dislocation so that the content of various—usually extreme—subgenres becomes a topic of controversy.

The black metal culture in early 1990s Norway offers a good example of this dynamic. Beginning as a small and marginal subculture, black metal eventually became a national—and to an extent, international—concern because of its violent imagery and themes. However, as Norwegian scholar of religion Asbjørn Dyrendal notes:

> What made Black Metal interesting news was not ideas as such, but an escalation in internal competition for transgressive, subcultural capital that ended in two murders, multiple church arsons and episodes of assault. This, combined with a militant, anti-Christian, anti-social attitude, made Black Metal an ideal example of the Satanism that the Evangelicals had warned about (Hjelm *et al.* 2009; see Kahn-Harris 2007).

This observation has two points that are relevant for the current argument. First, it was the deviant *actions* of the members of the black metal subculture that caused controversy, not the perceived deviance of black metal as such, which did not inspire that much public controversy until they were coupled with actual violent criminal activity. Church burnings and murder triggered the controversy and, by moving black metal from the arena of musical subcultures into the arena of crime, focused attention on a small group that most likely would have remained marginal without these events. Second, although black metal might not have been considered controversial as such before these actions, the trigger moments gave voice to an interest group

(Evangelical Christians) which held fixed beliefs about the evilness of heavy metal in a wider, absolute sense. The content of black metal did become a topic of controversy, but only after certain trigger moments (see Dyrendal and Lap 2008).

However, the idea of cultural dislocation is not exclusively about moving from the margins back to the mainstream. Arguing this would simplify the differences both between the subgenres of metal and between national contexts. For example, when the 'monster metal' group Lordi was voted to represent Finland in the 2006 Eurovision song contest, it was not the band's music or image as such that caused controversy. The band had sold double platinum with their first album in the domestic market, being thus very much in the mainstream. However, when the band moved to a cultural arena conventionally constituted as 'light pop', controversy arose. More importantly, it was widely considered inappropriate for a 'monster metal' band to represent Finland as a nation in an international contest. Thus, the question of content became controversial only after the band moved from the arena of commercial popular culture into the arena of national image and identity. However, because viewers in the Finnish qualifying rounds democratically voted the band, there was a discrepancy between the media accounts of the issue and popular sentiment. Perhaps not surprisingly, then, the tone of the media discourse took a full turn after the band returned victorious from the contest. National shame changed into national pride (see Nestingen 2008: 17–20; Häyhtiö and Rinne 2007).

The above said, it is important to acknowledge that controversy is not merely something ascribed to metal from outside. From its earliest days, when groups like Black Sabbath and Alice Cooper used occult themes and violent imagery and lyrics for clearly commercial purposes, metal has used controversy as a tool not merely of identity, but also of marketing. In this context, the deliberately offensive sonic landscapes, lyrical content, and physical imagery of some genres of metal are generated from within, not without; 'controversiality' is often also an intentional aspect of heavy metal bands. However, in order to grow into a controversy in the sense outlined above, trigger moments such as the above are required in the current Western cultural climate.

This does not mean that the cultural framework is fixed and irreversible. We still might see large-scale controversies such as the PMRC controversy in the 1980s, even if it looks unlikely at the moment. What is apparent is that as a consequence of the globalization of metal, situations analogous to the 1980s controversies over the content of metal have surfaced and will surface in contexts where the music, lyrics and imagery are in stark contrast to local cultural values, as in the contemporary campaigns against metalheads in Islamic countries (LeVine 2008).

Today it is the Muslim world where heavy metal faces the most persistent censorship, political repression and societal stigmatization. Metal arrived in the Middle East and North Africa in the late 1980s with satellite dishes and the movement of workers and other forms of migrants back and forth from the region to the West. However, it wasn't hair, glam or other 'lite' and commercial forms of metal that became popular; rather it has been classic groups such as Black Sabbath and Deep Purple, and more extreme subgenres such as death, thrash and various forms of black metal, that have inspired thriving scenes across the region. Not surprisingly, as the scenes became more popular, and in so doing, more public, they began to attract the attention of governments and conservative religious forces, who saw them as vehicles for the penetration of foreign, Western and even Satanic cultures that threatened the very fabric of their societies.

The situation became bad enough so that by the late 1990s the region witnessed 'Satanic metal' scares in countries including Morocco, Egypt, Lebanon and Iran, in which scores of metal fans and musicians were arrested, jailed, convicted of crimes against their religion, and even threatened with death by the highest religious authorities in their countries (LeVine 2008). In Southest Asia, countries like Malaysia and Indonesia have become home to innovative and increasingly popular scenes despite various attempts to rein them in or clamp down on the music.

Put simply, extreme metal has become popular across much of the Muslim majority world precisely because of its brutal vocals, intense, dissonant and powerful music, and violence-laden lyrics dealing with themes of corruption, war and oppression. These constitute a powerful vehicle for fans and musicians to critique the politics and social dynamics more broadly across their societies. Hip hop, and particularly political rap, has similarly become popular in the Muslim world and globally precisely for this reason. It too has done so at the same moment that, like metal, it lost its political edge in the US and Europe (LeVine 2008, 2011).

At the same time, the DIY ethic and close-knit solidarities of metal scenes globally, and in the region, have also encouraged them to become sites of subcultural and even countercultural production. Metal in the Middle East is the very antithesis of the far more popular, hyper-commercialized and corporatized Arab pop or the largely depoliticized and musically unchallenging religious pop that have attracted the attention of scholars in recent years. Not surprisingly, it is precisely these qualities that have led metal in the Muslim world to catch the attention of governments and religious forces, who until recently found convenient common cause in railing against and repressing the scenes.

Indeed, in countries across the region, and especially in Morocco, Tunisia and Egypt, metalheads have gone on to become major activists in pro-democracy movements as they've grown into adulthood, playing important roles in the revolutionary protests in Tunisia and Egypt. Alaa Abdel Fatah, one of Egypt's main first-generation metalheads, was arrested (and later released) by the post-Mubarak military junta because of his political activities. It is clear that the experience of being part of a marginalized but sophisticated subculture, in which merely going out in public looking like a metalhead would attract the opprobrium of other members of society, was a foundational experience that naturally led to more direct political action later on.

Yet, it's also worth noting that in recent years both governments and more mainstream Islamist movements have begun to adopt a more laissez vivre attitude towards metal, hip hop and other youth cultural scenes, as both sides have come to understand the importance of not alienating the 'new generation'. The growing acceptance of metal by mainstream society and governments in countries like Morocco, Egypt, and even Saudi Arabia and other Gulf countries reflects the broader, if still incipient, process of cultural liberalization they are presently experiencing. Yet the political activism of many members of scenes in countries now in the midst of often jarring transitions away from authoritarian and towards democratic cultures reminds us that these scenes remain, at their core, subversive of existing political orders.

Going back to the birthplace of metal, Europe and the USA, the first section—on metal as controversy—opens with Andy Brown's discussion of two 'moral panics' over heavy metal. Brown asks: how were the 'emo class of 2008' able to contest their media demonization, whereas the headbangers, burnouts or 'children of ZoSo' generation were not? He argues that compared to the PMRC panics of the 1980s (mentioned above), the British newspaper-induced panic over 'emo' culture was a 'failed moral panic'. Where the 1980s panics targeted working-class male youth who didn't have a voice in the media, the emos—mostly middle-class girls—were able to resist the labelling through the use of social media.

Brad Klypchak continues the theme of moral panics in his chapter. His focus is on 'reversioning', that is, how some of the most controversial metal acts of the 1970s and 1980s—Ozzy Osbourne, Alice Cooper and KISS—have become mainstream TV celebrities and heralds of corporate capitalism instead of rebellion. As suggested above and as Klypchak argues, despite the fact that modern extreme metal makes the above 'trinity' look tame in comparison, it was their dominance of the music market in the 1980s that made Ozzy, Alice and KISS a good target for the PMRC and others—something that fringe subgenres of today are only rarely able to accomplish on the merit of their sound, message or look alone. Klypchak argues that in their contemporary domesticated forms, the 'granddaddies of metal' seem to be saying 'I told you so' to mainstream audiences: They have become the positive role models of the very same corporate America they were seen to be threatening in their younger days.

One common perception—among fans especially—is that since its inception, metal has been dismissed as 'anti-taste' in the mainstream music press. Using Bourdieu as a guide, Hélène Laurin argues that this is not the whole story. She traces instances of 'valorization' of metal in the rock press and shows how during recent years previous 'stupid-rock' has become regarded as 'artful' and 'serious' in the press. At the same time as the bands berated as lowbrow since the 1970s have entered the mainstream, and in the process lost much of their controversiality, the rock press has started to treat metal as a legitimate form of expression.

Moving from mainstream metal to the definite underground, Lee Barron examines how 'porngrind', a particular subgenre of extreme metal, has appropriated the feminist critique of pornography exemplified by Andrea Dworkin's influential book *Pornography: Men Possessing Women* (1981), turning the feminist nightmare vision of pornography into a virtue. Porngrind is an example of how metal culture keeps pushing the boundaries of controversy and does so, as Barron argues, not necessarily because of an anti-feminist ideology, but rather in order to conform to the expectations of the extreme metal genre.

In his chapter, Marcus Moberg discusses the 'double controversy' of Christian metal, another scene on the margins of metal culture, and often literally positioned between two worlds. On the one hand metal's (real and imagined) connections with occultism and Satanism make the music suspect in the evangelical milieu from which many of the bands in the scene emerge. On the other hand, Christian metal has had a hard time breaking into the secular metal market. Thus, appropriate religious expression on the one hand and notions about authenticity and ideology on the other have made Christian metal doubly controversial. But, as Moberg explains in this volume, 'Christian metal has not only suffered from its double controversy; it has internalized it and managed to thrive on it as well'.

In the final chapter of Part I, Gérôme Guibert and Jedediah Sklower show that although evangelical Christians have lost much of their status as 'experts' of metal music (and its dangers), in local contexts religious sensibilities still play a part in constructing metal as controversial. Their chapter is an account of how one metal festival—the Hellfest organized in western France—struggled with legitimacy under pressure of condemnation from representatives of the Catholic Church, but managed to win the hearts of the local community despite initial reservations. The authors use the case to discuss how the 'controversiality' of metal is dependent on the social and cultural context and the interpretations that that context allows and enables.

Heavy metal as counterculture

Metal is not only a collection of musical sounds; it is inseparably connected to particular sets of cultural practices. As metal developed in the 1970s and 1980s a highly distinctive 'scene' emerged through which metal was disseminated, produced and discussed (Kahn-Harris 2007). Initially based around metal's male blue-collar Anglo-American core constituency, the metal scene became more diverse over time. Metal became one of the most commercially successful forms of rock music in the 1970s and 1980s, and metal bands were at the forefront of opening new touring circuits to 'western' bands, such as South America and Eastern Europe. Metal has come to be one of the most profoundly globalized musics, with vibrant scenes in most parts of the world (with the partial exception of sub-Saharan black Africa) (Wallach *et al.* 2012).

Central to the globalization of metal has been the development of a complex set of comparatively egalitarian institutions and practices with a high degree of autonomy from the mainstream music industry. In the 1980s, 'the underground' emerged as a decentralized, global scene that was interconnected by a dense network of letter writing, tape trading and small record labels (Kahn-Harris 2007). The underground was the principal space within which extreme metal developed as small groups of fans and musicians compensated for the lack of popularity of the music by connecting up with fellow scene members worldwide.

Crucially, the underground's egalitarianism ensured that bands from then marginal locations in the music industry, such as Brazil's Sepultura, were able to interact within the global scene on relatively equal terms (Harris 2000). In the 1990s and 2000s underground institutions such as tape trading were largely superseded by the internet, but extreme metal remains largely confined to the descendants of underground institutions and it is still the source of much of metal's innovations. Amongst these innovations has been the development of folk metal, in which bands create new hybrid metal styles through an encounter with 'local' musics.

While metal scenes are much more diverse than is often appreciated by outsiders, there remain imbalances of power and hierarchies. Some scenes, particularly in the US and Scandinavia, dominate metal globally. Racist attitudes exist, particular on black metal's right-wing fringe. Women remain underrepresented and 'out' homosexuals are rare. Metal is also a space of musical disagreement and there are fierce debates over the legitimacy of some metal genres such as nu metal and metalcore.

What binds metal together though is a relatively stable canon of artists—Iron Maiden, Judas Priest, Black Sabbath and Slayer being particularly revered—and a core of themes and preoccupations that are pursued across metal sub-genres. As mentioned above, metal tends to be dominated by a distinctive commitment to 'transgressive' themes. By transgression we mean the practice of boundary crossing, symbolically and/or practically, the practice of questioning and breaking taboos, the practice of questioning established values. This is particularly evident in extreme metal, as Kahn-Harris (2007) has shown: extreme metal bands transgress the boundaries of acceptable music, of acceptable discourses, of acceptable practice. Extreme metal provides the 'vanguard', the most systematic examples, of metal's commitment to transgression.

Metal bands explore themes such as sexual excess, the occult, death, violence and mutilation. They revel in myths that explore humanity's darker side, and in stories of human evil and degradation. Metal music has tested the boundaries of music, volume and sound itself. Metal fans and bands have thrown themselves into excess of all kinds and, on occasions (as in Norway in the early 1990s), extreme violence (Moynihan and Søderlind 1998). Such transgressive themes are present to varying degrees in metal music and culture and indeed they coexist, as Kahn-Harris points out, alongside an equally strong commitment to mundane community. But they can always be found somewhere, whether weakly or strongly, in metal music and culture.

It is to highlight this transgressive aspect of metal that we use the term 'counterculture' in the title of this introduction. Counterculture is a relatively unpopular term in social scientific research outside of specific times and places where the term has become ubiquitous, such as 1960s radicalism (e.g. Braunstein and Doyle 2001).[1] Social scientists who have looked at popular culture, popular music and metal have tended to prefer terms such as subculture and scene (for an overview, see Gelder 2005; Muggleton and Weinzierl 2003). Without going into the debates over such conceptual frameworks, we prefer counterculture in the particular context of this collection as a way of highlighting metal's antagonistic side. By this we do not mean simply active attempts to shock and provoke (although there have been plenty of those) but also those occasions when metal, by its very presence, is shocking. A genre that incessantly explores the dark side of humanity will always already be provocative to some sections of society, particularly in more conservative religious cultures. Whether scene members like it or not, metal will frequently become positioned as counterculture simply by existing.

In their chapter that draws on ethnographic work on metal scenes in Jakarta, Indonesia and Toledo, Ohio, Jeremy Wallach and Alexandra Levine outline a theory of metal scene formation. They argue that despite the very different contexts within which the scenes they describe operate, there are strong similarities between them and by extension with metal scenes elsewhere. While metal scenes have much in common with other global music scenes, they have unique features as well which recur repeatedly in a diversity of contexts. Broadly defining scenes as 'loosely bounded functional units containing a finite number of participants at any one time', they argue that metal scenes provide four 'critical functions' and outline seven generalizations about them. Their argument for the cross-cultural similarity of metal scenes is grounded in their argument that the materiality of the musical sounds of metal limit the parameters of musical meaning. Wallach and Levine therefore suggest that it is no accident that metal is controversial and counter-cultural in a variety of locations.

Benjamin Olson's contribution on National Socialist black metal (NSBM) demonstrates how certain forms of metal can be controversial and counter-cultural within the wider metal scene itself. In discursive terms, NSBM may fit in well with the pagan, Satanic and nationalist concerns of black metal; but as Olson argues, 'the majority of black metalers are unwilling to cross the threshold of the radical-right'. This is not necessarily because of any principled objection to racism, more because of a discomfort with the literalism and narrowness that would focus black metal's misanthropy onto any one subset of humanity. NSBM's political connotations also threaten black metal's cherished sense of independence and individualism. Olson argues that, even if black metal's symbolism will continue to be appropriated by the extreme right, NSBM is likely to remain a marginal phenomenon.

Michelle Phillipov's chapter begins by noting that many of the early scholars of metal concentrated on disavowing simplistic connections between metal and violence. Exploring the history of the early 1990s Norwegian black metal scene, she offers a subtle and cautious exploration of the connection between metal and violence. Although the church burning and violence of the early 1990s was not and is not the norm within black metal, it has a continued importance in defining what black metal is. More sophisticated black metal scene members, such as the band Emperor who Phillipov discusses, achieve success in part through their 'simultaneous promotion and disavowal of their involvement in violent crime'. This subtlety produces what Kahn-Harris (2007) argues is a 'balance' between the logics of mundanity and transgression that reproduce metal scenes.

Nicola Allett examines what it means to be a member of an extreme metal scene through a discussion of interviews with UK extreme metal scene members. She argues that in recent years extremity has been 'democratized' through the popular culture mainstream and that this 'threatens to disenfranchise Extreme Metal's extremity, because extremity does not have the cultural impact it once had'. In part as a response to this development, extreme metal fans emphasize their 'connoisseurship', their seriousness and their ability to make complex distinctions, in ways that recall the 'high' versus 'low' culture distinction—within a 'low' cultural form. The counter-cultural element of extreme metal is therefore maintained through scene members' projects of the self that affirm 'permanence, identification and status' against the hyper-individualism and fragmentation of late modernity.

For all of metal's globalization, metal is frequently associated with white, working-class men. Kevin Fellezs focuses attention on the African-American minority within US metal scenes, drawing on a case study of the all-black thrash metal band Stone Vengeance, who 'while enjoying a primarily white male audience, formed their aesthetic in recognition, even celebration, of their blackness'. The band face a predicament in how far to resist or to play with stereotypical constructions as blackness—embodied in the description of the band as 'lords of heavy metal soul'. Interviews with Stone Vengeance frontman Mike Coffey show how he both situates heavy metal within a tradition of black music and at the same time desires to locate himself simply as a heavy metal musician. This tension between individual empowerment and a commitment to the collective runs through the wider field of heavy metal.

Rosemary Overell confronts the construction of gender within metal, particularly the violent misogyny that can be found in some types of death metal and grindcore. Drawing on a case study of grindcore music in Melbourne, Australia, Overell explores the nature of 'brutality' that is identified by scene members as the essence of its affect. Grindcore offers an affective 'intensity' that partially transcends representations of gender, opening up possibilities for female scene members. While misogynistic rhetoric and representation may suffuse metal scenes, it is undermined and ironized in various ways.

Finally, Niall Scott's chapter focuses on the relationship of heavy metal to the political. The political is often rejected in heavy metal scenes in favour of a desired apolitical autonomy. At the same time, as Scott shows, there are also more political strains in metal, as in Napalm Death's anti-fascist stance for example. Drawing on the work of Herbert Marcuse, Scott affirms the potency and subversion inherent in metal's apolitical stance. Metal provides a 'liberated environment' in which the rejection of politics creates a space for community and art.

Conclusion

As third-generation metalheads begin to approach adulthood, first-generation metal scholarship has emerged. In some ways this could be taken as one more sign of the domestication of metal—metalheads turning an analytical and critical gaze on their own scene (almost all of the current scholars in the field are metalheads themselves). We believe, however, that as the remarks above and the chapters that follow below demonstrate, metal has retained a controversial edge precisely because controversy has been so deeply ingrained in the genre itself. As globalization deepens, metal enters new arenas of contestation, as has happened in the Middle East. But cultural pluralization also raises new questions about identities and the politics of identity in the traditional heartlands of metal. Metal is here to stay—whether you like it or not.

Note

1.   For an application of counterculture in a contemporary context see St John (2009).

Bibliography

Beckford, James A. 1985. *Cult Controversies: The Societal Response to the New Religious Movements*. London: Tavistock.

Braunstein, Peter, and Michael William Doyle, eds. 2001. *Imagine Nation: The American Counterculture of the 1960s*. London: Routledge.

Critcher, Chas. 2003. *Moral Panics and the Media*. Buckingham: Open University Press.

Dworkin, Andrea. 1981. *Pornography: Men Possessing Women*. London: The Women's Press.

Dyrendal, Asbjørn, and Amina Olander Lap. 2008. 'Satanism as a News Item in Denmark and Norway'. In *The Encyclopedic Sourcebook of Satanism*, ed. James R. Lewis and Jesper Aagaard Petersen, 327–60. Amherst, NY: Prometheus Books.

Fuller, Richard C., and Richard R. Myers. 1941. 'The Natural History of a Social Problem'. *American Sociological Review* 6(3): 320–28. http://dx.doi.org/10.2307/2086189

Gelder, Ken, ed. 2005. *The Subcultures Reader*. London: Routledge.

Goode, Erich, and Nachman Ben-Yehuda. 1994. *Moral Panics: The Social Construction of Deviance*. Oxford: Blackwell.

Harris, Keith. 2000. '"Roots"?: The Relationship between the Global and the Local within the Global Extreme Metal Scene'. *Popular Music* 19(1): 13–30. http://dx.doi.org/10.1017/S0261143000000052

Häyhtiö, Tapio, and Jarmo Rinne. 2007. 'Hard Rock Hallelujah! Empowering Reflexive Political Action on the Internet'. *Journal for Cultural Research* 11(4): 337–58.

Hjelm, Titus, Henrik Bogdan, Asbjørn Dyrendal and Jesper Petersen. 2009. 'Nordic Satanism and Satanism Scares: The Dark Side of the Secular Welfare State'. *Social Compass* 56(4): 515–29. http://dx.doi.org/10.1177/0037768609345972

Kahn-Harris, Keith. 2007. *Extreme Metal: Music and Culture on the Edge*. Oxford: Berg.

LeVine, Mark. 2008. *Heavy Metal Islam: Rock, Resistance, and the Struggle for the Soul of Islam*. New York: Random House/Three Rivers Press.

—2011. 'The New Hybridities of Arab Musical Intifadas'. *Jadaliyya* (29 October). http://www.jadaliyya.com/pages/index/3008/the-new-hybridities-of-arab-musical-intifadas

McDonald, James R. 1988. 'Censoring Rock Lyrics: A Historical Analysis of the Debate'. *Youth and Society* 19(3): 294–313. http://dx.doi.org/10.1177/0044118X88019003004

Moynihan, Michael, and Didrik Søderlind. 1998. *Lords of Chaos: The Bloody Rise of the Satanic Metal Underground*. Venice, CA: Feral House.

Muggleton, David, and Rupert Weinzierl, eds. 2003. *The Post-Subcultures Reader*. Oxford: Berg.

Nestingen, Andrew. 2008. *Crime and Fantasy in Scandinavia: Fiction, Film, and Social Change*. Seattle: University of Washington Press.

Schneider, Joseph W. 1985. 'Social Problems Theory: The Constructionist Perspective'. *Annual Review of Sociology* 11: 209–29. http://dx.doi.org/10.1146/annurev.so.11.080185.001233

Spector, Malcolm, and John I. Kitsuse. 2001 [1977]. *Constructing Social Problems*. New Brunswick, NJ: Transaction Publishers.

Springhall, John. 1998. *Youth, Popular Culture and Moral Panics: Penny Gaffs to Gansta-Rap, 1830–1996*. New York: St. Martin's Press.

St John, Graham. 2009. *Technomad: Global Raving Countercultures*. London: Equinox.

Wallach, Jeremy, Harris M. Berger, and Paul D. Greene, eds. 2012. *Metal Rules the Globe*. Durham, NC: Duke University Press.

Walser, Robert. 1993. *Running with the Devil: Power, Gender and Madness in Heavy Metal Music*. Hanover: Wesleyan University Press.

Wright, Robert. 2000. '"I'd Sell You Suicide": Pop Music and Moral Panic in the Age of Marilyn Manson'. *Popular Music* 19(3): 365–85. http://dx.doi.org/10.1017/S0261143000000222

Part I: Controversies

Suicide solutions?

Or, how the emo class of 2008 were able to contest their media demonization, whereas the headbangers, burnouts or 'children of ZoSo' generation were not

Andy R. Brown

Bath Spa University, UK

Drawing on historical and contemporary material, this chapter seeks to contrast the 'suicide epidemic' reporting that characterized the 'moral panic' press and media coverage of the popularity of heavy metal with white, suburban lower-class 80s youth in the United States (a group poignantly evoked by Donna Gaines' (1990) phrase, 'the children of ZoSo')[1] with a more recent episode, that surrounding the sensationalist press coverage of the 'emo subculture' in the UK, and its alleged promotion of teen self-harm and suicide, claimed to be found in the lyrics of *The Black Parade* (2006) album by 'emo' band, My Chemical Romance. Such a contrast allows an exploration of the factors that led, in the American case, to an escalation of such scares to the level of quasi-governmental advisory committees (involving an alliance between the national Parent Teacher Association (PTA) and the elite pressure group, Parents' Music Resource Center (PMRC), resulting in the 1985 Senate hearings and subsequent 'media trials' of leading metal bands, Judas Priest and Ozzy Osbourne, whose music was accused of triggering youth suicides (via 'backward' messaging communiqués whose music was on behalf of the devil). In the case of the emo-panic episode, a similar 'signification spiral' of reporting fails to gain the support of politicians and legislators, apparently because of a strategic contestation of such claims carried in subcultural-friendly niche and new media, which 'effectively' articulates the alternative voice of the emo fans.

The question I want to pose is whether the emo scare, initiated by the UK mid-market tabloid, the *Daily Mail*, reporting the death of teen 'self-harmer' Hannah Bond, and then coalescing around the malign influence of the *Black Parade* album, provides a contemporary example of a *failed* youth moral panic; or does it offer confirmation of factors that undermine the model? Central

to this question is the continued capacity of mainstream media to manufacture 'folk devils' out of youth style groups (which in the past seemed to occur
with the apparent 'consent' of majority audiences) in a transformed media
environment that McRobbie and Thornton describe as a 'labyrinthine web'
of niche and micro-media that complexly layer the space between big media
and society, allowing a 'multiplicity of voices [to] compete and contest the
meanings' set in play by moral panic coverage (2000: 181). If putative folk
devils have the means to contest their demonization or find that there are a
range of alternative forms of media that can do it for them, then Critcher's
assertion that the 'folk devil is more likely to be recruited from groups who
cannot speak for themselves and have nobody to speak for them' (2003: 145),
appears undermined. But does the idea of 'empowered folk devils' depend on
the social status and cultural resources of the stigmatized group itself? (de
Young 1998: 275). This is relevant because the emo subculture is largely a
middle-class phenomenon, as we will see, and this in itself reflects a diminished working class, who in the past were the typical material for the construction of youth folk devils (e.g. Cohen 1972: 9–11; 2002; Hall and Jefferson
1976, 2006).

Modus operandi: the comparative case study

What I will argue is that the case study on heavy metal music and its fans in
the 1983–87 period is an example of a *successful* moral panic episode that
demonized a section of blue-collar, white youth as 'folk devils'. This had consequences for many of them, from having to live with negative stereotypes
of themselves ('burnouts', 'dirtbags', etc.), to some being sectioned in psychi-
atric units and/or processed as delinquents (Rosenbaum and Prinsky 1991;
Pettinichio 1986). In addition, the Parental Advisory label on heavy metal
recordings initiated by the Recording Industry Association of America (RIAA)
in response to the panic meant that heavy metal music was harder to obtain,
since national chains refused to stock 'controversial' material. The case of emo,
originally a type of US hardcore punk—dubbed 'emotional hardcore' and then
simply emo[2]—I will argue, is an example of an *unsuccessful* moral panic. As I
have already suggested, it had all the ingredients to become a fully-fledged
panic but the amplification of the original press scare was not forthcoming.
The question is why?

   The model of moral panic that I will debate is the one derived from Stanley
Cohen's classic study (1972, 2002) and the account in Goode and Ben-Yehuda
(1994), but given something of a make-over by Chas Critcher (2003) recently.
Cohen's model of the moral panic process is usefully summarized in the opening paragraphs of his classic text:

> Societies appear to be subject, every now and then, to periods of moral panic. (1) A condition, episode, person or group of persons emerges to become defined as a threat to societal values and interests; (2) its nature is presented in a stylized and stereotypical fashion by the mass media; (3) the moral barricades are manned by editors, bishops, politicians and other right-thinking people; (4) socially accredited experts pronounce their diagnoses and solutions; (5) ways of coping are evolved or (more often) resorted to; (6) the condition then disappears, submerges or deteriorates and becomes more visible. Sometimes the object of the panic is quite novel and at other times it is something which has been in existence long enough, but suddenly appears in the limelight. Sometimes the panic passes over and is forgotten, except in folk-lore and collective memory; at other times it has more serious and long-lasting repercussions and might produce such changes as those in legal and social policy or even in the way the society conceives of itself (Cohen quoted in Critcher 2003: 9).

The numbers (added by Critcher) indicate that there are six stages to a moral panic cycle, although Cohen resists the idea that the model is sequential or overly determined, since each stage may enable or constrain progression to the next. Critcher suggests it is best defined as a 'processual model' (2003: 13), where each element needs to be present if a moral panic can be said to have occurred—although some elements need greater elaboration than Cohen originally afforded them. First, while the role of the media is crucial to stage 2 (exaggeration and distortion, prediction and symbolization), it could also be argued that it is also crucial to the progress of phases 3, 4, 5 and 6 and, therefore, is the key variable in the 'deviance amplification spiral'. This centrality implies that it does not always operate as a secondary definer, exaggerating and distorting the original event, episode or condition and symbolizing the nature of the folk devil but may also be the initial source of the panic, offering the primary definition of the social problem, incident or behaviour (carried in a report, editorial or commentary). Second, Cohen does not identify the folk devil as necessary to the process, which may amplify an 'episode' or 'condition' rather than a specific group; or indeed see the group as a victim of the former. In addition, Cohen fails to identify the police and the broader 'control culture', in stage 5, who may be called upon to offer or promote 'ways of coping' or controlling. Third, Cohen does not sufficiently consider the role of 'public opinion' in the mediated cycle. This element is important, not least because it is a central feature of what many see as the major alternative theorization of moral panics, Goode and Ben-Yehuda's (1994) 'social constructionist' or 'claims-making' model.

For these authors, a level of measurable 'public concern' has to be in play, one accompanied by evidence of hostility directed at a perceived 'enemy' of respectable society, who is clearly defined (the folk devil). There must also be a measure of consensus in the majority society, that the threat posed by this group is real and serious. Moral panic episodes are therefore highly disproportional societal reactions, involving collective behaviour and the public articulation of emotions, such as fear, anxiety, even hysteria; not surprisingly, therefore, they are also highly unstable public events that can quickly start and, just as suddenly, end. The fact that, from a rational perspective, moral panic episodes are 'contextual social constructions' requires identifying those agents and organizations who set in play claims that are successful in provoking a disproportionate reaction. Goode and Ben-Yehuda identify three: grassroots campaigns, which articulate a genuine but mistaken public concern; elites, who attempt to engineer fear and panic in the public, to displace concern over 'real' social problems, whose resolution may undermine their institutional power; and middle-order interest groups, such as professional organizations, police departments, the media, religious groups and educational organizations, who campaign to further their own interests in offering professional solutions to social problems that they have themselves defined. They conclude that elites do not have the power to determine the 'timing, content or direction' of morality panics, since the moral content at the heart of such campaigns requires 'fuel' or raw materials from the 'grassroots' that are then given 'focus, intensity and direction' by organized interest groups; that is, such groups 'co-opt and make use of grassroots morality and ideology' (1994: 43).

Two of Critcher's points of criticism of the 'claims-making' model seem compelling. First, Goode and Ben-Yehuda consistently underplay the role of the media in moral panic amplification, viewing it as a contributing interest group at best. Second, they consistently overplay the importance of 'public opinion' and therefore fail to consider how 'morality rhetorics', articulated by the media, may be less a reflection of the interests of the public and more that of the strategic concerns of elite groups. This has two aspects. First, the role of the press in coining a 'public idiom' through which it can communicate the nature of the problem to the public. Second, the way in which mediated reactions, staged by the media, are fed back to primary definers *as if* they are those of the public itself. Critcher argues, 'instead of attributing a hypothetical social anxiety to whole populations, we should examine the political mobilization of the rhetoric of morality among elite groups' (2003: 147). Evaluating these different models, Critcher recommends the concept of 'moral panic' should be retained as the most useful heuristic device (or 'ideal type' model) for the systematic investigation of mediated morality scares.

This judgement can be contrasted with those critics who argue for a root-and-branch revision of the concept or for its abandonment. Boethius (1995) argues that moral panics over youth and media have become less easy to sustain because of the explosion in new media and popular cultural forms; greater pluralism of moral and cultural values; decline in social and political tensions between classes; greater heterogeneity in the social composition of national populations and lifestyles. McRobbie (1994) and Thornton (1995; McRobbie and Thornton 2000) consistently emphasize three areas of weakness that they believe 'date' the model: that it operates with an 'excessively monolithic' view of the separation between elites, the media, experts and the control culture, on the one hand, and hapless deviants on the other; how youth culture itself is increasingly dependent upon and integrated into forms of media which communicate its values, perspectives and interests; that macro media forms are successful to the extent to which they misrepresent the nature of folk devils and social problems to a gullible and dependent audience, when actually media audiences are far from this, being both intelligent and active in a changed media environment that encourages their 'interactivity'. De Young (1998) argues that although the framework is useful it cannot account for folk devils fighting back, divided public opinion and ambiguous (or 'symbolic') resolutions. Ungar (2001) argues that accumulated knowledge about moral panics is suspect because it is based on the retrospective study of successful rather than unsuccessful or 'failed' examples. These points of debate, analysis and argument feed into the comparative case studies I offer next.

Heavy metal fallout: suicide, Satanism and symbolic censorship

The seeds of the panic can be traced to a middle-class father's complaint to his local paper, the *Cincinnati Enquirer*, in October 1983, about 'four letter words' on a Prince album that he had bought for his daughter. Acting on advice he took his case to the national PTA convention in the summer of 1984, where a majority of delegates, hearing the case, backed a resolution calling for 'accurate song lyrics to be printed on all record albums'. A letter was sent to 29 record companies and the trade organization RIAA, outlining their demands. The campaign met with little success until it found an ally in the newly formed PMRC, which Martin and Seagrave (1993: 292) describe as a 'grassroots organization composed of Washington D.C. wives and mothers who were for the most part wives of administration officials or of Conservative members of Congress'.[3]

The PMRC charged that rock music had become sexually explicit and pornographic. They produced a list of offending songs and identified five basic negative themes in such music: free love/sex, sadomasochism, rebellion, the occult, and drugs (Martin and Seagrave 1993). The group announced it wanted a rating system for records and mailed parents' groups and media to that effect. They soon found vocal support and their views were given prime space in the national media. For example, Kandy Stroud, a singer with the Washington Choral Arts Society, was given the guest editor page in *Newsweek* magazine, under the heading: 'Stop Pornographic Rock' (6 May 1985). Two weeks later David Gergen, a former White House communications director, in an editorial for the *U.S. News & World Report* on 'X-Rated Records', asked rhetorically: 'why do we allow this filth?' (20 May 1985). A similar editorial in the *Washington Post* applauded the wives for seeking to 'save children' from 'exposure to filth, violence, sado-masochism and explicit sex' (quoted in Martin and Seagrave 1993: 293–94).

In July 1985, PMRC members appeared on the *Donahue Show* as well as *CBS Morning News*, *Today* and the BBC. On 6 August, the Senate Commerce Committee announced a hearing on 'porn rock' was to be held the following month. The decision was a response to pressure from the PMRC, who had testified before the Justice Department's Commission on Pornography and made special presentations to senators on the evils of rock music. A standard tactic employed in such presentations was to quote 'explicit' lyrics and show 'objectionable' album covers from their 'rock file'. As Martin and Seagrave comment, the PMRC's 'bad list' contained an 'over representation of heavy metal groups' (1993: 299).

But it was the testimony of 'expert witnesses' during the Senate proceedings into record labelling (US Senate 1985: 99–259) that made the connection to heavy metal central and, along with it, the theme of youth suicide:

> Some rock artists actually seem to encourage teen suicide. Ozzy Osbourne sings 'Suicide Solution'. Blue Oyster Cult sings 'Don't Fear the Reaper', AC/DC sings 'Shoot to Thrill'. Just last week in Centerpoint, a small Texas town, a young man took his life while listening to the music of AC/DC. He was not the first (Susan Baker, quoted in Weinstein 2000: 250).

In support of their interpretation of the song 'Suicide Solution' the PMRC entered as evidence a publicity shot of Ozzy Osbourne, with a gun barrel in his mouth. PMRC expert consultant, Jeff Ling, followed up this imputed 'causal' connection, commenting: 'Steve died while listening to AC/DC's "Shoot to Thrill". Steve fired his father's gun into his mouth' (Weinstein 2000: 252–53). This was followed by reference to another case of a high school student who had hung himself while playing the same track. Ling concluded by declaring:

> Suicide has become epidemic in our country amongst teenagers. Some 6000 will take their lives this year. Many of these young people find encouragement from rock stars who present death as a positive, almost attractive alternative (quoted in Weinstein 2000: 253).

Despite the fact that this reasoning was highly speculative, continued press reporting on the connection, argues Weinstein, meant that the association between heavy metal music and youth suicide 'became fixed in public discourse' (2000: 254). This interpretation seems plausible when in October 1985, Ozzy Osbourne and his record company were sued by parents of a nineteen-year-old suicide victim, although the case never made it to trial. However, the case against Judas Priest and CBS records, brought by parents of two boys who acted out a suicide pact, did make it to court, in Reno, Nevada in the summer of 1990. The case gained national and international publicity. Richardson (1991: 212) argues that the reason why this case was able to proceed to trial was because of the 'novel' claim presented by the plaintiffs' council that 'subliminal messages were embedded in the music, and [such messages] were a major cause of the young men's actions'. Therefore, the band were not protected by the First Amendment, as subliminal messages 'should not be afforded the same constitutional protection granted supraliminal speech'. Such claims were already associated with scares about Satanism in youth culture (for example Raschke 1990: 171), and the activities of grassroots religious organizations, such as Parents Against Subliminal Seduction (PASS). These ideas were also rehearsed in the Senate Hearings (US Senate 1985: 15–16, 20–23) themselves. In August 1990, the judge found in favour of Judas Priest and against the plaintiffs' (although the band and label were required to pay the costs of the proceedings).

The outcome of the PMRC campaign was a 'voluntary agreement' between the RIAA and the pressure group, to the effect that record companies would self-label potentially 'offensive' records with a 'Parental Advisory: Explicit Lyrics' warning. This practice, agreed by the majority of labels under the umbrella of the RIAA, had come into force by 1986. It is now the industry standard practice and is to be found, not unsurprisingly, on mainly heavy metal and rap releases (Christenson 1992).

To the extent that a successful moral panic campaign requires a compelling event or object, then the highlighting of the link between heavy metal songs, specific youth suicide incidents and claims for an epidemic in youth suicide rates, clearly does seem to be the dominant emergent theme. These stories also prolong the life of the campaign, while drawing in other elements, such as Satanism, in the claims for 'backwards' or subliminal messaging (Richardson 1991). If there is a framing that can hold these largely incoherent themes together, it is the PMRC claim to be concerned for the protection of vulnerable children. What is unclear is how this claim informs understanding of the status of youth as both 'innocent' and 'possessed' by anti-social (media) influences. Certainly the object of the campaign is the regulation or control of music content, specifically lyrical content and 'messages' conveyed by it to minors. This raises the issue of how the 'folk devil' is to be understood, in that it could be claimed to be the bands and artists, the record company executives, the product itself and its youth consumers.

Examining the structure of the campaign cycle, the argument about the role of claims makers seems to be vindicated. There is evidence of grassroots activity, which is then taken up and pursued by organized interest groups. However it is also clear from the material that the role of the media is crucial. Press reporting in the period indicates a remarkable pattern of articulation of the views and actions of the elite protagonists and the shifts and turns in the campaign that resulted in the 'voluntary agreement' on labelling. Notable are items that articulate the position of the PMRC, carried in the tone of headlines and leader content. Many are a result of editorial space being given over to supporters or sympathizers of the PMRC campaign; it could also be argued that these pieces appear at strategic moments in the campaign. There is also evidence of niche coverage, carried in music magazines, and some evidence of the voice of heavy metal fans, carried in letters published on the issue (Weinstein 2000: 253). But there is no evidence of the coverage or impact of this at the macro media level. However, the appearance of the heavy metal musician, Dee Snider (Twisted Sister), at the Senate hearings and his 'surprisingly articulate' testimony did receive notable coverage (Goodchild 1986); as did the views of maverick rock musician, Frank Zappa. It is also clear that a number of industry trade-papers ran editorials supporting the autonomy of the music industry, against the PMRC proposals, towards the end of the campaign (Martin and Seagrave 1993: 297–98).

Despite the fact that the PMRC claimed to articulate grassroots feeling, the public expression of this mandate was more a rhetoric of morality, designed to appeal to, rather than reflect, majority opinions. Chastagner (1999; echoing Walser 1993) argues the PMRC campaign, whatever its original intentions, most closely resembles that of an elite-engineered strategy, to divert attention onto 'scapegoats' rather than focus public attention on more difficult economic and social problems facing lower-class youth. The fact that all the decisive aspects of the campaign were conducted within the confines of a narrow elite circle, which national media gave rhetorical access to, seems to underline this. Yet the victory of the forces of censorship were more symbolic than real, suggesting perhaps that the campaign was more about appealing to the newly emergent 'new right' forces, who sought to re-direct the state at this juncture. What is clear is that beneath the rhetorical power play of the campaign claims-makers and politicians was a functioning intermediary layer of public and private institutions that specialized in the treatment ('de-metalling') and regulation (30-day observational detention) of metal (and punk) kids who fitted the 'deviant' profile (Gaines 1990; Rosenbaum and Prinsky 1991) perpetuated by the campaign.

A much more dangerous teenage cult? Emo and the celebration of self-harm

The seeds of the emo panic can be traced to the publication of an exposé piece, by *Daily Mail* reporter Sarah Sands, entitled: 'EMO cult warning for parents'. It begins with a survey of the prevalence of a Goth look in fashion supplements, youth culture and even in the corporate world. It then shifts emphasis to announce the discovery of a 'new' and 'much more dangerous teenage cult, the Emos', who it is argued are a 'young sub-set of the Goths'. However,

> Although the look is similar, the point of distinction, frightening for schools and parents, is a celebration of self-harm. Emos exchange competitive messages on their teenage websites about the scars on their wrists and how best to display them. Girls' secondary schools have for some time been concerned about the increase in self-harm. One governor of a famous boarding school told me that it was as serious a problem as binge drinking, but rarely discussed for fear of encouraging more girls to do it. Although it is invariably described as a 'secret shame', there is actually a streak of exhibitionism to it (Sands 2006).

This piece is notable for characterizing the 'emo type'; identifying the style as middle-class ('Emos have a strong arts graduate bias') and predominantly female. It also locates the self-harm 'exhibitionism' of emos on 'teenage websites' and in 'dark and airless' bedrooms. It also notes emo bands, Green Day (*sic*), My Chemical Romance and Adam and Andrew (but MCR are not given especial prominence). It ends with a warning/prediction: 'What worries me is that teenagers are less equipped to manage strong emotions and a cult of suicide could have real and horrible consequences' (op. cit.).

This framing of the 'emo cult' is not taken up by any other papers until 7 May 2008, when the story of the suicide of 13-year-old schoolgirl, Hannah Bond, breaks.[4] A search of the UK and Ireland mainstream press, between 2000–2010 (Newsbank.com), reveals there were 157 pieces published on emo, prior to the *Mail* 'exposé' and before the suicide reporting. But none of these fit a moral panic framework. Of such items, only 25 could be said to be style or youth culture commentary, the vast majority (n=132) being music or arts/entertainment features, either reviews of new releases or live music. Such items refer to emo as a music genre or sub-genre category (emo-core, emotional rock, etc.); or employ the term as an adjectival pop-culture reference ('emo-punk angst'), usually when reporting on the growing success of emo bands, such as Jimmy Eat World, Panic! at the Disco, Hundred Reasons, Dashboard Confessional, You Me at Six, Funeral For a Friend, Death Cab for Cutie, and My Chemical Romance.

Employing a 'frame analysis' (Binder 1993: 756–57) of the 25 items that offered an editorial analysis, revealed the following frames of text-reader comprehension: a definitional or pop culture genre-mapping frame; recognition of new youth or subcultural style ('do you know your emo from your new goth'); identifying crossover-success and industry recognition (MCR); identifying key bands and album releases (*The Black Parade*); providing an instant cultural guide for readers (*The Bluffer's Guide to Emo*); and communicating a generational tolerance and 'panic' awareness ('It's self pity with knobs on, but we should listen to the emo-ters cries' (*The Observer*, 8 October 2006).

The panic phase begins: emo cult suicide press coverage

The would-be 'moral panic' phase of reporting can be organized, as follows:

First phase:

- Tragic emo teenager uses tie to hang herself. *The Evening Standard* (London) 7 May 2008.
- Popular school girl dies in 'emo suicide cult'. *The Daily Telegraph*, 7 May 2008.
- Girl, 13, hanged herself after becoming obsessed with 'emo'. *The Times*, 8 May 2008.
- Suicide of Hannah, 13, the secret 'emo'. *The Sun*, 8 May 2008.
- Girl hanged herself to impress 'emo' cult. *The Daily Telegraph*, 8 May 2008.
- 20th SUICIDE IN BRIDGEND. *The Daily Mirror*, 8 May 2008.
- Suicide of girl, 13, hooked by cult that glamorizes death. *The Daily Mail*, 8 May 2008.
- Hannah was a happy 13-year-old until she became an 'emo', part of a sinister teenage craze that romanticizes death. *The Daily Mail*, 15 May 2008.
- Why no child is safe from the sinister cult of emo. *The Daily Mail*, 16 May 2008.

What is most striking about the first phase of 'moral panic' reporting in the mainstream, mainly tabloid press, is its disconnection from the pop culture coverage that precedes it. The Sands (2006) piece, linking emo to a suicide and self-harm culture, defines emo as a sub-set of goth culture, which the music coverage in the *Mail*, and elsewhere, clearly contradicts. On closer inspection the cover-stories do recycle some of the descriptive phrases but these are re-framed within the 'emo cult' or 'sinister teenage craze' idea, suggesting this is an exposé of a teen world that is completely unknown to parent-readers. This idea of a 'secret life' and behaviour, hidden to the parents of the deceased girl, fits the 'warning' frame of the earlier Sands piece. Typically, it is the *Mail* that reinforces this framing ('sinister cult' and 'sinister teenage craze') in their follow-up pieces (15 and 16 May), announcing that 'no child is safe'. All the papers attribute the alleged role of emo in the death to the coroner's comments. But these, in turn, summarize the testimony of parents at the inquest and the problem of accounting for why a 'model school girl' would take her own life. The term 'cult', mentioned in eight of the nine cover stories, is not present in the coroners' report but drawn from the Sands piece. It is also notable that neither claims makers nor experts, beyond the coroner and a brief comment from a 'child clinician' (in the *Mail* coverage), are mentioned. The *Mail* does go on to suggest that self-harm often leads to suicide and to offering data that suggests a dramatic rise in rates. Yet the story run by the *Mirror* attempting to link the suicide verdict with the ongoing story of a spate of suicides in Bridgend, South Wales (8 May 2008) is not picked up by any other papers.

Clearly the 'condition, episode or person' requirement of the moral panic framework is present in the coverage, discovering or identifying a threat or danger to 'normal' society. However, this framing can only be sustained in terms of the idea that this 'deviant' activity or behaviour is 'hidden' and therefore unknown to the public. As we will see, the specific claims of the panic, that the victim was a 'secret' fan of the band My Chemical Romance and listened obsessively to the album, *The Black Parade* ('apparently a place where emos go when they die'), are rapidly undermined by the second phase of reporting. As with the heavy metal campaign, what is even more highlighted here is the problem of how the folk devil is to be defined? Is it the secret bedroom cult of the emo teenager, transforming well-adjusted teens into self-harmers obsessed with the glamour of suicide? Or is it the music of bands such as My Chemical Romance and therefore the musicians themselves? Or the record companies who record and distribute the 'dangerous' materials? Or is it the social-networking forums, where emos gather to talk suicide? What is most notable about this coverage is that there is no attempt to identify a 'solution' to this condition or to quote the opinions of claims-makers who represent a view on the source or cause of the 'danger' to children. But clearly the theme of vulnerable children who might become *monstrous* is emergent in the coverage and also the theme of internet-media, which will re-emerge later as a potential campaign focus.

Second phase:

- Maligned emo fans to march on *Daily Mail. The Guardian*, 22 May 2008.
- Reasons to be cheerful. *The Independent*, 23 May 2008.
- EMO. *The Independent*, 23 May 2008.
- Mail's chemical reaction. *The Observer*, 25 May 2008.
- The kids who march in the black parade. *The Times*, 30 May 2008.
- Black parade of teen angst. *Irish Independent*, 31 May 2008.
- Is emo a suicide cult? *The Guardian*, 31 May 2008.
- Emo fans protest at 'suicide cult' label. *The Observer*, 1 June 2008.
- SUICIDE newspaper under siege as fans of emo music protest at 'suicide cult' coverage of teenager's death. *Independent on Sunday*, 1 June 2008.

What is remarkable about this phase of the emo panic is that it is entirely unexplainable within the classic framework. The 'event' that coheres the coverage and acts as its object and rationale is the march on the offices of the *Daily Mail*, of '200' emo fans protesting their depiction as a 'suicide cult' and defending the music of emo bands, such as My Chemical Romance. What is also noteworthy about the coverage is that it is almost entirely made up of broadsheet titles covering a story of popular criticism of 'moral panic' type reporting, particularly in the *Daily Mail* but also in the tabloid press generally. Indeed, an examination of the coverage reveals that at least half of the items report the announcement and planning of the march *before it happens*, thereby acknowledging the existence of alternative, internet-based 'viral' media as the source of the anti-*Mail* campaign.[5]

Also noteworthy is that even mid-market tabloids, such as *The Daily Telegraph*, satirize the *Mail* coverage in its arts/pop culture features ('Don't panic! Here comes Emo', 26 October 2006) in the period between the Sands exposé and the first phase of reporting. All of which suggests that McRobbie and Thornton's (2000) criticism that successful moral panics require a model of 'monolithic' media is greatly justified. And as for the teen 'folk devils' made possible by such a model, the marchers on the *Mail* are far from 'inarticulate'. For example, Anni Smith, the 16-year-old organizer of the protest, claimed the *Mail* coverage was: 'badly researched journalism in danger of promoting irresponsible stereotyping' (quoted in *The Independent*, 23 May 2008). So unexpected was this 'news event' and its publicly articulated criticism, that the *Mail* was compelled to release a statement defending itself, claiming its coverage had been 'balanced, restrained and, above all, in the public interest' (reported in *The Guardian*, 2 June 2008).

Third phase:

- 13-year-old suicide over 'emo' cult bullying. *The Daily Telegraph*, 11 June 2008.
- BULLIED TO DEATH AT 13 FOR LOVING EMO MUSIC. *Daily Mirror*, 12 June 2008.
- Boy bullied over taste in music hangs himself. *The Daily Express*, 12 June 2008.
- Bebo bullies kill emo lad. *The Sun*, 12 June 2008.
- Boy found hanged suffered website abuse say family. *The Guardian*, 12 June 2008.
- Bullies blamed for suicide of 'emo' music fan. *The Independent*, 12 June 2008.
- Emo 'teen 'hanged himself after bullying'. *Western Mail*, 12 June 2008.
- EMO GIRL HANGED. *The Daily Mirror*, 19 June 2008.
- HANGED GIRL, 12, WAS USING EMO WEBSITES. *The Daily Mirror*, 19 June 2008.
- Girl, 12, hanged herself as 'emo' music played. *The Daily Telegraph*, 19 June 2008.
- Girl found hanged in bedroom had become obsessed with 'emo culture'. *The Times*, 19 June 2008.
- Web bullies 'killed' boy. *Daily Post* (Liverpool), 25 June 2008.
- 'Terrorist' bullies of emo lad. *The Sun*, 25 June 2008.

The third phase, coming only ten days after the emo protest march, was clearly made possible by the coroner's report on the suicide cases. Notable here also is the shift in emphasis towards the idea of cyber-bullying of 'alternative' or emo-types, which includes the idea of 'sensitive' boys as well as girls. But again this characterization rests on the testimony of parents, which could be said to be the key 'grassroots' feature in the emo panic cycle. However, there is very little evidence of a concerted shift towards a view of the need for controls or regulation of internet media, although the comments of a Bebo 'spokesman' does feature in one story. This cycle ends with the comments of a 'local vicar' fulminating against 'cyber terrorists'. But this claim is not amplified or endorsed by more establishment spokespeople.

Fourth phase:

- Goths 'ate girl in pie'. *The Daily Mirror*, 5 February 2009.
- 'Hungry, so we cooked and ate my girlfriend'. *The Express*, 5 February 2009.
- Prozac boy killed father in hammer attack frenzy. *The Daily Mail*, 7 February 2009.
- Prozac is blamed after lad kills dad. *The Sun*, 7 February 2009.
- Prozac teen stabbed dad to death. *The Daily Mirror*, 7 February 2009.
- Killer son given life. *The Sun*, 31 March 2009.
- We must listen to our children. *Bristol Evening Post*, 24 September 2009.
- Teens under pressure. *Irish Times*, 27 October 2009.
- TRAIL OF ONLINE SUICIDES. *News of the World*, 15 November 2009.
- BULLIED BEYOND THE GRAVE. *News of the World*, 6 December 2009.

This phase is characterized by a lack of focus, although it does conclude with a reconnection to the theme of internet-bullying. The other stories are the vaguely bizarre and too-distant tales of deviance to reanimate the emo panic, which can be said to have exhausted itself by this point.

Emo vs. the media: the role of niche and alternative media in the campaign

In comparison to the suggestion of opposition from metal magazines and their letters pages in the panic over heavy metal, there is clear evidence that the niche music press played a strategic role in the outcome of the emo panic in the UK. This is so on two counts. First, niche weekly music titles, *Kerrang!* and *NME*, competed for championship of the emo music wave, through their review and coverage of new and breaking bands identified with the genre label. This bid for ownership and definitional expertise is reflected in macro media music coverage of emo, where reviewers often quote or refer to this niche media endorsement as proof of the significance of emo bands as 'new music' with a significant subcultural or audience demographic.

Secondly, once the macro-media panic began to break, the niche music media titles were galvanized into a 'fan centred' response. *Kerrang!*, for example, ran a double-page feature ('EMO under fire') in its news section which reproduced the tabloid coverage, noting that the band My Chemical Romance were singled out for especial infamy, and asked for a reader response (17 May 2008). This came in the next issue of the letter's page (24 May 2008), which was entirely devoted (9 letters) to reader reactions, ranging from a generalized rejection ('the teenage generation do not need the press to interpret our music') (Letter 6), to specific criticism of the *Daily Mail* (Letter 2) and the 'ever intellectual' *Sun* (Letter 1). The *NME* letters page of the same week began with the sub-heading, 'Emo in the dock again', featuring a response from a fan as its letter of the week (24 May 2008: 14). It went on to refer readers to the 'huge response' to the issue on its website, nme.com.

All of which suggests that the critics of the moral panic framework, McRobbie and Thornton in particular, are right on many counts. Their point that, following a surge of growth in the 1980s, 'some 30 (UK) magazines now target and speak up for youth' (2000: 190), was borne out not only in the niche coverage of the *misrepresentation* of the mainstream press but also the incorporation of many of these views within the broadsheet criticisms of the *Mail's* campaign. Yet this stance did not prevent many broadsheet titles from joining in on the reporting of further suicide stories in the third phase. In addition, McRobbie and Thornton's account of the magazine sector itself needs updating, particularly the impact of the tabloidization of the music magazine sector (Forde 2001) which has resulted in the increasing branding and brand sponsorship of titles (Brown 2007; 2010) and, in particular, net-based add-ons (such as *NME* 'shockwaves'). There is also some evidence that titles, like the *NME*, now behave more like tabloids, not just in how they look, but in their editorial strategies. For example, the *NME*'s coverage of (stimulation of?) 'anti-emo' comments from leading 'indie' bands is surely a case in point (e.g. 'Kasabian slam My Chemical Romance', *NME*, 14 October 2006; 'My Chemical Romance Respond', 24 January 2007)? When the *Mail* 'panic' piece was first published, the magazine re-examined its position on emo, though it did not abandon its sensationalist cover style: 'Bottled at Reading, attacked by tabloids, threatened in the streets... WAR ON EMO: whose side are you on?' (16 September 2006).

Conclusions

Even if judged in terms of Critcher's revised model, the emo panic that briefly flared across the pages of the UK national press was an unqualified failure: its lurid vignettes of darkly-clothed, emo-fringed schoolgirls, self-harming in darkened bedrooms to the soundtrack of *The Black Parade* album, did not provoke a national outcry of worried parents or self-appointed moral guardians calling for legislation to censor or regulate teen-access to this life-threatening music cult. Indeed, the coverage, although it did include the condemnation of one bona-fide vicar, was notable for the absence of any recognizable campaigning claims-makers or politicians. This was not the case with the campaign waged against heavy metal music and its alleged culture of Satanism, suicide ideation and sexual depravity, by the PMRC elite pressure-group and its supporters, which received high-profile national press and media coverage in the United States in the 1983–1987 period, resulting in both real and 'symbolic' costs to its stigmatized, subcultural consumers.

Could it be that the image of the deviant, oppositional or dangerous, lower-class youth 'folk devil' (teds, mods, rockers, skins and punks), so prominent in earlier bouts of moral panic media coverage, is no longer able to symbolically mark the divide between 'normal society' and deviancy, because youth cultural creation is no longer exclusively a working-class practice? The wide-scale influx of middle-class youth into the youth culture market, clearly evident by the early 80s (Roberts and Parsell 1994), suggests that heavy metal, particularly the revived form of it (NWOBHM,[6] speed, thrash and death metal), marked the symbolic last stand of a white, male, working-class-oriented youth culture. The procession of youth cultural formations since this time, including goth, new romantics, post-punk, grunge, indie, acid house and rave, nu-metal and emo, announce themselves as 'classless' and are more concerned with the defence of style distinctions operating *within* the social space of youth itself, such as 'mainstream' vs. 'underground' or 'cool' vs. 'conformist' modes of consumption (Thornton 1995).

The other significant factor to consider is that of gender. It is surely an obvious point that the putative folk devils of the respective campaigns were strongly marked by *gendered* representations, contrasting the white male (working-class) headbanger or metalhead with that of the white female (middle-class) emo fan. Here it might be argued that this representational discourse suggested the headbanger as a danger to others (and therefore the wider society), whereas emo girls were a danger to *themselves* and their families.

Lastly, the growth and complexity of youth media forms since the 1980s (Osgerby 2004) appears significant. Not only has the music magazine sector mushroomed into a niche-defined and branded marketplace, commodifying musical tastes into a plethora of types of 'life-style' consumption (Forde 2001) but there has also been an exponential growth in the internet and web 2.0 new media forms (Gauntlett and Horsley 2004), facilitating the increased interaction of youth on social media forums concerned with the definition, promotion and discussion of new music and consumer (and anti-consumer) style practices (Heath and Potter 2005), beyond the 'reach' of old-media.

It is my conclusion that it was the mediated impact of these social and technological factors that undermined the significatory power of the *Mail*'s divisive youth exposé piece to provoke a disproportionate reaction, in either its readership or the agents and representatives of the 'control culture'. It should also be noted that the *Daily Mail*, once considered the 'voice of middle England', is now the leading daily newspaper in the UK, having recruited a new self-identifying, 'middle-class' majority of readers, who would most likely have recognized the *misrepresentation* of their own teens' consumer affiliations, in the panic coverage.[7] Finally, what seems in retrospect to be a significant factor is the migration of the music journalism and pop-culture commentary of the niche magazine sector to the media-culture pages, style guides and supplements of the mainstream press, from the 1990s onwards.

Notes

1. The phrase 'ZoSo' relates to the four symbols or ancient runes found on the spine of Led Zeppelin's fourth album, which is otherwise untitled.
2. There is a good deal of controversy surrounding the relationship of the successful emo bands to hardcore punk and to metal, more generally. This controversy, even hostility among some metal fans, is not dissimilar to that accompanying the nu-metal style that achieved chart success, prior to emo. Both genre styles achieved cross-over success, particularly through attracting female fans, leading to the accusation that they were industry-based genres rather than scene-based ones. This criticism was also levelled at glam or 'big hair' metal, one of the styles at the centre of the 80s panic.
3. Given the elite social and political locale from which the members of the PMRC were drawn, Martin and Seagraves' description of them as a 'grassroots' organization seems risible.
4. Although there is an isolated story, covered in *The Sun* (22 April 2008), concerning 'hoardes of make-up wearing' emo fans being attacked by 'punks and metal heads', in Mexico.
5. http://www.independent.co.uk/arts-entertainment/music/features/emo-welcome-to-the-black-parade-832854.html; http://www.bebo.com/Profile.jsp?MemberId=6842052119; http://www.youtube.com/watch?v=6RbteHntnLk; buzznet. com
6. NWOBHM refers to the New Wave of British Heavy Metal. The phrase was coined by Sounds journalist, Geoff 'deaf' Barton, to characterize the resurgence of a louder, faster, more aggressive form of heavy metal in the wake of punk, in the 1980–1984 period in the UK.
7. For example, *Kerrang!* magazine, an early and consistent champion of the emo music wave, has a entry link on its website, for fans of 12 years and under. In addition, my survey of reader's letters, from 2006–2008 (Brown 2009) revealed that not only were the majority of letter writers female but many thanked mums and dads for taking them to concerts. Also, a significant number of letters written by parents to *Kerrang!* and the mainstream press referred to their own former teenage styles or its negative coverage at the time.

Bibliography

Binder, Amy. 1993. 'Constructing Racial Rhetoric: Media Depictions of Harm in Heavy Metal and Rap Music'. *American Sociological Review* 58(6): 753–67. http://dx.doi. org/10.2307/2095949

Boethieus, Ulf. 1995. 'Youth, the Media and Moral Panics'. In *Youth Culture in Late Modernity*, ed. Johan Fornas and Goran Bolin, 39–57. London: Sage.

Brown, Andy R. 2007. '"Everything Louder than Everything Else": The Contemporary Metal Music Magazine and its Cultural Appeal'. *Journalism Studies* 8(3): 642–55. http://dx. doi.org/10.1080/14616700701412209

—2009. '"Girls Like Metal, Too!": Female Readers' Engagement with the Masculinist Culture of the Tabloid Metal Magazine'. Paper presented at the Heavy Metal and Gender conference, University of Music and Dance, Cologne, Germany, 8–10 October 2009.

—2010. 'The Importance of Being "Metal": The Metal Music Tabloid and Youth Identity Construction'. In *The Metal Void: First Gatherings*, ed. Niall Scott and Imke Von Helden, 105–134. Oxford: Inter-Disciplinary Press.

Chastagner, Claude. 1999. 'The Parents' Music Resource Centre: From Information to Censorship'. *Popular Music* 18(2): 179–92. http://dx.doi.org/10.1017/S02611430 0000903X

Christenson, Peter. 1992. 'The Effects of Parent Advisory Labels on Adolescent Music Preferences'. *Journal of Communication* 42(1): 106–113.

Cohen, Stanley. 2002 [1972]. *Folk Devils and Moral Panics: The Creation of Mods and Rockers*. 3rd edn. St. Albans: Paladin.

Critcher, Chas. 2003. *Moral Panics and the Media*. Buckingham: Open University Press.

de Young, Mary. 1998. 'Another Look at Moral Panics: The Case of Satanic Day Care Centers'. *Deviant Behaviour: An Interdisciplinary Journal* 19(3): 257–78.

Forde, Eamon. 2001. 'From Polyglottism to Branding: On the Decline of Personality Journalism in the British Music Press'. *Journalism* 2(1): 23–43. http://dx.doi.org/10.1177/ 146488490100200108

Gaines, Donna. 1990. *Teenage Wasteland*. New York: Harper Collins.

Gauntlett, David, and Ross Horsley, eds. 2004. *Web.Studies*. 2nd edn. London: Hodder Education.

Goodchild, Seth. 1986. 'Twisted Sister, Washington Wives, and the First Amendment: The Movement to Clamp Down on Rock Music'. *Entertainment & Sports Law Journal* 3: 131–96.

Goode, Erich, and Nachman Ben-Yehuda. 1994. *Moral Panics: The Social Construction of Deviance*. Oxford: Blackwell.

Hall, Stuart, and Tony Jefferson, eds. 2006 [1976]. *Resistance through Rituals: Youth Subcultures in Post-War Britain*. 2nd edn. London: Hutchinson.

Heath, Joseph, and Andrew Potter. 2005. *The Rebel Sell: How the Counter Culture Became the Consumer Culture*. Chichester, West Sussex: Capstone Wiley.

Martin, Linda, and Kerry Seagrave. 1993 [1988]. *Anti-Rock: The Opposition to Rock 'n' Roll*. New York: Da Capo Press.

McRobbie, Angela. 1994. *Postmodernism and Popular Culture*. London: Routledge. http:// dx.doi.org/10.4324/9780203168332

McRobbie, Angela, and Sarah L. Thornton. 2000. 'Re-thinking "Moral Panic" for Multi-Mediated Social Worlds'. In *Feminism and Youth Culture*, ed. Angela McRobbie, 180–97. London: Macmillan.

Osgerby, Bill. 2004. *Youth Media.* London: Routledge. http://dx.doi.org/10.4324/978020 3343630

Pettinichio, Darlyne. 1986. *The Back in Control Centre Presents the Punk Rock and Heavy Metal Handbook* (pamphlet). Fullerton, CA: Back in Control.

Raschke, Carl L. 1990. *Painted Black: From Drug Killings to Heavy Metal—the Alarming True Story of How Satanism is Terrorizing Our Communities.* New York: Harper Collins.

Richardson, James T. 1991. 'Satanism in the Courts: From Murder to Heavy Metal'. In *The Satanism Scare*, ed. James T. Richardson, Joel Best and David G. Bromley, 205–217. New York: Aldine De Gruyter.

Roberts, Ken, and Glennys Parsell. 1994. 'Youth Cultures in Britain: The Middle Class Take-over'. *Leisure Studies* 13(1): 33–48. http://dx.doi.org/10.1080/02614369400390031

Rosenbaum, Jill Leslie, and Lorraine Prinsky. 1991. 'The Presumption of Influence: Recent Responses to Popular Music Subcultures'. *Crime and Delinquency* 37(4): 528–35. http://dx.doi.org/10.1177/0011128791037004007

Sands, Sarah. 2006. 'EMO Cult Warning to Parents'. *The Daily Mail*, 16 August.

Thornton, Sarah. 1995. *Club Cultures: Music, Media and Subcultural Capital.* Cambridge: Polity.

Ungar, Sheldon. 2001. 'Moral Panic versus the Risk Society: The Implications of the Changing Sites of Social Anxiety'. *British Journal of Sociology* 52(2): 272–91.

US Senate. 1985. Record Labeling. Hearing Before the Committee on Commerce, Science and Transportation, United States Senate. First Session on Contents of Music and the Lyrics of Records, 19 September. US Government Printing Office, Washington. http://www.joesapt.net/superlink/shrg99-529/index.html

Walser, Robert. 1993. 'Professing Censorship: Academic Attacks on Heavy Metal'. *Journal of Popular Music Studies* 5: 68–78. http://dx.doi.org/10.1111/j.1533-1598.1993.tb00083.x

Weinstein, Deena. 2000. *Heavy Metal: The Music and its Culture.* New York: Da Capo Press.

'How you gonna see me now'

Recontextualizing metal artists and moral panics

Brad Klypchak

Texas A&M University-Commerce, USA

In heavy metal's formative stages, three acts, Alice Cooper, Black Sabbath, and KISS, proved tremendously influential in terms of musical and performative innovations which would come to help establish the genre, its artistic potentials, and its subcultural standing. Coincidentally, these three acts initiated another of metal's longstanding traditions, inciting those who found the imagery or lyrical content of metal to be obscene, blasphemous, or threatening to youthful members of metal's audience to protestation, proposed prohibition, and attempts at political action. Considerable publicity, including a number of urban legends, followed, and a moral panic surrounding heavy metal music ensued. During this time, Black Sabbath, Alice Cooper, and KISS were specifically targeted by metal's detractors as being among the most objectionable of the whole.

In light of this contextual history, it seems anomalous that, roughly thirty years later, the very targets of parental scorn have become ubiquitous in mainstream popular culture. Both Gene Simmons from KISS and former Black Sabbath vocalist Ozzy Osbourne have participated in a number of television series. Alice Cooper is now a restaurateur, a renowned participant in celebrity golf tournaments, and the host of a syndicated radio show. Advertising campaigns for products ranging from hotel chains to carbonated beverages have featured these artists. To arguably the greatest extreme, in September 2009, the city of West Hollywood, California celebrated 'Ozzy Osbourne Day', a far cry from the past when many a community sought to prohibit Osbourne performances in their town.

This chapter examines the scope of such anomalous recontextualizations by situating the past controversies within the present day and its blend of nostalgic reversioning of past actions. The recontextualizations are also considered in light of contemporary creative works offered by each of the respective artists, thereby adding further significations to the reversioning process as a whole. In the case of the new musical and musically performative works, choices which could evoke potentially panic-worthy responses are still engaged. However, the creative and commercial endeavours beyond music offer enough of a stabilizing buffer to overcome such concerns.

Situating the past to the present—metal and its connection to moral panics

When viewed with historical hindsight, one may well argue that the entirety of the KISS, Osbourne, or Cooper catalogue falls outside the scope of what metal has come to represent stylistically and subculturally. Certainly, the music differs considerably in terms of tempo and tenor when juxtaposed to more recent releases, particularly those from metal subgenres like black metal, death metal, or grindcore. Similarly, in comparison to the content presented by a Behemoth concert or a Lividity lyric sheet, the degree of perceived societal moral threat represented by the Sabbath's occultist themes or Cooper's use of a snake in stage shows seems far removed from the realms of extreme metal's explorations. With this in mind, I offer that the historical significance of Cooper, Simmons, and Osbourne as connected to moral panic holds a skewed point of relevancy in ways in which the arguably more transgressive extreme metal acts come to be encountered, and for the most part, overlooked by contemporary mainstream purview.

In his canonical text *Folk Devils and Moral Panics*, Stanley Cohen offers moral panic as existing when

> a condition, episode, person, or group emerges to become defined as a threat to societal values and interests; its nature is presented in a stylized and stereotypical fashion by the mass media; the moral barricades are manned by editors, bishops, politicians and other right-thinking people; socially accredited experts pronounce their diagnoses and solutions; ways of coping are evolved or (more often) resorted to; the condition then disappears, submerges or deteriorates and becomes more visible (Cohen 2002: 1).

Considerable scholarly and popular attention has situated the origins of heavy metal music and its thematic scope as fitting such a scenario (see, for example, Weinstein 2000; Walser 1993 and Nuzum 2001 among others).

In large part, the diversification of rock music as an industry and the advent of diverse publicity outlets have changed the ways in which metal moral panics have proceeded and the responses both within and outside the metal community have transpired (as Andy Brown's chapter in this volume may well attest). That the initial moral panic surrounding Cooper, Osbourne, and Simmons occurred in an era of far more centralized music and media practices, greater potential connection to mainstream awareness could result. For example, an era like that described in E. Ann Kaplan's (1987) deconstruction of MTV and the potential impact of music videos in the early 1980s differs considerably from the diversity of outlets vying for mainstream commercial attention. Be it on the publicity side (including but not limited to webpages, social media, podcasts, peer-to-peer sharing, and the diversification of specialized niche content in television, radio, publishing, and computer-based outlets) or the production side (for example, the reduced role of limited distribution channels, the increased ease of do-it-yourself recording and mixing, and reduced reliance upon major label funding and support), the opportunity for any single niche performance or artist to extend to mainstream awareness is considerably more challenging to achieve in comparison to the era in which metal origins emerged.

Contrarily, there was far less collective distance from the rock charts and the most popular touring acts of the 1970s and 1980s and those outside the subcultural confines of rock and/or metal fandom. Innovators and trendsetters like Alice Cooper, Black Sabbath, and KISS were far more distinctively recognizable to the mainstream since there were far fewer publicity and advertising outlets available. Carnivalesque publicity ploys (for example, the 'breakdown' of a truck advertising Alice Cooper in Wembley Square or the band members' blood being added to the ink for KISS comics) received mainstream attention. As a result, stories recounting such 'news' became the fodder through which urban legends surrounding the bands arose and the capital of representing youthful rebellion was manufactured. In doing so, the same patterns as described by Dick Hebdige regarding punk could be seen with metal: 'these statements, no matter how strangely constructed, were cast in a language which was generally available...for both the members of the subculture and its opponents, and for the success of the punk subculture as spectacle' (Hebdige 1979: 87).

The language of the original metal moral panics has become an inherent component of metal's own self-definition and ongoing historical narrative. Though KISS, Osbourne, or Cooper may not necessarily reflect contemporary metal today, their nostalgically-celebrated contributions to metal's nascent stages affords them canonical respect and inclusion into metal discourse. Perhaps more significantly in terms of the mainstream however, the oft-repeated criticisms of metal in these early stages have become the commodifiably recognizable images of popular metal moral panic. Much like rock moral panics hearken back to Elvis's pelvis or the Everly Brothers' Susie needing to wake up, metal's detractors inevitably rekindle their criticisms of the foundational metal acts in establishing their adversarial position.

For Cooper, Simmons, and Osbourne, subcultural capital could then be selectively utilized. As an example, both Simmons and Osbourne's involvement in the film *Trick or Treat* (1986) self-referentially positioned the rock stars in line to their moral panicked personas. For Osbourne in particular, the inversion of rock star portraying a conservative preacher condemning satanic rock bands (and his eventual death) offers a lampooning mockery of the very rhetoric which the moral panics embraced—a point which metalhead consumers of the film most certainly would have appreciated. In Hebdige's terms, the commodity form of rebellion becomes 'simultaneously returned' (Hebdige 1979: 94), and in doing so, the performers become 'frozen' in the subculture's own history as 'rebellious' and 'innovators'. Each successive metalhead generation then reinforces this frozen connection by repeating the same stories of past rebellion and further solidifying the performers as canonical regardless of the relative connectedness to contemporary metal practices.

Reversioning

Elsewhere, I have written of the phenomenon wherein popular cultural entities become understood not only from their initial appearance within a cultural milieu, but also become consciously rescripted as historical appropriations of the past with current agendas and current ideologies (Klypchak 2007a, 2009). The changed meaning from original experience through each subsequent version of experience adds additional layers of meanings thereby creating new hybrids of what the entity itself comes to signify, a process I term a 'reversion'. Paralleling what psychologists term 'reconstructed memories', a significant action is not necessarily remembered for the moment itself, but for the moment and each subsequent retrieval and rehearsal of the moment. From original experience through each subsequent version of experience, additional layers of meanings occur. In reversioning, the process is extended beyond mere recollection as the popular cultural entity itself becomes reengaged in some predicated fashion.

As an example, the trend to reissue albums in 'remastered' forms, typically supplemented by new packaging and liner notes, reversions the meanings for what the original album itself connotes. Going a step further, the promotional cycle of an artist may well refer to the album over a span of multiple years and may well alter the narrative meanings attributed by the artist to the work—the 'best album we've ever done' becomes condemned as 'what the label made us do' and then may well be favoured again once the 25th anniversary of the release comes around. Similarly, the historic understanding of a band may well be changed as a result of various reversions via lineup changes (examples like the two competing versions of L.A. Guns or Saxon come to mind), contradictory narratives across publicity vehicles (such as changed tales found in the Mötley Crüe book, *The Dirt*), altered or manipulated releases (remasters or remixes, changed track orders, new recordings or studio additions) and the like.

Regardless of the mechanisms, whatever the initial understanding and interpretation of the entity had been remains as informing the whole (and as has been historically practised and rehearsed), but the subsequent engagements give rise not only to potentially new interpretations of the initial moment, but also the constructs of the contemporary happening as well; new versions of what the entity itself comes to signify reversions the previous construction. For rock performers with historical legacies like Alice Cooper, KISS or Ozzy Osbourne, each subsequent presentation of the band as a nostalgic yet contemporary entity reversions the ways in which the whole of the respective band's past comes to be understood, often times through the very selective manipulation of the artists or the record companies themselves. Inevitably, the later versions of presentation often offer contrasting details, emphases, or remembrances of what was expressed during those original moments. What had initially been claimed as factual in publicity materials concurrent with an album's release become challenged through twenty years of retellings of stories and subsequent reversioning.

Recalling Hebdige, the frozen commodity form can then become manipulated in such ways as to reinforce the selective utility for the performer. For canonical metal artists like KISS, Alice Cooper or Black Sabbath, emphasizing their respective roles within metal's initial moral panics reaffirms their contemporary inclusion to metal, even though metal itself has diversified well beyond the performative styles the artists themselves enacted. This historic association inherently writes the bands into deeper discussions of emergent moral panic (be it as seen through associations like Cooper's performative style and the Columbine/Manson panic or 'Suicide Solution' to the 1994 civil lawsuit against Deicide and Cannibal Corpse) thereby rekindling connections to rebellious standing. Similarly, subcultural recognitions such as being labelled as iconic, being chronicled in retrospective 'Top Metal Artists of All Time' articles, being the subjects of 'tribute' records, and being referenced as influences to newer bands, all work to further mark the nostalgic past as being relevant to the contemporary form, regardless to whether or not there is resemblance to the contemporary form.

For my explicit purposes here, the treatment of urban legends attributed to performers like Simmons, Cooper, or Osbourne offer a form of reversioning which proves meaningful in recontexualization. As Cooper himself noted, 'as the Alice Cooper circus pulled into the next city, there were four or five new fables of gore and excess waiting for us' (Cooper *et al.* 2007: 85). To those seeking inflammatory reasons to condemn the performers, the stories became prime sources of evidence. Whether it be the salaciousness of KISS signifying 'Knights in Satan's Service', Cooper's refusal to go on stage without an animal sacrifice, or Osbourne's being a satanic practitioner of black magic, the reputation of taboo or threat manifested regardless of actual validity, and spurned moral panic reactions all the more. To the performers, stories circulating of their own accord simply enticed sensational reaction and subsequent press coverage. Keeping in mind the advice given to Alice Cooper from mentor Frank Zappa regarding the various versions of the chicken sacrifice rumour: 'well don't tell anybody! Everyone hates you—that means the kids will love you' (Cooper *et al.* 2007: 80), to debunk the urban legends at the time would undermine the rebellious capital being so conveniently generated. According to Cooper, the chicken incident, which 'the overground and underground press blew...way out of proportion', marks the 'beginning of national notoriety' for the band and is 'still one of the first questions asked me today' (80). That Cooper has selectively retold stories of the infamous Toronto show (which in itself fuelled the subsequent rumour mill) countless times since it happened in 1970 affords opportunity to reversion its elements, be they factual or fictional, and create a regenerated history that reflects both past and present significations.

In terms of the moral panic reactions to controversial artists, the ability to reflectively look back and reassess the rhetorical arguments being put forth by those rock dissenters often show considerable instances of conflation, insinuation, exaggeration, misrepresentation, and/or misinformation. For present-day interpretations of artists like Cooper, Simmons, and Osbourne, the factual shortcomings of the initial panic argument offer a historic recontextualization which positions those voices of past authority as objects of scorn. Since folks like the Peters Brothers earned coverage on *Nightline* and Darlyne Pettinicchio had a featured segment in the film *Decline of Western Civilization II*, the anti-rock movement held a degree of authoritative respect. Now, revisiting the rhetoric in hindsight (be it the proclaimed seriousness of subliminal messages and baskmasking in rock recordings, the satanic threat of the 'metal horns' gesture, the influence of performers on the 'prepubescent youth' claimed to be targeted by rock artists, or the call for record album bonfires or 'demetalling' treatments), many of the impassioned pleas are undermined and the Jerry Falwells and Tipper Gores of the era are resituated as overzealous attention seekers.

From this vantage point, the relative impact of the moral panic may well be diminished in perceived threat, but additional relative causes of parental, governmental, or religious concern did not magically disappear—the records, videos, and album art still presented taboo subject matters to a consuming public. The artists still created controversies that challenged the moral standards and still generated public outcry regarding issues such as explicit lyrics, gratuitous violence and/or salacious sexuality, all topics that continue to recur in parenting discourses through contemporary times. During the formative metal era, rock resistances ranging from local protests to cancelled concerts to outright bans of select artists in certain cities were commonly initiated. Though less prevalent in contemporary times, the problematics of KISS being too sexually forward, Alice Cooper being too violent or Ozzy Osbourne being satanic and foul-mouthed still recur and regenerate the rhetoric of moral panics of the past (for examples, see LoBello 2008, Blabbermouth 2008 and Malone 2009 respectively). What becomes curious is how the interpretation of these artists and the degree of threat had changed over time even though each has continued to incorporate the same motifs deemed threatening in the past.

Alice Cooper

By the point of the release of 1976's *From the Inside*, Alice Cooper had accrued considerable notoriety. As a rock musician, the former Vincent Furnier led his band in an elaborate series of performative choices accessing both the sublime shock of the Grand Guignol and the mundane challenges of the teenage boy, yet doing so in a manner that adhered to rock's ethos of rebellion, celebration and excess. Unsurprisingly, not all accepted Cooper's creations with enthusiasm. The 'ever deepening stages of perversion' (Larson 1987: 151) of 'gruesome' (Peters *et al.* 1984: 137) stage shows 'that make Dante's descriptions of hell look like a nursery school playground' (Gore 1987: 148) tempted 'hundreds of thousands of adoring teenagers eager for Alice's own peculiar brand of sadistic thrills' (Godwin 1985: 82). Cooper's choice to mock critics in the song 'Go to Hell' revels in such reactions and in the misperceptions put forth by 'all of the decent citizens [Cooper] enraged'. The result was a perfect storm of rock moral panic—challenges to established authority in slickly enticing packaging that scoffed at parents' sense of decorum as readily as the paper panties which accompanied the *School's Out* record.

Even so, the pressure of being a key cog in an entertainment machine while embracing the role of public enemy number one took its toll, and Cooper institutionalized himself to come to grips with his alcohol problems. The *From the Inside* record depicts the experience and features the ballad single, 'How You Gonna See Me Now'. While the song specifically addresses Cooper's uncertainty at resuming life as both performer and husband in a sober state, the song also precursors the first steps at reversioning the Alice Cooper past. Though the stage show continued to include both the controversial songs and problema-tized depictions of baby decapitations, necrophilia, and Cooper's beheading, Cooper begins to formally acknowledge, at this point, the division between the stage character and the 'real' person he seeks to provide the public.

With the release of the autobiography, *Me Alice* (1976), Cooper publicly declares how Alice is a stage persona, the character which he becomes and who embodies the symbolic villain getting carried out on stage. Off stage, Cooper becomes 'Coop', the relatively shy 'regular' guy fighting addiction and seeking balance and security in day-to-day life. The choice to humanize 'Coop' and to refer to Alice in the third person acts to reversion the meanings of the stage show and song messages. The displacement between the character and the person offers Coop as being less culpable for the mayhem on stage. Simi-larly, Cooper's choices to take part in public performances in the Coop guise (with or without stage makeup) offered a second form of image for compari-son. Hosting the *Muppet Show* in 1978 and appearing on the *Hollywood Squares* game show and in films like *Roadie* and *Wayne's World* supplemented the division of Alice from Coop. Declaring his born-again Christianity and being highly visible in charity work in the Phoenix area added layers of contrasting safeness all the more.

Contemporary Cooper still performs songs like 'Poison' and 'I Love the Dead' deemed lyrically problematic in the past. The guillotine, the gallows or some other deathly device remains as a key performance prop. The blood-packs squirt from mannequins and Cooper's own daughter is the victim of simulated violence every night. Despite parallel content from the moral panic era, Cooper's ongoing prominence as Coop counterbalances the core threat of the stage show. As a representative example, a Marriott Inns commer-cial portrays Coop in makeup and leathers providing parenting advice to an unsuspecting suburban father. At the commercial's end, Coop and two little girls play together, reciting rhymes while jumping rope. Inverting the threat of Alice's past in favour of being a family-friendly icon allows for the historic past to be referenced, but the allusion mitigates the contemporary understanding of that past. Sure, Alice remains a scary-looking monster, but a safely com-partmentalized one who happens to favour the lifestyles of the golfing guys at the country club.

Gene Simmons

KISS bassist Gene Simmons has historically revelled in generating atten-tion for his band and his favourite cause, 'power and the pursuit of it' (Sim-mons 2008: 2). Attributes and actions from his Demon character prompted the lion's share of moral panic criticism targeted toward KISS as a whole. The 'sexually-glutted lyrics' and 'crude sadomasochism' (Peters *et al.* 1984: 69) presented by these 'demented charlatans and cradle robbers' (Godwin 1985: 131) who 'exhibited psychic powers' (Larson 1987: 164) were made all the more threatening by Simmons's unabashed declarations of sexual conquests (with Polaroid proof of the four-thousand plus encounters), and his penchant for tongue waggling, fire breathing, blood spitting, and even more skirt chasing.

Though the band itself has altered personnel and has fluctuated between employing iconic makeup or not, KISS has stayed consistent in recording and performing music along the same anthemic themes as their initial recording in 1973. Their recent release, 2009's *Sonic Boom*, offers yet another round of Simmons in Demon-guise as sex-crazed misogynist, as a song like 'Russian Roulette' illustrates. While Simmons did venture beyond the scope of the band through acting in films like *Runaway* and *Trick of Treat*, many of his extracurricular activities and projects remained consistent with his usual bravado and constructed persona. Unlike the Alice/Coop division, Simmons remained Simmons, the guy bemoaning marriage as a denial of his rightful desire to get laid—although since 2011 married to long-time partner Shannon Tweed—and merchandising anything and everything that would add dollars to the KISS coffers (like KISS coffins) and perhaps best exemplified by the title of his second book *Sex, Money, Kiss* (2003).

In essence, Simmons never really changed from the persona which fuelled the moral panic reactions initially. If anything, he simply added more potential fuel to the flame with every interview in which he went out of his way to announce his 'sex, money, kiss' decree. However, that very tactic seems to have worked to his reputation's favour. To hold consistent to the portrayal was to become a known and predictable commodity. Simmons can then be seen as a caricature, a sexist oaf that is relegated to 'dirty old man' status epitomized on his website's 'Ladies in Waiting' area where female fans submit seductive photos of themselves. Yet, for *Sonic Boom* to be solely distributed via the notoriously conservative Walmart, the seemingly repeated sexualized messages must somehow lose their threat or become countered in some fashion. Even Simmons himself admits, 'many corporations around the country were scared of an association with us' (2002: 256). In this regard, the money focus of Simmons seems to offer the most explanatory power of getting those like Walmart to buy in.

Merchandising has long been a passion for KISS/Simmons. The desire to create a recognition and following as 'iconic as Disney' (2002: 118) superseded any lone musical or performative intentions. Years of promotional and corporate tie-ins offered Simmons opportunities to cultivate his image as business mogul, an image which often countered that of the sexual hedonist. His short-run appearance on *The Celebrity Apprentice* (2008) illustrates both Simmons's inventive marketing mindset and his steadfast (and successful) dedication to his business principles. While the exposure of the show offered a connection between Simmons and charity, the additional publicity afford Simmons a more desirable outcome, seeking access to new markets through which to spread the KISS brand. Historically, Simmons actively sought ventures tied to youth thereby generating inroads for potential new fans, but also reinvigorating connections to those parents which may have lost touch with KISS as they progressed to adulthood. In this specific pursuit, Simmons has reversioned aspects about his past and has reframed himself and the KISS experience in such a way that, despite the moral panic arguments, family-centred fun is really what KISS represents.

Beyond the assorted products ranging from Halloween costumes to games, toys, and comic book and video game series, the area in which Simmons has arguably offered the greatest entrée to family-acceptable reversioning is through television. *Gene Simmons' Rock School* (2005) essentially duplicated the plot of the film *School of Rock* with Simmons taking on the Jack Black role of teacher and mentor at a British boarding school. The Teletoon cartoon series *My Dad the Rock Star* (2003) focuses on how a young boy, Willy, negotiates having a rock celebrity as a father. The publicity for the show specifically frames Simmons who, as a child, held a remarkably close bond with his mother and is now a dedicated father in his own right. Re-presenting his relationship with his children, Simmons eliminated the animated fictionalization and developed and sold *Gene Simmons [sic] Family Jewels* (2006) as a reality show. Here, despite the usual Simmons sex and money components, Simmons becomes the butt of his children's jokes, and long-time partner Shannon Tweed exposes the hypocrisy of Simmons as he clings to the very conservative family values he resisted so adamantly in the past. The show, entering its fourth season of the same father-as-foil formula, humanizes the oaf character into something more conservatively palatable, an atypical yet typical father figure.

Ozzy Osbourne

The third component to the formerly unholy trinity, Ozzy Osbourne, represents a blend of both Cooper and Simmons reversioning. Similar to Cooper, Osbourne incorporated rhetoric of born-again Christianity into his later interviews and in his show performances ('God bless you's' rival 'I love you all's' and 'get fuckin' crazy's' in stage rap proclivity) and has explicitly drawn attention to the harm his prior substance abuse has caused. While the legacy of the 'Madman' and the 'Prince of Fuckin' Darkness' continues, it is now delivered in a forum intermixed with twelve-step tenets and calls for just saying no. Similar to Simmons, Osbourne's embrace of portraying foul-mouthed father-as-foil has propelled the whole of the Osbourne family to popular iconic status. In demonstrating a doddering Osbourne as 'just another beleaguered suburban dad' (Crowley 2003: 42), the show does manage to offer moments of cross-generational parenting nonetheless. Osbourne's confessionals about drug use or getting tattoos to his children provide the same messages of abstinence and open communication that Tipper Gore herself advocated in her 1987 moral panic text *Raising PG Kids in an X-Rated Society*.

It is partly the result of the doddering quality that one might see Osbourne as fostering a 'Coop'-like persona. Knowing that the foil image was driving the show's popularity, Osbourne's embrace of the fool becomes a running parody of himself. As an example, a 2008 Samsung cell phone commercial featuring Osbourne mocks his incomprehensibility, be it attributed to dialect or carryover slurring from past overindulgences. In other ads from the campaign, Osbourne lampoons his technological inabilities and his problematized relationship to the occult by attributing a keyboard which changes its layout dependent on the direction one holds the apparatus as 'black magic'. He also undermines his own profession by evaluating a demo video clip from a Samsung employee that happens not to be human; Osbourne's day job is so easy a chimp could do it apparently.

The result of this fatherly-dolt who still retains his wildman unpredictability allows Osbourne the freedom to own his past problematics. His autobiography, *I Am Ozzy* (2009), offers further examples of the same sort of sensational story-telling couched in reframed, parentally savvy messages. The rock cultural capital for his madness and hedonistic indulgences remain, but become reframed in a rhetoric of regret and reticence, yet open up the possibilities that some of the past antics were just as contrived and calculated as those of the Samsung ads—performances of 'Ozzy' by an actor far more shrewd than the character he elects to perform.

Conclusion

Lawrence Grossberg describes the period of early hard rock and heavy metal moral panics as a paradox; attacks on rock music surged at the same time rock music emerged as a dominant mainstream cultural form. In Grossberg's argument, he notes how rock music has been 'colonized by the economic interests of capital' in such a way that questions whether rock fans were ever 'politically active, let alone radical' (Grossberg 1988: 31). He concludes that rock itself in this time represents a 'conservative' resistance against the New Right's restrictive moralities and simply seeks to maintain the culturally dominant position of the industry maintaining the economic status quo (34).

Ultimately, it is a position like Grossberg's that I find myself coming back to. The moral panics of the past no longer come to represent the selective threat as they once might have appeared or become selectively remembered in ways that create distance from initial worries. After all, as Grossberg notes, the PMRC folks advocated a return to the clean and wholesome classic rock styles of the past, those very same times when Chuck Berry played with his ding-a-ling. To revisit those past arguments seems anachronistically jarring. For example, the Westboro Baptist Church's decision to picket outside the funeral for Ronnie James Dio sparked more controversy for being linked to hate speech and poor taste than Dio's past associations to occultism. Rekindling the same zealous fervour out of seemingly nowhere for an issue twenty-five years hibernated failed to re-incite the panic. If anything, the panic itself was shown to be all the more innocuous.

Specifically tied to Osbourne, Simmons and Cooper, their selective reversioning strategies come to reflect a similar reaction. When framed through humour and self-referential parody, the very arguments presented by the Fred Phelps of the world are made all the more ludicrous. Cooper's jump-roping with children, Osbourne's bumbling with technology, and Simmons's over-the-top sexism being usurped by family commitment each recollect the frozen commodity form, but its reversioned significations only account for rebellion in a co-opted and commercially viable form. There is a superficial sense of 'madman', 'macabre' and 'marauder' still lingering, but it is done through such predictably known nostalgic territories that there is little concern about its presentation.

Robert Wright posits that the metal moral panic itself has altered in its fundamental construction. Whereas in the past, moral panics were 'spearheaded by special interest groups' (Wright 2000: 366), Wright sees reactions to the new breed of panic sensations, epitomized by Marilyn Manson, as resonating in a far more culturally inclusive scope; the neoconservative reactions of the eighties have been reconceived as a 'kind of "received wisdom" or even "common sense" that obviates the need' (Wright 2000: 366) for the public notoriety groups like the Moral Majority or the PMRC incited. In light of this presumptive mindset, a Foucauldian sense of self-policing ensues. The panic becomes internalized in such a way that one assesses and judges for oneself. However, by doing so, the hegemonic foundations inscribed within the status quo become all the more powerful. Discursive steps are skipped over and the tenets of conservative norms are presumed to be the comparative standard.

The combination of reversioned images, the historical distance and desensitized comfort with what might have shocked previously, and the addition of culturally conservative values—be they tied to celebrating nuclear family, material capitalism, just saying no, or some combination therein—reflect rock as a colonized commodity form. As commonly argued elsewhere (as examples, see Walser 1993; Weinstein 2000; Klypchak 2007b; or Halnon 2004) much of the problematized hard rock/heavy metal of the seventies and eighties might be understood as serving the hegemonic purpose of regulating deviance on the level of the individual, whether it be the decadent performer or the failed parent not disciplined enough to prevent their children from such immoral exposures. Thirty years later, those very children who sought out the taboos their parents feared are now those in the position of authority figures doing the watching and surveying themselves.

Jeff Bostic and his colleagues suggest that the anti-heroic rock icon appeals as a means for developing an independency from parental systems of regulatory order. The rigidity of 'defensive paternalism' (Bostic *et al.* 2003: 58) and its strict reactions toward any perceived threat on the child (such as those of the moral panicked metal acts) initiates a break from the child's blind acceptance of parental authority: 'Finding flaws in the existing adult social order helps the adolescent shift more time and loyalty away from the value system of adults' (56). Carried over into their own parenthood, the teens of the seventies and eighties can resituate their own experiences. As such, their past fandom emerges as all the less threatening since, presumably, they themselves have become well-adjusted societal members reflective of the status quo. Cooper, Simmons and Osbourne, as desirable marketing vehicles for corporate America, not only recontextualize both hard rock/heavy metal as panic-worthless but becomes a retrospective 'I told you so', a belated victory over one's parents who suggested their idols were not the positive role models they have come culturally reversioned to be.

Bibliography

Blabbermouth. 2008 'Alice Cooper: Still Censored After All These Years' (30 September), http://www.roadrunnerrecords.com/blabbermouth.net/news.aspx?mode=Article&newsitemID=105900 (accessed 5 July 2010).

Bostic, Jeff Q., Steve Schlozman, Caroly Pataki, Carel Risuccua, Eugene V. Beresin and Andrés Martin. 2003. 'From Alice Cooper to Marilyn Manson: The Significance of Adolescent Antiheroes'. *Academic Psychiatry* 27(1): 54–62. http://dx.doi.org/10.1176/appi.ap.27.1.54

Cohen, Stanley. 2002. *Moral Panics and Folk Devils*. 3rd edn. New York: Routledge.

Cooper. Alice. 1976. 'Go To Hell'. *Alice Cooper Goes To Hell*. Warner Brothers. 2986, CD.

Cooper, Alice, and Stephen Gaines. 1976. *Me, Alice: The Autobiography of Alice Cooper*. New York: G. E. Putnam & Sons.

Cooper, Alice, Keith Zimmerman and Kent Zimmerman. 2007. *Alice Cooper, Golf Monster*. London: Aurum Press.

Crowley, Michael. 2003. 'Ad Share'. *New Republic*, 10 February.

Godwin, Jeff. 1985. *The Devil's Disciples: The Truth About Rock*. Chino, CA: Chick Publications.

Gore, Tipper. 1987. *Raising PG Kids in an X-Rated Society*. Nashville, TN: Abington Press.

Grossberg, Lawrence. 1988. 'Rock Resistance and the Resistance to Rock'. In *Rock Music: Politics and Policy*, ed. Tony Bennett, 29–42. Gold Coast, Queensland: Griffith University Institute for Cultural Policy Studies.

Halnon, Karen Bettez. 2004. 'Inside Shock Music Carnival: Spectacle as Contested Terrain'. *Critical Sociology* 30(3): 743–79. http://dx.doi.org/10.1163/1569163042119868

Hebdige, Dick. 1979. *Subculture: The Meaning of Style*. London: Methuen & Co. http://dx.doi.org/10.4324/9780203139943

Kaplan, E. Ann. 1987. *Rocking Around the Clock: Music Television, Postmodernism, and Consumer Culture*. New York: Routledge.

Klypchak, Brad. 2007a. '"All on Account of Pullin' a Trigger": Violence, the Media, and the Historical Contextualization of Clint Eastwood's *Unforgiven*'. In *Clint Eastwood Actor and Director: New Perspectives*, ed. Leonard Engel, 157–70. Salt Lake City: University of Utah Press.

—2007b. *Performed Identity: Heavy Metal Musicians Between 1984 and 1991*. Saarbrücken, Germany: VDM Verlag.

—2009. 'What's in a Name? Lineup Changes and Perceived Authenticity in Hard Rock and Heavy Metal'. Paper presented at the American Studies Association of Texas Conference, San Angelo, TX, 12-13 November.

Larson, Bob. 1987. *Larson's Book of Rock*. Wheaton, IL: Tyndale House.

LoBello, Lia. 2008 'A&E Flashing *Gene Simmons' Family Jewels* in All the Wrong Ways'. *The Huffington Post*, 13 March. http://www.huffingtonpost.com/lia-lobello/ae-flashing-gene-simmons-_b_91458.html.

Malone, Michael. 2009. 'Some Fox Affils Keep "Osbournes" Off'. *Broadcasting & Cable*, 1 April. http://www.broadcastingcable.com/article/191084-Some_Fox_Affils_Keep_Osbournes_Off.php.

Nuzum, Eric. 2001. *Parental Advisory: Music Censorship in America*. New York: Harper Collins.

Osbourne, Ozzy, and Chris Ayres. 2009. *I Am Ozzy*. New York: Grand Central Publishing.

Peters, Dan, Steve Peters, and Cher Mirrell. 1984. *Why Knock Rock?* Minneapolis: Bethany House.

Simmons, Gene. 2002. *Kiss and Make-Up*. New York: Three Rivers Press.

—2003. *Sex, Money, Kiss*. Beverly Hills, CA: New Millennium Press.

Walser, Robert. 1993. *Running with the Devil: Power, Gender, and Madness in Heavy Metal Music*. Middletown, CT: Wesleyan University Press.

Weinstein, Deena. 2000. *Heavy Metal: The Music and Its Culture*. Boulder, CO: Da Capo Press.

Wright, Robert. 2000. '"I'd Sell You Suicide": Pop Music and Moral Panic in the Age of Marilyn Manson'. *Popular Music* 19(3): 365–85. http://dx.doi.org/10.1017/S026114300000000222

Triumph of the maggots?

Valorization of metal in the rock press

Hélène Laurin

McGill University, Montreal, Canada

Although the perception is changing, it is generally agreed that metal is, by and large, dismissed by the rock press. This apparent consensus has existed for at least 25 years (if not since metal's inception, in the early 1970s), and thus has deep roots. To many, metal represents an 'anti-taste', something one has to hate in order to understand 'the good taste' (Lindberg *et al.* 2005). This anti-taste has been partly shaped by the established, most important voices of rock writing (Gendron 2002; Straw 1990). In part, metal is considered to be an anti-taste because it is often linked with low culture and poor people, something most people do not want to be associated with (Bryson 1996). Apparently, rock critics 'have helped to shape the dominant stereotype of heavy metal as brutishly simple, debilitatingly negative and violent, and artistically monotonous and impoverished' (Walser 1993: 24). Seemingly, rock critics consider metal to be:

> musically simplistic, 'primitive', and unsophisticated; and that its lyrical themes are sexist paeans to hedonism and militate against hope for the future. Metal is 'the beast that refuses to die', maintaining its traditions as other music-based subcultures change or become extinct (Weinstein 2000: 240–41).

Is this perception that metal has been hated and denigrated by the rock press since its inception based in reality? I would like to address the nuances of this consensus, as it appears that the attitude rock writers have reserved for metal has changed over the years.

Metal: rejection and solidarity

The idea that metal has been rejected by the rock press is also shared by metal fans. Metal fans are very important to metal subculture: actually they sometimes seem more important than the music itself. In short, metal is shaped and cast into a music, a culture and a lifestyle that embody 'the last rebellious music on Earth', uniting outcasts of today and yesterday. Many metal fans feel they must defend their music against accusations of being unsophisticated or being 'noise'. As rejection is key in creating a sentiment of solidarity, the perceived accusations pointing to the supposed 'inferiority of metal' contribute to unifying the metal community.

Furthermore, many metal fans portray themselves as going against the grain of society, and this happens all over the world. As explained in Sam Dunn and Scot McFadyen's documentaries, *Metal: A Headbanger's Journey* (2005) and *Global Metal* (2007), metal fans and musicians see themselves as outsiders, 'badasses', 'weird kids', who confront what the rest of society would rather ignore: themes such as death, violence, pain, forces of evil, and fear. Hence, metal fans commonly feel righteous because they are part of a culture that embodies the negation of a sick, sad, boring world (the 'regular' world)—a negation in which they revel. There are also many 'casual headbangers', particularly fans of bands that have crossed over to mainstream rock culture. These are the bands that I have decided to study.

In order to analyse critical discourses expressed in the rock press, I chose metal bands that are well-known enough in the rock culture to be treated as the topic of features or reviews, small or big. Hence, I made the choice to cover groups that crossed over to the rock mainstream culture, such as Black Sabbath, Metallica, Mötley Crüe, Marilyn Manson, Slipknot and a few others. Some of these bands have been—and still are—controversial in metal culture, because of their level of success and fame. They don't necessarily embody the rebellion and the negation of the sick, sad world anymore, as they are fully integrated into the society they originally fought against. However, as I want to examine valorization processes articulated in the rock press, and as these groups are acknowledged as *metal* in mainstream rock culture, studying them will illuminate changes in the discourses about metal articulated by rock writers.

The rock press

The rock press can be viewed as a field. Pierre Bourdieu defines a field as a 'universe' where social actors play along certain rules, such as patterns of domination, legitimate opinions and valorizing instances (Bourdieu 2001). These rules are always already defined by actors and institutions populating the field, even though these agents are not necessarily aware of playing such games. On the field is a battle—a debate—in which various agents are engaged, and this creates a system of relationships. In the case of the field of the rock press, the main struggle over the years has been the construction and the establishment of the idea of good taste in popular music; I will return to this after this short history of the rock press field.

A number of actors and institutions have shaped the rock press field since the mid-to-late 1960s. Even though *Melody Maker* was launched in 1926 (at first, mostly a jazz and swing magazine) and the *New Musical Express* (concerned with teenage pop music) in 1952, serious journalism about rock music written by strong individual voices emerged with titles like *Crawdaddy!* (1966), *Rolling Stone* (1967) and *Creem* (1969) (Nunes 2004; Lindberg *et al.* 2005; Frith 1981). Eventually, the *Melody Maker* and the *New Musical Express* would both change their editorial practices to treat rock as a serious music and they joined the ranks of the most important voices in rock press. Over the years, some newspapers and magazines proved to be more read, more prestigious, more influential and more symbolically powerful within the field. It is those magazines and newspapers in particular that I include in my corpus: *Rolling Stone*, *Spin, Creem, Sounds, Q, New Musical Express, Melody Maker, Village Voice, Billboard*, etc., those whose archives can be accessed via their own websites, *Rock's Backpages* or the *International Index to Music Periodicals* (IIMP).

Although somewhat stable over the years, the rock press has changed a lot since its inception: topics of discussion; the ways articles are written; writers' statuses; different outlets for journalists; relationships between journalists, musicians and publicists; magazines' and newspapers' ownerships, etc. Establishing good taste, what counts as *good music*, has been, and still is, the rock press field's main debate. However, this debate has known many forms. First, rock was legitimated as an art form, around the mid-sixties (Gendron 2002). Then, during the late 1960s and early 1970s, some journalists debated about a 'revivalist' 1950s aesthetic (somewhat distorted by hindsight) in order to determine what 'good music' was: good music was perceived to be physically direct and energetic; by and for the people; authentic; unpretentious; unmediated; and created by auteurs (Gendron 2002; Guðmundsson *et al.* 2002). Later, punk fuelled another debate concerning the co-existence of art and commerce in rock music (Frith and Horne 1987; Gendron 2002; Lindberg *et al.* 2005). These debates eventually found resolution in a 'double aesthetic' for rock: romantic authenticity, with ideas of community, sincerity and directness; and modernist authenticity, putting forward ideas of artifice, irony and style (Lindberg *et al.* 2005; Keightley 2001). During the 1980s and 1990s, good taste was built on a sense of canonization in rock culture. A short list of recurrent musicians now seemingly inspire what counts as good music: The Beatles, the Rolling Stones, Bob Dylan, the Sex Pistols, Nirvana and Radiohead appear repeatedly in lists crowning best albums (Wyn Jones 2008). Rock canonization brings unity and stability to the rock press and to the rock field. However, this unity can be disturbed by the impact of the internet. The abundance of self-defined 'rock writers', through the accessibility and user-friendliness of blogs, the ubiquity of social networking and an abundance of information sources shake not only the foundation of good taste, but also the foundations of the rock writing profession.[1] In other words, nowadays, the leading question in the field concerns who has the right to decide what good music is. For professional rock writers the solution is to display more cultural capital.

As a matter of fact, how the internet has become an issue for rock writers shows how good taste is articulated with and by cultural capital. According to Bourdieu, capital is composed of all the different types of resources available, material and immaterial (Bourdieu 1979, 2001). Cultural capital, more specifically, comprises non-financial means that somebody possesses, hence it leans more towards the social, intellectual, even scholarly, spheres of life. For Bourdieu, what one knows, and the display of this knowledge, is the key to social mobility. Symbolic capital—the acknowledged prestige, honour and power other people give to one individual—derives partly from cultural capital. The field of the rock press and its uniting debate over good taste have been (and still are) articulated via rock writers' knowledge of rock and how they frame it in their writing. What causes music to be considered good or bad has been shaped by rock writers' struggles for cultural capital, their editorial choices and by the way they write: fitting in comparisons with other musicians; references to trends of the past; and learned adjectives: all of this happening without necessarily becoming a 'knowledge fight' between writers (even though it is hard to imagine a rock writer *not* being knowledgeable about rock music and its history). In other words, rock writers' cultural capital has shaped the rock press field.

Cultural capital can be displayed in many instances. Rock writers, as mediators between the record industry (constituted of musicians and record companies) and listeners, guide the latter, advising them as to what is supposedly best for them (Lindberg *et al.* 2005; Frith 1996). In the process, not only do rock writers legitimize themselves and their own endeavour (Gendron 2002) via the creation of their own symbolic power, but they also legitimize rock musicians and rock culture more generally. By legitimizing rock as an art form, rock writers have created (now highly consensual) 'truths' about rock music, 'truths' that are part of a full-blown 'rock mythology' (Regev 1994; Lindberg *et al.* 2005). Rock writing is a major player in the formation and the duration of consensus over the history and culture of rock, its meanings and its values (Shuker 1994). In other words, rock writers have the symbolic power to 'knight' and 'un-knight' particular recordings, musicians, scenes and phenomena.

From hated to recommended?

As rock writers have had such an influence in shaping rock culture, it is worth looking at how they have rated metal over the years in order to see how the perceptions that metal has always been hated hold up. For analytical purposes, I have divided rock writing discourses into three categories: authenticity strategies (how metal musicians prove their authenticity to show their legitimacy); historiographical (re)writings (how metal's story is told and retold somewhat positively through the years and how it is differentiated from other genres and made unique); and self-consciousness and art in metal (how metal gradually came to be described as art created by self-conscious, involved, musicians). These categories generally converge towards positive assessments of metal, contrary to the usual consensus (although there are obviously negative commentaries about various metal bands and subgenres over the years).

Authenticity strategies

One of most valued musical attributes, to rock writers, is authenticity. Of course, being authentic is not judged using an evaluative grid: rock writers each form and constantly redefine their own ideas of authenticity (Fornäs 1994). This cloudiness, however, does not mean that the concept of authenticity is not deeply rooted in rock culture. Showing authenticity often means being '*believable* relative to a more or less explicit model, and at the same time being *original*, that is, not being an imitation of the model' (Peterson 1997: 220, original italics). Authenticity is the value mobilized in order to demonstrate rock's validity and legitimacy (Keightley 2001). Rock is a 'good' music, a 'right' music, because it is 'true' and 'authentic', (supposedly) kept pure, away from commerce and business (Fornäs 1994). To the rock community, the opposite of authenticity resides in the 'sell-out' who makes music for commercial purposes. Hence, a series of binaries fuel the different distinctions: authentic versus sell-out; sincere versus poseur; art versus entertainment; 'mainstream versus independent; ... commercialism versus creativity' (Shuker 1994: 36). Rock values equate authenticity with independence and excellence; and commercialism with mediocrity and pretence.

As seen earlier, it is important to note that there are two major strands of authenticity, especially since punk: 'romantic authenticity' and 'modernist authenticity' (Keightley 2001). Even though these two authenticities can hardly be compared and are based on different assets, they represent the same preoccupations: sincerity and integrity in and of the artistic process, which has led to the notion of 'meta-authenticity' (Lindberg *et al.* 2005). Subversiveness is also a very important criterion and it has been portrayed as going hand in hand with authenticity: being authentic means being rebellious. Subversiveness can express itself in two ways: negation and resistance to routine, and a celebration of hedonism (Regev 1994). Accordingly, the less a musician (apparently) cares, the more praise s/he gets. Demonstrating authenticity requires strategies, employed consciously or not, in order to increase the worthiness of one's art. Thus, through authenticity strategies, metal musicians valorize themselves, the metal genre, and its culture and lifestyle.

First strategy: metal musicians pride themselves on making 'good music'. The quality of the music buttresses against possible accusations of being sellouts, even during periods of tremendous popular success. Thus, good music might equate to being 'real' or being 'valid'. Consider this quote from *Billboard* magazine: 'While the musical similarities between Papa Roach and Iron Maiden are there for the discerning fan, all most music lovers care about is if it's "real" and that it rocks' (Turman 2000: 84). However, there is another strand of discourse, equalling good (thus 'real') music with popular success. For example, Dave Mustaine, leader of Megadeth, states: 'There are so many different ways that people are trying to take apart the music industry and figure it out. It's really simple: Good music sells' (Mustaine, quoted in Reesman 2001: 34). This is quite contradictory. As a matter of fact, selling a vast amount of records can easily lead to accusations of inauthenticity, as this might make it seem like a musician or a band 'plays the industry's game'. So if 'good music' is 'real' and 'sells' at the same time, there's an inherent contradiction in this particular reasoning about authenticity. So how do the musicians 'who sell' get away with it?

To counter accusations of inauthenticity and to valorize themselves in the eyes of the rock press, metal musicians display a nonchalant attitude towards commercial success; this is the second strategy. Whether or not they really care about record sales is not important because metal musicians can shape their reception through interviews where the subject matter is music rather than financial success. For example, Mötley Crüe's bassist and primary songwriter Nikki Sixx says: 'I'd never even thought about things like number-one albums' (Sixx quoted in Kuipers 1990: 50). By expressing a specific idea of what success is (e.g. making good music, fulfilling dreams, being with friends on the road, putting on a show, etc.) and by not caring (or, at least, pretending not to care) about the business side of their career, metal musicians—especially those successful in the mainstream popular music sphere—avoid losing too much credibility in favour of the 'malevolent industry'. Therefore, they also valorize themselves by implying how involved they are in their music, how removed they are from pecuniary matters, and, ultimately, from everything 'rational' in the music (Stratton 1982, 1983). We will come back to this notion of involvement in the last section.

Consider for example Lars Ulrich, Metallica's drummer. His lawsuit against online peer-to-peer file-sharing service Napster, in 1999, has been framed not only as a dismissal of fans, but also as pure greed. Metallica's reputation among rock critics was not so favourable during the late 1990s and early 2000s (of course, the Napster story is only one of the threads explaining Metallica's bad press during this time). Contrasting this consideration in favour of the business side of music is Black Sabbath, as reported by Keith Altham:

> 'I must admit to being biased about [Black] Sabbath after meeting them for the first time—they struck me as *four typical Northern lads without pretention or affectation* who are busily playing *hard, exciting rock* and enjoying themselves while others enjoy their music' (Altham 1971, italics added).

Seemingly, being concerned with music and good times is a sign of success and authenticity that is valued by rock writers. Hence, making good music equates to being authentic and is often opposed to caring too much about what doesn't count: specifically the music business, but, more generally, anything that is not music. In rock press discourse, the contradiction inherent in the idea of 'good music that sells' is resolved in the *object* of involvement.

The third authenticity strategy deployed by metal musicians, and caught on by rock writers, is a sense of rebellion. Actually, going against the grain for metal musicians is determinant in their authenticity strategies, as metal culture is shaped for and by outcasts. Even actors in the metal subgenre retrospectively the most linked with mainstream rock culture, pop metal, portray themselves as rebels. Jani Lane, lead singer and songwriter for pop metal group Warrant, explains the pop metal comeback in the late 1990s like this:

> 'It sounds so cliche to say that hard rock is about rebellion, but it is. [...] It's like, "Screw you; we're gonna see what's big now and go the complete opposite way!" It's like, "Now we're gonna dress up again, 'cause we're sick of you flannel guys"' (Ali 1997).

By posturing themselves as mavericks, metal musicians oppose the 'dreaded' music industry (in Lane's words: 'what's big now'), but also distinguish themselves from discourses that might position them—and metal culture more generally—as being part of 'regular, boring and sick' society, the same society against which metal musicians and fans rebel.

A fourth authenticity strategy contributing to the valorization of metal culture is the sincerity and genuineness put forward by musicians. More than any other, this strategy is intertwined with the preceding ones. Making 'good music' is quite often paired with being genuine and credible:

> 'There was this big bulldozer that took any band that came out in the '80s, pushed them in a ditch and covered them with the dirt of Nirvana and Alice in Chains', [radio host Eddie] Trunk observes. 'But what was forgotten was that some of these bands were real, credible bands that never were about image and hair' (Miller 2001: 36).

Here, credibility, sincerity and writing good music are opposed to caring about 'image and hair', thus playing the 'business game'. Finally, a 'true' connection with the fans guarantees sincerity and credibility.

> 'None of the bands have sold out', he [Earache Records president and founder Digby Pearson] states. 'They are true to themselves, and the kids recognize and respect that. That's why this sound will stick around, because the bands have made a connection with the kids'. The health of hard rock and metal is, though, based not just on innovation and integrity but also its sense of tradition (Clark-Meads 1999: H–36).

In this quote, a 'sense of tradition' is identified as necessary in order for an artist to be 'true' to metal; being conscious that one is a part of a longer history of metal enhances credibility and sincerity in the making of 'authentic' metal music. This is what I will discuss in the next section.

Historiographical understandings of metal

Historiographical understandings of metal concern the different revisions, rearticulations and affiliations rock writers have endowed metal with over the years. Histories of rock are constantly being shaped, as they are constantly rewritten in consideration of current happenings within the field. With hindsight, we are able to judge the activities, the values and the culture of a particular period. We can compare and associate older values with more current ones, emphasizing what was relevant, thus (re)writing earlier accepted histories (Williams 1961). Rock writers often display historiographical reflexivity by selecting what they view as the most important past events in light of current trends (Straw 1990). This is important because rock writers have the symbolic power to shape rock culture and rock history, and, hence, what is important to know about them (Regev 1994; Shuker 1994).

As metal's story is retold and its historiographical understandings change, the question of its sustained economical success arises. Current metal histories tend to state that at its inception, early metal bands, such as Black Sabbath, Led Zeppelin and Grand Funk Railroad, enjoyed popularity as indicated by record and ticket sales. The 1980s are often described as a 'golden age' for pop metal acts, outselling any other genres: 'From the mid-'80s to the early part of '91, metal owned the land—everyone else was just paying rent' (Moses and Kaye 1999: H10). In the 1990s, this changes, although it is told that the scene was still financially lucrative: some metal superstars were still selling millions of records or enjoying back catalogue sales (Reesman 1999: H–44). Although 'wealth does not seem to be the prime motivator for the heavy metal band'

(Weinstein 2000: 87), financial success, embodied in record and ticket sales, are constantly used as indicators of the genre's longevity, durability, enduring power and, ultimately, its cultural legitimacy. Within a capitalist value system, long-term profitability demonstrates that a particular popular music genre can be sustainable over time: 'as popularity and robust sales maintain themselves in the *perceived* long run, the evaluations of critics often noticeably improve and stabilize. Longevity in economic accreditation pays dividends in aesthetic accreditation' (Gendron 2002: 175, original italics). In other words, a 'fad' ceases to be labelled as such when it makes enough money in the long run and becomes a 'real' cultural movement to be considered seriously; it then becomes 'here to stay', socially important and deserving of more thoughtful commentaries. Today, metal has proven to be a durable genre, undeniably present in the big rock mosaic due to its sustained selling power.

Also, rock journalists retrospectively distinguish metal from other genres, thus contributing to its social acknowledgement and cultural uniqueness. A genre oftentimes invoked to account for the 'birth' of metal is blues. Following a heavily stabilized version of history, blues 'naturally' evolved into metal:

> We all know that heavy metal came from the blues, we know that Willie Dixon, Muddy Waters, and B. B. King kicked the whole thing off, that white guys amped it a bit louder, that Jimi Hendrix twisted it into new shapes, and then Jimmy Page added malevolence to the mix and...eureka! Heavy metal (Sharpe-Young 2007: 8).

The association with blues appears as a founding act, attaching metal firmly to rock tradition and claiming its worthiness.

Metal's classical roots have also been remarked upon and discussed. Musical virtuosity and complexity, often derived from classical music, are highly valued in the world of metal. By insisting on these classical roots, in which the blues element gets somewhat purged, metal writers contribute to making metal an acknowledged 'higher' form of musical expression, as Walser (1993) has noticed. Rewriting metal this way has contributed to its acknowledgement as a unique genre.

Punk is another genre with which metal has been intertwined throughout the years, sometimes diametrically opposed, sometimes fused together. The comparisons and associations with punk reveal much of what is appreciated and unappreciated in metal. As early as the late 1970s, when UK punk emerged, metal (as well as progressive rock) was labelled as 'dinosaur rock', seemingly for its lack of excitement and, some say, innovation. In the words of rock journalist Sean Egan: 'When punk came along, all of metal's abundant flaws were embarrassingly exposed... Unlike heavy metal, it [punk] boasted an exciting tempo, no musical self-indulgence, a social conscience and lack of hostility to women' (Egan 2001: 57). However, it is interesting to note that, in other stories, metal and punk not only share the same characteristics, but that the former positively influenced the latter. If we are to believe the first champions of metal, Lester Bangs, Dave Marsh and Mike Saunders, early metal owes a great deal to punk rock, as it was conceived in the first half of the 1970s. This garage-style, pubescent, inept music shared a crude energy with early metal (Bangs 1992).[2] And it is not the only occasion that metal is likened to punk. Sean Egan, in the article quoted earlier, remarks that 'like heavy metal, punk was a form of music defined by riffs, razor-edged instrumentation and howling self-assertion' (Egan 2001: 57). Strangely, punk, with all its comparisons to metal, is consistently a winning genre. Judging from the discourse of rock writers, punk seems to be the embodiment of an 'ideal' genre: fast, crude, authentic, root-based.[3] These distinctions from and associations with blues, classical music and punk[4] define metal, pointing out metal's (good or bad) salient characteristics depending on the genre with which it is associated or against which it is discriminated.

Self-consciousness and artistry in metal

Critical reception of metal has changed due to a metamorphosis in the perception of what generally constitutes self-consciousness and artistry in metal and rock culture. Notions of self-consciousness and artistry rest on the judgement values developed and applied by rock critics; when one knows what is well received, one can make him/herself fit with whatever this is, somewhat deliberately. Earlier I noted that musicians are judged for their authenticity, but also on their subversiveness. This authenticity and subversion, however, must be qualified. Involvement could be considered as encompassing both authenticity and subversion (Stratton 1982; 1983). The rock press, having a separate economic system from the record industry, emphasizes the discursive aspect of music, representing it as a cultural artefact rather than a commercial product. In doing so, perhaps paradoxically, rock writing 'also emphasise[s] the non-analysability of the music from a rational, capitalist perspective' (Stratton 1983: 296). In other words, in as much as rock is defined as 'irrational' from a capitalist point of view in the rock press, the issue becomes about involvement: 'the most important criterion defining rock music centres around the idea of the emotional involvement of the artist with the music; ideally recognition of this will be achieved by the hearers on an intuitive, which is to say emotional level' (Stratton 1982: 281). Hence, this is a very instinctive notion, one that is hard to pin down, conjuring ideas of presence, of dedication, even enthusiasm.

For musicians, perceiving this involvement (rationally or not) is important, because they can curve their personas and their music towards constructing, maintaining and transmitting it. We have seen earlier how metal musicians often display a nonchalant attitude towards commercial success. This is actually involvement at work: this idea of dedication is mainly put forward through a priority given to the music, and anything else is seen as less important. If it is perceived that a musician's first priority is not music (such as megalomaniac ambitions, politics, drugs, sex, money), rock writers tend to judge him/her negatively. It is mainly a question of credibility.

This self-consciousness, rooted in involvement, is also a characteristic of the artistic attitude shaped in rock music. The idea that rock is art has been around at least since the 1960s, having its roots in art school teachings in the United Kingdom which resulted in students infusing their music with romantic values such as artistic freedom, individualism, authenticity and rebelliousness (Frith and Horne 1987). As they perceived themselves as artists, and as these musicians greatly shaped the sounds upon which future rock would rest,[5] the idea that rock is art emerged. However, as we have seen earlier, punk altered not only the ways in which value-judgements about contemporary popular music were articulated, but also the ways in which rock music itself was created and thought about. Many studies of popular music portray the punk movement, occurring during the late 1970s, as a great shifting moment when irony, post-modernity, avant-garde and artificiality converged (Grossberg 1990; Gendron 2002; Frith and Horne 1987). In short, the sources of emotional involvement, an important foundation upon which to judge music, changed. The punk movement introduced a plurality of ways of creating and appreciating art with less hierarchy between these aesthetics.

With this change in aesthetics resulting from the fallout of punk, metal, first described as stupid, inept, and non-artistic, gradually metamorphosed as serious, sophisticated and artful music. Some rock critics positively valued the ineptness in metal music during the 1970s and early 1980s while others did not. Similarly, sophistication in metal during the 1980s, 1990s and early 2000s was appreciated by some critics and loathed by others. For example, on the one hand Mike Saunders, in the early 1970s, thought highly of metal:

> Black Sabbath are one hell of a good rock and roll band. Their music is based on the same formula great rock'n'roll has always risen from (from Little Richard to the Stones to the Stooges), that of crude unrefined street clatter. There's absolutely nothing superfluous about Black Sabbath's music, as distinctly opposed to the school of Cream/Jeff Beck/Ten Years After egomania and interchangeable ten-minute jerk-off guitar solos (Saunders 1971a).

Rock writer legend Lester Bangs, known for his love of inept music, also likes it: 'As its detractors have always claimed, heavy-metal rock is nothing more than a bunch of noise; it is not music, it's distortion—and that is precisely why its adherents find it appealing' (Bangs 1992: 459). On the other hand, Mick Farren disparaged metal, precisely because of its ineptitude:

> At this point the fact has to be faced that Black Sabbath are simply low consciousness music. (At this point the ingratiating critic slips in a disclaimer.) There is nothing essentially wrong with a low consciousness. It's simply that I find it hard to relate to. I don't have one... This has to be atrophy music (Farren 1975).

The same for the influential Robert Christgau:

> The worst of the counterculture on a plastic platter—bullshit necromancy, drug-impaired reaction time, long solos, everything... I've been worried something like this was going to happen since the first time I saw a numerology column in an underground newspaper. C– (Christgau 1970).

It has to be noted that these writers made these comments before punk happened; they like or dislike metal precisely because it is 'stupid-rock' (Saunders 1971b).

But metal is generally not considered stupid anymore. The pluralism motivated indirectly by punk and a certain kind of post-modernism in rock culture put forward a movement where the artistry of this music is no longer questioned. Today, metal music is worthy of being taken seriously. Even though it is sometimes undervalued, its compound character is acknowledged:

> MTV X [hard-rock music television channel] is dominated by that nearly lame horse called, for reasons unknown to me, nü metal... It's just a convenient tag for hard rock that uses metal riffs and crunch, hardcore punk barking occasional ersatz rapping (although this seems to be disappearing), and occasional new-wave crooning over synths and electronics (Seward 2001: 71).

Today, it seems like there is no question that metal is considered to be art among rock critics. For example, Strauss writes:

> Never has there been a rock star quite as complex as Marilyn Manson, frontman of the band of the same name... When it comes to getting serious about his work, Manson is among the most eloquent and artful musicians... *Antichrist Superstar*, recorded during eight months with Reznor in New Orleans, is an incredible leap of

prowess, a technically, musically and lyrically sophisticated album (Strauss 1997).

Furthermore, metal musicians claim the seriousness they put into their art. For example, Shawn Crahan, one of Slipknot's percussionists, points it out:

> We're not here to follow. We're here to break the monotony and the rules of efficiency. An artist's job is to be out of their mind to help the evolution of the species. I'm tired of wisecracks about us—we are serious and take this shit seriously (Crahan, quoted in Bozza 2001).

Hence, there appears to have been a change in the reception of metal after the punk movement. Metal underwent a change of status: it went from 'stupid' and 'unsophisticated' music to 'artful' and 'serious'.

Conclusion

It seems as if the idea that metal has always been hated by the rock press is more based on perceptions than on facts. However, the reasons why it has been received positively from its inception until now have changed since the 1970s. Not only has the foundation for assessing authenticity changed, but the struggles uniting the rock press field have also shifted. Good taste is not necessarily embodied by a 'revivalist aesthetic' anymore (which metal embodied quite well, for some writers), but it is also defined by canonization. Since metal has remained in the field of rock production for forty years, it is perhaps justifiably canonized: Black Sabbath entered the Rock and Roll Hall of Fame in 2006. However, metal is still perceived as a persecuted genre by some. Why? One possible reason is that metal requires a sense of rejection, especially for fans, in order to thrive; because acknowledging its mainstream acceptance would mean its death by inauthenticity. Moreover, the impression that metal is rejected by the mainstream unites headbangers, thus increasing the strength and appeal of the subculture for those who feel they do not 'fit in'. To paraphrase members of Slipknot, could this be the triumph of the maggots, of headbangers? With metal's valorization in the rock press, and its everlasting outsider status, metal might just have the best of both worlds.

Notes

1. For more details, read the articles composing the 'Music Journalism R.I.P.?' feature of *Drowned In Sound* (July 2009)—see bibliography below.
2. What is particularly interesting with punk is that it was a discursive formation before being a musical genre. 'Punk' as a musical label has been around since the

early 1970s, made famous by Lester Bangs, Lenny Kaye, Greg Shaw and Dave Marsh, and referring then to a type of 'garage' music done by American teenagers during the mid-1960s (Gendron 2002; Waksman 2009). The label eventually changed to refer to the rebellious, mostly-UK, minimalist musical movement in the late 1970s (and now to even a more confusing composite), although there are some formal and substantial links to be made between this late 1970s movement and American mid-1960s 'garage' music (Gendron 2002).

3.   A closer inspection of the critical discourses about punk could demonstrate or qualify this claim.

4.   Other genre distinctions are at work when rock writers discuss metal: progressive rock and grunge are also very important genres against which metal was—and still is—defined.

5.   Important musicians such as John Lennon, Keith Richards, Eric Clapton, Pete Townshend, Jeff Beck, Eric Burdon, Freddie Mercury, Syd Barrett and Cat Stevens all attended UK art schools (Frith and Horne 1987).

Bibliography

Ali, Lorraine. 1997. 'Rock & Roll: Devil's Haircut'. *Rolling Stone*, 21 August.

Altham, Keith. 1971. 'Black Sabbath: Nobody but the Public Digs Sabbath'. *Record Mirror*, 30 January.

Bangs, Lester. 1992. 'Heavy Metal'. In *The Rolling Stone Illustrated History of Rock & Roll*, ed. Anthony DeCurtis, James Henke and Holly George-Warren, 459–63. New York: Random House.

Bourdieu, Pierre. 1979. *La distinction: critique sociale du changement*. Paris: Éditions de Minuit.

—2001. *Langage et pouvoir symbolique*. Paris: Éditions Fayard.

Bozza, Anthony. 2001. 'Highway to Hell'. *Rolling Stone*, 11 October.

Bryson, Bethany. 1996. '"Anything but Heavy Metal": Symbolic Exclusion and Musical Tastes'. *American Sociological Review* 61(5): 884–99. http://dx.doi.org/10.2307/2096459

Christgau, Robert. 1970. 'Black Sabbath'. *Robert Christgau: Dean of American Rock Critics*. http://www.robertchristgau.com/get_artist.php?name=black+sabbath.

Clark-Meads, Jeff. 1999. 'Smoke Across the Water: Brits Fire Up'. *Billboard*, 5 June.

Drowned in Sound. 'Music Journalism R.I.P?' http://drownedinsound.com/lists/ismusic-journalismdead.

Egan, Sean. 2001. 'Heavy Metal Thunder: The Roots of a 35-Year-Old Genre'. *Goldmine*, 1 June.

Farren, Mick. 1975. 'Black Sabbath—Sabotage'. *New Musical Express*, 11 October.

Fornäs, Johan. 1994. 'Listen to Your Voice! Authenticity and Reflexivity in Rock, Rap and Techno Music'. *New Formations* 24: 155–73.

Frith, Simon. 1981. *Sound Effects: Youth, Leisure, and the Politics of Rock 'n' Roll*. New York: Pantheon Books.

—1996. *Performing Rites: On the Value of Popular Music*. Cambridge, MA: Harvard University Press.

Frith, Simon, and Howard Horne. 1987. *Art into Pop*. London: Methuen.

Gendron, Bernard. 2002. *Between Montmartre and the Mudd Club: Popular Music and the Avant-Garde.* Chicago: University of Chicago Press.

Grossberg, Lawrence. 1990. 'Is There Rock after Punk?' In *On Record: Rock, Pop and the Written Word*, ed. Simon Frith and Andrew Goodwin, 111–23. London and New York: Routledge.

Guðmundsson, Gestur, Ulf Lindberg, Morten Michelsen and Hans Weisethaunet. 2002. 'Brit Crit: Turning Points in British Rock Criticism, 1960–1990'. In *Pop Music and the Press*, ed. Steve Jones, 41–64. Philadelphia: Temple University Press.

Jones, Carys Win. 2008. *The Rock Canon: Canonical Values in the Reception of Rock Albums.* Burlington, VT: Ashgate.

Keightley, Keir. 2001. 'Reconsidering Rock'. In *The Cambridge Companion to Pop and Rock*, ed. Simon Frith, Will Straw and John Street, 109–42. Cambridge: Cambridge University Press. http://dx.doi.org/10.1017/CCOL9780521553698.008

Kuipers, Dean. 1990. 'Beyond the Valley of the Ultra Glam Boys'. *Spin*, January.

Lindberg, Ulf, Gestur Guðmundsson, Morten Michelsen and Hans Weisethaunet. 2005. *Rock Criticism from the Beginning: Amusers, Bruisers, and Cool-Headed Cruisers.* New York: Peter Lang.

Miller, Geri. 2001. 'Still Rockin' after All These Years'. *Billboard*, 23 June.

Moses, Michael, and Don Kaye. 1999. 'What Did You Do in the War, Daddy?' *Billboard*, 5 June.

Nunes, P. 2004. 'Popular Music and the Public Sphere: The Case of Portuguese Music Journalism'. PhD dissertation, Stirling University.

Peterson, Richard. 1997. *Creating Country Music: Fabricating Authenticity.* Chicago: University of Chicago Press.

Reesman, Bryan. 1999. 'Big Hair, Big Comeback: '80s Metal Rocks Anew'. *Billboard*, 5 June.

—2001. 'Hard Music: Sustaining the Success'. *Billboard*, 23 June.

Regev, Motti. 1994. 'Producing Artistic Value: The Case of Rock Music'. *Sociological Quarterly* 35(1): 85–102. http://dx.doi.org/10.1111/j.1533-8525.1994.tb00400.x

Saunders, Mike. 1971a. 'Black Sabbath: Master of Reality'. *The Rag*, 20 September.

—1971b. 'Sir Lord Baltimore—Kingdom Come'. *Creem*, May.

Seward, Scott. 2001. 'Heard it on the X'. *Village Voice*, 28 August.

Sharpe-Young, Garry. 2007. *Metal: The Definitive Guide.* London: Jawbone Press.

Shuker, Roy. 1994. *Understanding Popular Music.* London and New York: Routledge.

Stratton, Jon. 1982. 'Between Two Worlds: Art and Commercialism in the Record Industry'. *The Sociological Review* 30(2): 267–83. http://dx.doi.org/10.1111/j.1467-954X.1982.tb00757.x

—1983. 'What is "Popular Music"?' *The Sociological Review* 31(2): 293–309. http://dx.doi.org/10.1111/j.1467-954X.1983.tb00391.x

Strauss, Neil. 1997. 'Sympathy for the Devil'. *Rolling Stone*, 23 January.

Straw, Will. 1990. 'Characterizing Rock Music Culture: The Case of Heavy Metal'. In *On Record: Rock, Pop and the Written Word*, ed. Simon Frith and Andrew Goodwin, 97–110. London and New York: Routledge.

Turman, Katherine. 2000. 'Where Does it Go from Here?' *Billboard*, 2 December.

Waksman, Steve. 2009. *This Ain't the Summer of Love: Conflict and Crossover in Heavy Metal and Punk.* Berkeley: University of California Press.

Walser, Robert. 1993. *Running with the Devil: Power, Gender and Madness in Heavy Metal Music*. Middletown, CT: Wesleyan University Press.

Weinstein, Deena. 2000. *Heavy Metal: The Music and its Culture*. Cambridge and New York: Da Capo Press.

Williams, Raymond. 1961. *The Long Revolution*. New York: Columbia University Press.

Videography

Dunn, Sam, Scot McFadyen, and Jessica Joy Wise. 2005. *Metal: A Headbanger's Journey*. Produced by Sam Dunn and Scot McFadyen. Canada: Banger Films.

Dunn, Sam, and Scot McFadyen. 2007. *Global Metal*. Produced by Sam Dunn, Scot McFadyen and Victoria Hirst. Canada: Banger Films.

Dworkin's nightmare

Porngrind as the sound of feminist fears

Lee Barron

Northumbria University, UK

> METAL SIDE: Feminism is in my opinion one of the most dangerous sickness (*sic*) of the contemporary mind. Would you agree with me?
>
> WACO JESUS: With a song title like 'blast you in the face with my semen, then I blast you in the face with my fist', what would you think (*sic*).

This chapter explores the relationship between extreme metal and gender, and specifically the sexual representation of women in a relatively obscure 'underground' metal subgenre that developed in the 1990s—porngrind. With a sound rooted within punk-tinged UK grindcore and more specifically death metal, a subgenre characterized by its 'unbridled sonic brutality and lyrical glorification of all things morbid and decaying' (Moynihan and Søderlind 2003: 29), porngrind fuses the gore/death lyrical content of such forms with a sustained focus on sexual explicitness, sexual violence and misogyny. Initially associated with the German grindcore bands, Gut, and Cock and Ball Torture, a multitude of bands would emerge to constitute this distinctive subgenre ultimately dubbed 'porngrind' due to its focus upon pornographic imagery. While not exhaustive, porngrind is typified by bands such as: Soldered Poon, Anal Penetration, Spermswamp, Anal Whore, AxHxPxPx, Waco Jesus, Lividity, and Meatshits. Although displaying some differing sonic approaches (many bands favour a death/grindcore sound, while others employ techno/rap influences), they are all bands that are thematically united via their use of extreme pornographic imagery and themes. Commercially, porngrind arguably errs towards the 'underground' and its proponents do not typically enjoy the cultural visibility of other extreme metal bands (Cannibal Corpse, for example). Indeed, while qualitative indicators of popularity from convergent platforms such as YouTube show song hit rates ranging from the hundreds to the tens of thousands, Shane Botten, the singer with Waco Jesus, ably illustrates the underground nature of the form, stating that he has a dual identity, that of extreme metal musician and a construction worker, 'because people who play this type of music sure the fuck aren't doing it for the money' (Brutalism.com). Moreover, while a precise number of bands falling beneath the porngrind tag may be difficult to articulate, unlike death metal, it is a smaller and more exclusive subgenre, with the primary examples numbering no more than double figures. Therefore, the form of metal music to be explored within this chapter is a little-discussed one (Purcell [2003] makes a brief mention of it but does not explore the form in detail).

However, the theme and argument of this chapter is the relationship between porngrind and feminist positions on pornography. While this may appear inevitable given the subject-matter of the music, this chapter will analyse porngrind in direct relation to the approach of Andrea Dworkin, the now-classic anti-pornography feminist writer whose trenchant critique of pornography rests upon the assertion it represents nothing less than the debasement and victimization of women; that it is a mode of cultural practice that is complicit with male sexual violence, and the murder and rape of women. Dworkin's anti-pornography perspective has been subject to extensive critique and re-evaluation since publication in terms of censorship, female sexuality, and the authoritarian nature of her critique (Vance 1984; Assiter 1989; Wilson 1991; Segal 1993; Thompson 1994; Judges 1995; Kipnis 1996; Shellrude 2001; Marinucci 2005; Snyder-Hall 2010). Furthermore, debates concerning the cultural visibility of sexuality, sexual identity and pornography have developed extensively, from the proliferation of queer theory to research that suggests that pornographic consumption is not solely the preserve of males, nor is it conclusively 'harmful' (Williams 1990; Strossen 1994; Attwood 2002; Attwood and Smith 2010). However, having acknowledged such developments, I will use Dworkin's arguments as a reference point in a deliberate manner. Although the pornography/feminism debate has long-since transcended her position, there remains a distinctive correlation between Dworkin's articulation of pornography and that which is conveyed by numerous porngrind bands. As such, I will argue that porngrind centrally reflects the salient perceptions Dworkin levels at pornography within her seminal text, *Pornography: Men Possessing Women* (1981): that it expresses patriarchal oppression, that it constitutes a manual for rape, and that it can involve violence against women as a form of male gratification. As such, porngrind frequently appears as if its purveyors are versed with Dworkin's work, and have set out to purposely represent the worst excesses of her perception of the 'reality' of pornography. Additionally, this chapter will also suggest that the subject-matter of porngrind also points to a degree of proximity between it and Dworkin. Although it represents her nightmarish vision of pornography, the ways in which porngrind bands emphasize the male perspective with regards to sexual acts, and regard sex as an act of domination, brutal oppression and triumphant 'possession' of women's bodies actually accords with Dworkin's perception of the association of sex, sexual acts and violence within male sexuality and as expressed within pornography.

Metal, feminism and pornography

From its beginnings, heavy metal music has been continually dismissed by critics who have concluded that it is a 'genre' thematically dominated by 'violence and aggression, raping and carnage' (Bangs 1992: 459), a musical form that has long been perceived as a source of social fears with its apparent advocacy of violence, social harm, murder, drug-abuse, and nihilism (Arnett 1992; Binder 1993; Wright 2000; Wilson 2008). Furthermore, heavy metal has consistently been read as a bastion of sexism and patriarchal oppression in terms of lyrical content, album imagery and video performance. Walser, for instance, argues that classic heavy metal is a discourse that directly reflects patriarchy and patriarchal values. As he states in relation to bands such as Guns 'N' Roses, Poison, W.A.S.P., Whitesnake, and Mötley Crüe: 'for much of its history metal has been appreciated and supported primarily by a teenage, male audience' (1993: 154), and consistently expresses 'exscription'—the denial of any gender angst 'through the articulation of fantastic worlds without women' (1993: 155). Although Walser's research is now somewhat dated, the male-centredness of metal fandom and the issue of the marginality of women within metal scenes, either as fans or performers, has remained a significant and persistent factor (Krenshe and McKay 2000; Kahn-Harris 2007; Selfhout, Delsing and ter Bogt 2008). However, Walser does draw an interesting comparison between metal and pornography, stressing that both tend to eschew representations of sexual violence because of the demands and pressures of patriarchal hegemony. Consequently, gender violence within pornography (and metal) music would act as a disruptive force, damaging the patriarchal ideology that transmits the naturalness of sexual relations and their foundations in love. Walser argues that due to their normalizing patriarchal patterns, both pornography and metal seldom link sex with violence. But this is not the case with regard to extreme metal subgenres. It is present within death metal, and it is the defining feature of porngrind—a metal form that consistently equates sex with violence. Although the pervasive source of imagery and lyrical inspiration within extreme expressions of heavy metal music (thrash, grindcore, death or black) tends to find inspiration from horror fiction, and especially the horror film (Arnett 1996; Weinstein 2000; Barron and Inglis 2009), porngrind (as the appellation unambiguously indicates) takes its inspiration from pornographic imagery, and exactly the perception of pornography that fuels a feminist anti-pornography position based upon the assertion that all forms of pornographic imagery is synonymous with violence, sexual oppression, female dehumanization, humiliation, rape and murder.

Although the feminist critique of pornography includes a number of commentators (Gloria Steinem, Robin Morgan and Catherine MacKinnon, for example), it was Andrea Dworkin's 1981 book, *Pornography: Men Possessing Women*, which would be the leading critical work, and Dworkin the primary advocate for the total censorship of pornography. In Dworkin's analysis, the foremost theme of pornography lies in male power, because male sexuality is inherently related to domination, the objectification of women and violence. Accordingly, pornography exposes the extent to which 'male pleasure is inextricably tied to victimizing, hurting, exploiting; that sexual fun and sexual passion in the privacy of the male imagination are inseparable from the brutality of male history' (1981: 69). Consequently, male supremacy is dependent upon the capacity of men to perceive women as purely sexual objects. Indeed, the link between pornography and female degradation is rooted within its etymology. As Dworkin states, the word 'pornography' is rooted in the Greek words 'porne' and 'graphos', which translates as 'writing about whores'. Furthermore, little has changed with regard to this 'slavish' meaning in contemporary culture, and its dissemination (from graphos/writing to photography, film and video) consists of images and scenes in which 'real women are tied-up, stretched, hanged, fucked, gang-banged, whipped, beaten, and begging for more' (1981: 201).

So, according to Dworkin, pornography is the primary expression of male sexual power, and it is suffused with violence, and even sexual murder. Diana Russell concurs: 'some pornography celebrates extreme torture, mutilation, and sexualised "Femicide"—the misogynist killing of women by males for sexual gratification' (1998: 39). In this analysis, pornography plays a central causal role within rape and sexual assault, and Dworkin attributes the blame to de Sade, who she identifies as the primary influence on modern pornography, and who, through his lurid tales of eroticism fused with torture, inextricably linked sex with brutality and violence. Although Dworkin claims that *all* pornography is degrading and steeped in violence, she cites a particular example that seemingly proved that male oppression was being given expression in murderous pornographic form: the 'snuff film'. According to Dworkin, in the mid-1970s in the United States, 'organised crime reportedly sold "snuff" films to private collectors of pornography. In these films, women actually were maimed, sliced into pieces, fucked, and killed' (1981: 71). Although accorded the status of a moral panic (Thompson 1994), the themes raised by the snuff panic would be perpetuated within porngrind, and Dworkin's strident articulation of the nature of pornography.

Porngrind, misogyny and anti-feminism

For Williams (2004), the essence of pornography is that it represents sexual acts and fantasies that seek to arouse viewers, and fails as a pornographic text if it does not do this. Porngrind, as I will discuss, although music, nevertheless is invariably packaged as a pornographic 'text'. It is an example of popular music that takes pornography as its inspirational source, However, in addition to painted artworks, the consistent thread that runs throughout porngrind is the extensive use of photographs that displays extreme imagery of female bodies, sexual scenarios, genital penetration, fellatio and other sexual acts, many evidently drawn from pornographic texts, and often displaying 'underground' or fetish images (anal sex, oral sex, S&M, and the use of faeces, urine, vomit or mucus). Hence, pornography and pornographic imagery are not causal or tangential reference points; rather, they are the essence of porngrind. Moreover, they keenly articulate sexual explicitness and violence in such a way that reflects the anti-pornography feminist position, sometimes by happenstance, but also as a deliberate strategy, as the key examples discussed in this chapter will illustrate.

But what does porngrind look and sound like as a subgenre? A striking characteristic is that its sound can vary markedly. For example, while some bands favouring a death/grindcore sound and consist of full bands (guitars, bass, drums, vocals), others employ 'techno' sounds achieved via drum machines, sequencers and sampling, or consist of one member driven by frenetic drum-machine beats. However, the subgenre coalesces via their use of extreme pornographic imagery and their aggressive approach to the representation of women. Thus, the intrinsic connection between pornography and extreme violence that typifies Dworkin's argument can be readily located within porngrind. For instance, the international band Soldered Poon (from Morocco, Belgium and Israel) fuse explicit album imagery with song titles that consist of bizarre sexual scenarios aligned with pornographic themes and images, all beneath a moniker that conjures a horrific image of female bodily mutilation. While albums such as *Chapter of Maliciousness* and *A Chapter of Pornography* display images that combine sexuality, sadism, submission, murder and graphic nudity, the former consisting of an artwork that displays a zombie dismembering a bound woman, the latter takes the form of an S&M rear-view image of a naked woman who is gagged and strapped to a wooden post, and in a post-coital condition as suggested by the semen-like substance dripping from her exposed vagina. Yet, while the pornographic features of the albums are unequivocal and extreme, the songs range from the sexually macabre—'Death From Anal Orgasm' and 'Quadruple Anal Penetration'—to the ludicrous: 'Masturbating In Front Of Old Ladies On Wheelchairs', 'Masturbating With A Cactus Dildo', 'Masturbating To A Photo Of Your Dead Cat', and 'Masturbating With Your Grandma's Ashes Under Your Foreskin'. On the one hand, there is an obvious degree of humour present, a sense of deliberate excess that Kipnis (1996) locates within pornography, for example the 'carnivalesque' anti-authority and excessive (but deliberate) content of *Hustler* magazine. As such, Soldered Poon's song titles can invite laughter. However, on the other hand, the graphic imagery of the album art works to destabilize such a reading from a feminist perspective. The song titles may be ridiculous, but the imagery unequivocally links sexuality and the female with, at worse, violence and murder, but more conventionally, submissiveness and graphic representation drawn from S&M pornography.

In a similar manner, Anal Penetration, a Dutch one-man-band created by 'Nydoom', also expresses humour with regard to sexual subject matters conveyed by a sound that consists of a relentless distorted guitar-driven assault, propelled by an incessant 'machine-gun-like' drum-machine percussion—a key distinguishing factor that separates many porngrind bands from the 'organic' musical instruments of grindcore/death metal. The songs are further punctuated by vocals that shift from a gurgling growl to high-pitched screams and shrill tones. Akin to Soldered Poon, Anal Penetration albums such as *Dutch Depravity* contains songs with the sexually bizarre titles of 'At The Bestiality Farm', 'Sodomized By A Domestic Goat', 'Locked Up In A Testicle', and 'Fucked With A Clog'. However, later recordings lack this 'comedic' edge, focusing more firmly on misogyny and sexual violence. For example, the *Spray For Jesus* album displays 'sacrilegious' artwork that consists of Nydoom's face superimposed onto a statue of Christ against a background photograph of a naked woman urinating, visually (and graphically) emphasizing the pun of the title. Beginning with a sampled extract from a pornographic film, the album consists of songs that routinely equate sex with domination and violence, as evidenced by titles such as: 'Baise Moi', 'Where Next To Fuck Her', 'Cheap Ass Bitches', 'Suck Or Die', 'Power Of My Cock' and 'Beatings From My Evil Sword'. In terms of sexual semantics and posturing, the latter song perfectly adheres to Dworkin's assertion that within male culture, the penis is perceived and used as 'a weapon, especially a sword' (1981: 56). Hence, sexuality is centred upon male physical domination and the expression of power. As such, 'Beatings From My Evil Sword' reflects exactly Dworkin's assessment of the sexual act as an instance of violence and violation—the exercise of male power, and nothing else.

Violence in relation to explicit sexuality and extreme pornography are also further central with reference to the bands that can be argued to represent 'pure' porngrind, such as Canada's Spermswamp. As such, their *Extreme Cream* mixes images of female nudity and sexual acts with a sci-fi theme (the cover depicts an alien ejaculating green semen over a compliant naked woman), but also features an acknowledgements list that consists exclusively of the names of contemporary female porn actresses (including: Jenna Jameson, Jill Kelly, Asia Carrera, Tera Patrick and Aurora Snow); demonstrating an acute awareness of the pornography scene and registering their fandom of it. However, the German one-man-band outfit, Anal Whore's album, *Pornorama*, contains a disclaimer announcing that it represents '100% Noisy Porn Grind', reflexively tagging itself within this subgenre, and confirming that the subgenre exists. This is a claim validated by album imagery that is dominated by photographs of naked women, exposed female genitals, lesbian bondage, and scenes of women performing fellatio. Indeed, the graphic and unrestrained nature of the band is aptly illustrated by the way in which its band's album-cover insignia, an A and W, is spelled out by rear-view shots of two naked women who contort their bodies to mimic the letters. In terms of sound, Anal Whore demonstrates a unique aspect of the porngrind form. This is signified at one level by the extensive use of samples, a central technique within rap and hip hop (Miyakawa 2005), but here used to insert audio clips from pornographic movies. However, the vocal style is also of significance. Unlike the 'demonic', guttural and 'inhuman' cadence of grindcore and death metal bands, the vocals of Anal Whore consist of a gurgling, liquid rattle that is utterly incomprehensible, and consequently completely indecipherable (Soldered Poon exhibit a similar quality)—meaning that the explicit nature of the lyrics is masked. But the song titles unambiguously stress that the representation of pornography is intimately linked with misogyny and sexual violence. Hence, the album contains a large number of (frequently abruptly short) songs bearing titles like: 'Adrenaline pumps through my veins as i (*sic*) punch the bitch in the face and fuck her at the same time', 'Sex mixed with violence—who said this can't be fun?', 'Absolute Obedience', 'There will be pain as much as there will be pleasure', 'Why do women bleed once a month? Because they deserve it' and 'Snuff bitch superstar'.

However, it could be argued that the extremism of porngrind is not intrinsically linked with anti-feminist attitudes, but rather reflects the nature of a form of music that displays a marked tendency to 'nihilistically wallow in the depths of taboo' (Baddeley 1999: 168). Consequently, porngrind may be simply conforming to the expectations of extreme metal: sub-generic offshoots that base their identity upon purposely shocking imagery, effacing moral boundaries while producing severe sounds. In this regard, 'Andy Baby', the sole member of Anal Whore, provides a statement within the inner-sleeve notes of *Pornorama* that (albeit in a non-politically correct fashion) claims that: 'THIS IS

ONLY MUSIC', suggesting a deliberate employment of sexual excess. Support- ing this, the idea of performativity and play with regard to offensive lyrics or images is found elsewhere within extreme metal. As Kahn-Harris states of the charges of racism and fascism made in relation to the Norwegian black metal band, Darkthrone, though many songs invite such critiques, the band claimed that they were non-political in nature, thus, they were arguably 'cynically uti- lizing reflexive anti-reflexivity in order to maximize the transgressive poten- tial of racist discourse' (2007: 152). As such, Andy Baby's disavowal could be read in a similar manner: it is all game-play and deliberate transgression— shock tactics to maximize visibility and bestow a clear sense of extreme iden- tity to the band. In spite of that, in relation to the nature of the imagery that adorns the albums, this renunciation of any 'real' sexism is inadequate from many feminist perspectives because the images conform centrally to a porno- graphic discourse that objectifies women from an aggressive and belligerent male point-of-view.

This latter view is supported in relation to albums such as *XXX Ways*, featur- ing the Belgian band, AxHxPxPx. The imagery that dominates this album deliber- ately apes pornographic magazines, and specialist pornography as it possesses an explicit cover that consists of images of naked women, and scenes of pen- etrative anal sex; while the inner sleeve continues with its uninhibited visual approach, with its close-up images of vaginal penetration, exposed female genitals, oral sex, and masturbation. Although *XXX Ways* displays a magazine- like declaration that it is '100% Porn', songs such as 'Raped and Happy' work to further reinforce the tendency within porngrind to equate sexual activ- ity and pornographic presentation with lyrical content that emphasizes male violence and rape fantasy. Therefore, within porngrind, pornography seldom equates to sex. It rarely merely concerns desire or even voyeurism. It is, alter- natively, about the worst excesses of sexuality and routinely links the practice of sex with acts of brutality and violence. Indeed, the idea of 'snuff', Dworkin's apparent 'proof' of the violent/murderous nature of pornography, is preva- lent, from song titles to band names (Snuff Fetish and Snuffgrinder, for exam- ple). Therefore, the graphic images and sexually aggressive sensibilities located within porngrind reflect those offered by Dworkin within the pages of *Pornog- raphy: Men Possessing Women*. But there are further examples that cement the porn/violence link far more explicitly, and which render a reflexive or excessive approach problematic.

Sonically, many exponents of porngrind are indebted to the lyrical and stylistic tropes of death metal, particularly that produced by the American bands, Lividity and Waco Jesus. Taking Lividity's *The Age of Clitoral Decay* album as a prime example of their output, with the shared vocals of Matt Bishop and Dave Kibler alternating between 'demonic' guttural death-style growls and high-pitched shrieking, complete with blast beats and relentless guitar riffs, Lividity blend the pornographic with horror, utilizing dialogue samples drawn from horror and pornographic films. The album artwork represents a similar combination of the pornographic and the horrific, or combinations of this theme. For instance, the cover image depicts a naked woman displaying a 'vagina dentata' in the form of fanged snakes emerging from her sexual organ, while the inner sleeve imagery consists of a montage of band photographs intermingled with explicit photographic images of female genitalia. Signifying their death metal influences, the inner sleeve also contains an original artwork depicting zombies sexually assaulting and murdering a woman in a graveyard. Lyrically, within songs such as: 'The Urge To Splurge', 'Anal Action Wife', 'Oozing Vaginal Discharge', 'Dismembering Her Lifeless Corpse' and 'Sodomy Ritual', sex, pornography, torture and murder are habitually intermingled, with a frequent emphasis within the lyrics upon acts of rape, cannibalism and necrophilia. Consequently, the 'world' conjured by Lividity is one in which women are consigned the status of 'whores' and sexuality is unremittingly from the violent perspective of the male: women are forcibly 'taken', and there is no hint of mutual pleasure in the sex act. Subsequently, there is little space for any self-consciously transgressive reading; instead the pornographic onus of these songs serves to reflect Dworkin's perception of both pornography and male sexuality: that they equate to violence, domination and nothing else.

Opponents of Dworkin's approach have attacked it on numerous fronts: for its anecdotal methodological approach, to its narrow focus upon the issue of pornography as the root of all gender ills, to the detriment of economics and culture (Segal 2004). Furthermore, it is argued that Dworkin denies women any status as sexual agents and portrays women as passive and helpless victims—thus disempowering femininity (Kendrick 1996; Brown 2006), that her 'fundamentalist' analysis is divisive, heterophobic and denies any possibility of 'female sexual pleasure and desire' (Heartney 1991: 17). However, while Dworkin's vision of pornography was difficult to culturally locate in terms of general pornographic production, porngrind does represent it. Within this brand of metal music, sex *is* synonymous with the penis, the penis is a 'weapon' of terror, and (agreeing with Dworkin) female desire is irrelevant. Thus, for Dworkin and for bands such as Lividity, sex is a male preserve that inevitably involves violence and degradation. As such, porngrind's utilization of explicit imagery is its central component, and they are related (if not frequently identical) to the images found within hardcore pornographic magazines.

Numerous porngrind recordings feature graphic photography and artwork that display woman's faces extensively daubed with semen, or, in the case of the five-way band release—appropriately entitled *Facial Humiliation*—cover art consisting of a photograph of a young woman's face being urinated upon simultaneously by two men. In other instances, inner artwork features photographs of women ejecting mucus and vomit into the mouths of other women as a sexual spectacle. There is also a seam of porngrind that depicts graphic images of sexual acts that involve coprophilia (the sexual use of excrement), an act that the British Home Office, in reviewing pornographic production, stated involved 'the total degradation of the person subject of such acts...enjoyed by sadists' (Attwood and Smith 2010: 173–74). Accordingly, in addition to songs that centrally deal with coprophilic themes, such issues are graphically presented in album imagery. For example, the nine-way and one hundred-way albums, *Splatter Fetish* and *Uncontrollable Laxative Abuse*, both feature artwork that explicitly and vividly depict excessive coprophilic images of excretion and the consumption of excrement. However, these are painted artworks, whereas Waco Jesus' 1999 album, *The Destruction of Commercial Scum*, contains a series of photographs of sexual acts and submissive poses that intimately involve faeces (consumption, photographs of defecation, men and women's faces smeared with excrement). Similarly, their *Filth* album displays a close-up image of a women's anus while she is in the throes of defecation. As with the *Facial Humiliation* album and various images of bodily fluids, Waco Jesus' artworks are real pornographic images, not simulations that display extreme scatological pornographic images. However, Waco Jesus also expresses an ideological message that consciously links such pornographic images with sexual violence and a defiantly anti-feminist rhetoric. Such sentiments are present within *The Destruction of Commercial Scum*, an album which, in addition to its startlingly graphic imagery, also contains a number of songs that are unequivocal in their misogyny and aggressive perception of sex, principally: 'Mass Pussy Obliteration', 'Strangled Then Revived', 'Virgin Assassin', and 'Cunt Killer'. Furthermore, the sexual violence of *The Destruction of Commercial Scum* would be similarly expressed in the band's 2006 recording, *Receptive When Beaten*, with the addition of a patent anti-woman/anti-feminist stance, as illustrated by the songs 'The War On Women', 'Receptive When Beaten', and 'Respect The Fist...Bitch'. These compositions, as the titles unambiguously indicate, chart a masculine eagerness and delight in the inflicting of violence on women, with lyrics that stress the normative nature of this approach. Such sentiments of violence are compounded by the inner-sleeve imagery in which each band member's profile is represented by the image of a woman, with a disclaimer that states their sexual submissiveness to each musician (e.g. 'I'm only in heaven when I'm mounting Kevin'). The album also contains mock pornographic magazine-style sex-line advertisements. So, while the musical style is rooted within a direct grindcore tonal approach, the substantive character of the band expresses a confrontational misogyny that valorizes male aggression and the naturalness of violence against women—all framed within references to the conventions of pornographic publications.

The explicit citation of feminism and a mocking position taken with regard to the idea of female empowerment evident within Waco Jesus is reinforced by the American band, Meatshits, an outfit that produce music demonstrably misogynistic, and critically names and rejects feminism itself. On albums such as *Fuck Frenzy* and *Gorenography*, in addition to the songs dedicated exclusively to violence, misogyny and pornography ('Sodomized', 'Anal Lust', 'Pornoholic', 'Massacre of Genitals', 'Cunt'), the albums are filled with artistically-rendered images of sexual acts, with a consistent emphasis on the act of rape. Meanwhile, *Gorenography*'s artwork consists of a Japanese Anime-style art cover that represents a 'snuff' image—that of a suitcase that contains the carefully-packed body parts of a young woman. Consequently, while the snuff anxiety may have been an unsubstantiated moral panic (Thompson 1994), porngrind consistently keeps the idea within cultural circulation, and adheres to (and revels in) the male 'pleasure principle' that Dworkin argued lay behind pornography—the sexual gratification of witnessing the mutilating and murder of women. But more significantly, Meatshits take an overtly anti-feminist position, one that not merely confronts and apparently confirms Dworkin's argument, but that also castigates any expression of feminist empowerment. Thus, the provocative masculine 'political' stance of their album and song, 'Violence Against Feminist Cunts', which, aside from its deliberate and confrontational designate, consists of a blunt and aggressive rejection of feminism itself, dismissively dubbed a 'worthless cause'—a lyrical message that is reinforced by album artwork that consists of the archetypal Dworkin scenario: the (computer-generated) image of a woman, bound and beaten, being raped, and, arguably, conforming to the assessment of the Dworkin-inspired Jensen, that 'we live in a culture in which sexualised violence...is so routine that it has to be considered "normal"' (Dines, Jensen and Russo 1998: 6).

Porngrind: Dworkin's pornography?

In a culture that has seen the dividing lines between art, pornography and popular culture blur in the last two decades, creating what commentators have dubbed the cultural process of 'pornographication', whereby pop music videos, advertising billboards and high street stores routinely display images that reflect pornographic tropes or 'porn chic' (McNair 2002; Attwood 2004;

Smith 2010), porngrind may be a further example of this phenomenon, albeit of an extreme form. However, it is very different from Britney Spears' scantily-clad pop performances, or naked Sophie Dahl billboard fragrance advertisements. Porngrind draws upon the hardcore world and is infused with an ideology that sustains the critiques raised by anti-pornography commentators, in addition to popularizing the patriarchal and misogynistic elements that have long been identified to exist within heavy metal. It does so in a way that centrally reflects the worst excesses of misogyny that feminists argued is a defining characteristic of pornography, particularly those associated with violence and rape (Ramos 2000). So, while O'Toole states that the truth of hardcore pornography is that, while a multi-layered phenomenon, it is ultimately 'simply pictures and films of people having sex together' (1999: 38); the view of Dworkin (and fellow anti-pornography feminists) is that it is a source of 'harm'; that it constitutes dehumanization, sexual exploitation, forced sex, physical injury and 'inferiority presented as entertainment' (Thompson 1994: 96)—factors all present within porngrind. Subsequently, even though considered unfashionable and outmoded, I argue that it is Dworkin's view of pornography that is best positioned to reflect the pornographic world that porngrind conveys, because it appears as if it is a deliberate response to her position. All of the nightmarish horrors Dworkin attributes to pornography and the male sexuality that drives it is luridly and graphically represented.

While Dworkin's view has been criticized and augmented by research that suggests significant levels of pornographic consumption by women (Attwood 2002), it does have contemporary academic expression. In the context of British regulatory responses to pornography (the Criminal Justice and Immigration Act 2008—the 'Dangerous Pictures Act', for instance), calls are made to criminalize extreme pornography based upon the continuing perception that 'pornography can nurture real injustice and ruin real lives', underpinned by contemporary anti-feminist academics such as Catherine Itzin (Attwood and Smith 2010: 172). Meanwhile, in the US, commentators such as Pamela Paul (2006) argue that pornography is a personally and socially damaging force. So, the Dworkin-style anti-pornography tradition has not disappeared from feminist discourse in relation to pornography. Similarly, the view that pornography is dangerous and implicitly connected with violence is also evident within popular media commentary. Thus, Decca Aitkenhead of *The Observer* newspaper cites a porn addict's quest for the perfect porn image as being 'really about looking for death' (Attwood 2007: 6). But while Attwood is critical of a return to the 'effects' view of pornography, nevertheless, the censorial 'fear' approach to pornography is still evident within contemporary feminist debate, and porngrind does little to abate this.

While bands such as Anal Whore make overtures to claim that the misogyny is simply for effect, there is scant evidence of any reflexive attitude within the music and imagery of bands such as Lividity, Waco Jesus, AxHxPxPx or Meatshits. Conversely, the message is unequivocal: violence and sex are identical, and pornography constitutes the complete objectification of women. In this regard, porngrind projects a world in which there are no boundaries with regard to how women may be treated and abused: a patriarchal fantasy in which women must be submissive, and must be physically compelled to be if they resist. Referring back to Kahn-Harris's Darkthrone example and racial politics raised earlier, as the Waco Jesus interview extract at the beginning of this chapter illustrates, the idea that feminism is a 'dangerous sickness' is not denied, nor is any playful taboo-baiting sensibility suggested; rather, it is confirmed. And while this may be posturing, it may not. However, it is not my suggestion that porngrind, due to its imagery and lyrical content, is specifically a male preserve in terms of consumption. For instance, Waco Jesus' album sleeves contain concert images that show female members of the audience actively engaged in the 'mosh-pit'. Thus, the anti-female messages can be negotiated or offset by female extreme metal fans attracted to the music, the scene or the extremity of the bands. Kahn-Harris (2003), referring to Cannibal Corpse's song, 'Fucked With A Knife', cites examples of female fans who are fans of the band, with female scene member interviewees maintaining a sense of 'open mindedness' about music that should offend them. However, within extreme music circles, the misogynistic attitudes that are prevalent in many bands do raise concerns with regard to lyrical content and gender. As Angela Gossow, lead singer with Arch Enemy, and one of the most prominent female figures within extreme metal stated of the band, Cannibal Corpse, and the general prevalence of violence against women expressed within extreme metal:

> I loved Cannibal Corpse's *Eaten Back to Life*, because it was so extreme at the time when I was a kid, but I didn't sing along with those lyrics... It's somehow just a bit intimidating. It's so much about violence against women. It's not a guy who's being totally shredded—it's always women... I just don't know how they can justify that (Mudrian 2004: 251).

Of course, while alternative musical genres such as gangsta rap are similarly lyrically dominated by misogyny, rape and sexual violence (Armstrong 2001), porngrind expresses such themes within the context of a specific cultural referent—pornographic texts, and the extreme pornography of 'specialist' markets such as anal sex and coprophilia or 'scat'. Moreover, if, as Kahn-Harris

(2003) suggests, death metal and extreme metal forms are invariably 'invisible' to wider culture, and thus able to escape censorship, porngrind is especially 'below the radar'. Indeed (as I discovered in the course of my research), many recordings, due to the explicitness of their cover art, have a similar 'under-the-counter' quality that is associated with 'specialist' pornography. Porngrind albums are not readily available from mainstream stores, and must either rely upon independent record stores, or be bought directly from the independent record labels that produce them (Last House on the Right records, for example). As such, within popular music, the feminist fears that have been articulated in relation to the nature of pornography do find expression, albeit with a curious symmetry existing between porngrind and Dworkin.

While Dworkin's essentialist and polemical position has been extensively criticized from within feminism itself, and the debate has developed into more sophisticated and balanced forms, the view that pornography represents the symbolic expression of a patriarchal society persists, as does the view that it is intrinsically linked with violence and male aggression against women. To some degree, the same assumptions continue to be made: pornography is read as a monolithic form, with no acknowledgement of nuance or consumption patterns and no discernment is made between online rape fantasy sites and *Playboy* magazine (Attwood and Smith 2010: 172). However, Dworkin would similarly see no dividing line, nor any between sex, pornography and masculinity. As she asserts: 'violence is male; the male is the penis; violence is the penis or the sperm ejaculated from it' (1981: 55). But, while this view has been dismissed as little more than 'fire and brimstone' rhetoric (Segal 2004: 59), it is the actually the defining characteristic of porngrind. In consequence, it is somewhat ironic that there is a meeting point between radical feminism and pornographically inspired popular culture: the proponents of porngrind and Dworkin share common ground in their sex/male violence matrix. Indeed, the misogynistic nature of porngrind is equally reflected by the misandry of Dworkin, as Young (2005) states: 'in Dworkin's world view, the Marquis de Sade and Jack the Ripper seem to be representative of all men', and in the music produced by porngrind bands, they are.

Consequently, porngrind, I argue, represents *exactly* what Dworkin always thought pornography is, and O'Toole's dismissive evaluation of radical anti-pornography feminism, that it is filled with nothing more than 'fantastic tales of porn "violence"' (1999: 48), works to reflect the nature of porngrind perfectly. As such, at one level, the patriarchal nature of metal music identified by Walser in its earlier days has arguably been intensified in variants of extreme metal, and most energetically by porngrind. Thus, although her position has been largely discredited, she is the primary figure inspired by the music because

Porngrind conforms to Dworkin's perception of the brutality of pornographic images and ideology, within popular culture, at least. This may simply reinforce the view that her version of pornography was a fantasy, and that the only consistent representation of it exists within the underground popular cultural world of porngrind. And yet, there is the reference to an anti-feminist ideology that ensures that porngrind cannot be emphatically read as taboo-breaking transgression, and which cannot disavow Dworkin entirely. This is because it is politically ambiguous with regard to intention. Therefore, while demonstrating the countless ways in which metal music sub-divides itself, it is also fitting that, due to its extreme nature, the feminist critic who is most apposite to apply to it is equally extreme to the extent that poring through the pages of *Pornography* and listening to Soldered Poon, Anal Whore, Lividity, Waco Jesus or Meatshits is a similar experience. Both conjure lurid images of violent excess, blunt sexual language and an unerring focus upon sexual violence. So, if Dworkin had looked to the underground world of extreme metal, she would have found porngrind—producing exactly the stuff of her feminist nightmares, but in a manner uncannily similar to her own particular pornographic vision.

Bibliography

Armstrong, Edward. G. 2001. 'Gangsta Misogyny: A Content Analysis of the Portrayals of Violence against Women in Rap Music, 1987–1993'. *Journal of Criminal Justice and Popular Culture* 8(2): 96–126.

Arnett, Jeffrey Jensen. 1992. 'Soundtrack of Recklessness: Musical Preferences and Reckless Behaviour among Adolescents'. *Journal of Adolescent Research* 7(3): 313–31. http://dx.doi.org/10.1177/074355489273003

—1996. *Metalheads: Heavy Metal Music and Adolescent Alienation*. Boulder, CO: Westview.

Assiter, Alison. 1989. *Pornography, Feminism and the Individual*. London: Pluto.

Attwood, Feona. 2002. 'Reading Porn: The Paradigm Shift in Pornography Research'. *Sexualities* 5(1): 91–105. http://dx.doi.org/10.1177/1363460702005001005

—2004. 'Pornography and Objectification: Re-reading "The Picture that Divided Britain"'. *Feminist Media Studies* 4(1): 7–19. http://dx.doi.org/10.1080/14680770410001674617

—2007. '"Other" or "One of Us?" The Porn User in Public and Academic Discourse'. *Particip@tions* 4(1): 1–23.

Attwood, Feona, and Clarissa Smith. 2010. 'Extreme Concern: Regulating "Dangerous Pictures" in the United Kingdom'. *Journal of Law and Society* 37(1): 171–88. http://dx.doi.org/10.1111/j.1467-6478.2010.00500.x

Baddeley, Gavin. 1999. *Lucifer Rising: Sin, Devil Worship and Rock'n'Roll*. London: Plexus.

Bangs, Lester. 1992. 'Heavy Metal'. In *The Rolling Stone Illustrated History of Rock & Roll*, ed. Anthony De Curtis and James Henke, 459–63. New York: Random House.

Barron, Lee, and Ian Inglis. 2009. 'Scary Movies, Scary Music: Uses and Unities of Heavy Metal'. In *Terror Tracks: Music, Sound and Horror Cinema*, ed. Philip Hayward, 186–98. London: Equinox.

Binder, Amy. 1993. 'Constructing Racial Rhetoric: Media Depictions of Harm in Heavy Metal and Rap Music'. *American Sociological Review* 58: 753–67. http://dx.doi.org/10.2307/2095949

Brown, Wendy. 2006. 'American Nightmare: Neoliberalism, Neoconservativism and De-Democratization'. *Political Theory* 34(6): 690–714. http://dx.doi.org/10.1177/0090591706293016

Brutalism.com. 2003. 'Waco Jesus and the Numerous Fuck Yous'. http://brutalism.com/content/waco-jesus-0.

Dines, Gail, Robert Jensen and Ann Russo. 1998. *Pornography: The Production and Consumption of Inequality.* New York and London: Routledge.

Dworkin, Andrea. 1981. *Pornography: Men Possessing Women.* London: The Women's Press.

Heartney, Eleanor. 1991. 'Pornography'. *Art Journal* 50(4): 16–19. http://dx.doi.org/10.2307/777318

Judges, Donald. P. 1995. 'When Silence Speaks Louder than Words: Authoritarianism and the Feminist Antipornography Movement'. *Psychology, Public Policy, and Law* 3: 643–13. http://dx.doi.org/10.1037/1076-8971.1.3.643

Kahn-Harris, Keith. 2003. 'Death Metal and the Limits of Musical Expression'. In *Policing Pop*, ed. Martin Cloonan and Reebee Garofalo, 81–100. Philadelphia: Temple University Press.

—2007. *Extreme Metal: Music and Culture on the Edge.* Oxford and New York: Berg.

Kendrick, Walter. 1996. *The Secret Museum: Pornography in Modern Culture.* Berkeley: University of California Press.

Kipnis, Laura. 1996. *Bound and Gagged: Pornography and the Politics of Fantasy in America.* New York: Grove Press.

Krenshe, Leigh, and Jim McKay. 2000. '"Hard and Heavy": Gender and Power in a Heavy Metal Music Subculture'. *Gender, Place and Culture* 7(3): 287–304.

Marinucci, Mimi. 2005. 'Television, Generation X, and Third Wave Feminism: A Contextual Analysis of The Brady Bunch'. *Journal of Popular Culture* 38(3): 505–524. http://dx.doi.org/10.1111/j.0022-3840.2005.00126.x

McNair, Brian. 2002. *Striptease Culture: Sex, Media and the Democratization of Desire.* London: Routledge. http://dx.doi.org/10.4324/9780203469378

Miyakawa, Felicia. M. 2005. *Five Percenter Rap: God Hop's Music, Message, and Black Muslim Mission.* Bloomington and Indianapolis: Indiana University Press.

Moynihan, Michael, and Didrik Söderlind. 2003. *Lords of Chaos: The Bloody Rise of the Satanic Metal Underground.* Washington: Feral House.

Mudrian, Albert. 2004. *Choosing Death: The Improbable History of Death Metal and Grindcore.* Los Angeles: Feral House.

O'Toole, Laurence. 1999. *Pornocopia: Porn, Sex, Technology and Desire.* London: Serpent's Tail.

Paul, Pamela. 2006. *Pornified: How Pornography is Damaging our Lives, our Relationships, and our Families.* London: Times Books.

Purcell, Natalie. J. 2003. *Death Metal Music: The Passion and Politics of a Subculture.* Jefferson, MI and London: McFarland & Company, Inc.

Ramos, Norma. 2000. 'Pornography is a Social Justice Issue'. In *Feminism and Pornography,* ed. Drucilla Cornwell, 45–48. Oxford: Oxford University Press.

Russell, Diana. E. H. 1998. *Dangerous Relationships: Pornography, Misogyny, and Rape.* London: Sage.

Segal, Lynne. 1993. 'Does Pornography Cause Violence? The Search for Evidence'. In *Dirty Looks: Women, Pornography and Power*, ed. Pamela Church Gibson and Roma Gibson, 5–22. London: BFI.

—2004. 'Only the Literal: The Contradictions of Anti-Pornography Feminism'. In *More Dirty Looks: Gender, Pornography and Power*, ed. Pamela Church Gibson, 59–71. London: BFI.

Selfhout, Maarten H. W., Marc J. M. H. Delsing and Tom F. M. ter Bogt. 2008. 'Heavy Metal and Hip-Hop Style Preferences and Externalizing Problem Behavior: A Two-Wave Longitudinal Study'. *Youth & Society* 39(4): 435–52. http://dx.doi.org/10.1177/0044118X07308069

Shellrude, Kathleen. 2001. 'Coming Between the Lines: A Fresh Look at the Writings of Anti-Porn and Whore Feminists'. *Canadian Woman Studies* 20(4): 41–45.

Smith, Clarissa. 2010. 'Pornographication: A Discourse for All Seasons'. *International Journal of Media and Cultural Politics* 6(1): 103–108. http://dx.doi.org/10.1386/macp.6.1.103/3

Snyder-Hall, Claire, R. 2010. 'Third Wave Feminism and the Defense of "Choice"'. *Perspectives on Politics* 8(1): 255–61. http://dx.doi.org/10.1017/S1537592709992842

Strossen, Nadine. 1994. *Defending Pornography: Free Speech, Sex, and the Fight for Women's Rights*. New York: New York University Press.

Thompson, Bill. 1994. *Soft Core: Moral Crusades against Pornography in Britain and America*. London: Cassell.

Vance, Carole. S. 1984. *Pleasure and Danger: Exploring Female Sexuality*. London and New York: Routledge & Kegan Paul.

Walser, Robert. 1993. 'Forging Masculinity: Heavy Metal Sounds and Images of Gender'. In *Sound and Vision: The Music Video Reader*, ed. Simon Frith, Andrew Goodwin and Lawrence Grossberg, 153–85. London and New York: Routledge.

Weinstein, Deena. 2000. *Heavy Metal: The Music and its Culture*. New York: Da Capo Press.

Williams, Linda. 1990. *Hard Core: Power, Pleasure and the "Frenzy of the Visible"*. London: Pandora.

—2004. 'Second Thoughts on *Hard Core*: American Obscenity Law and the Scapegoating of Deviance'. In *More Dirty Looks: Gender, Pornography and Power*, ed. Pamela Church Gibson, 165–76. London: BFI.

Wilson, Scott. 2008. *Great Satan's Rage: American Negativity and Rap/Metal in the Age of Supercapitalism*. Manchester: Manchester University Press.

Wilson, Elizabeth. 1991. *Pornography and Feminism: The Case against Censorship*. London: Lawrence & Wishart.

Wright, Robert. 2000. '"I'd Sell You Suicide": Pop Music and Moral Panic in the Age of Marilyn Manson'. *Popular Music* 9(3): 365–385. http://dx.doi.org/10.1017/S0261143000000222

Young, Cathy. 2005. 'Women's Hating: The Misdirected Passion of Andrea Dworkin'. *Reason Magazine*. http://reason.com/archives/2005/04/19/womans-hating.

The 'double controversy' of Christian metal

Marcus Moberg

Åbo Akademie University, Finland

Christian metal has always occupied a peculiar position within the wider world of metal music. Yet, despite its marginal status, its existence still tends to be widely known and frequently contested among secular metal audiences. As a phenomenon, Christian metal (earlier also called white metal) came into being in the early 1980s when US bands such as Stryper, Messiah Prophet and Saint, as well as Leviticus from Sweden, appeared with a full-blown metal sound and look and an expressed intent of spreading the Christian message among secular metal audiences (Moberg 2009: 128).

This was also a time during which the popularity of metal, particularly in its shock and glam metal variants, had reached unprecedented heights (e.g. Weinstein 2000: 249). And, it was also a time during which metal *as a genre* was starting to become the subject of growing controversy, debate and moral panic within the wider context of the US 'culture wars' of the 1980s and 1990s (e.g. Luhr 2009; Hunter 1991).

Critical debates surrounding metal reached a peak in relation to the concentrated campaign against popular music's perceived negative moral influence on youth spearheaded by the Parents Music Resource Center (in cooperation with other groups such as the Parent-Teacher Association) in 1985. This particular campaign successfully managed to cement the association of metal with the promotion of violence, self-destructive behaviour, suicide, sexual promiscuity and perversion, extreme rebellion, juvenile delinquency and the 'occult' in wider public discourse (e.g. Walser 1993: 139; Weinstein 2000: 254). Indeed, the key concerns of this campaign—the preservation of traditional 'family values', parental authority and the morality of youth—have historically often stood at the very centre of wider critical conversations about popular culture (e.g. Clark 2003: 47; Walser 1993: 138).

These types of concerns were, however, not the sole property of secular parental lobbying groups such as the PMRC and the PTA. For slightly different reasons, they were also very much shared by many Protestant conservative Christian, evangelical and fundamentalist groups alike. Conservative Christians of various strands were quick to join the wider crusade against immorality in popular music (often believed to have become epitomized in metal) that was gaining momentum in the mid 1980s. Through their engagement in these wider debates, the issue of 'Satanism' also started figuring ever more frequently in critical debates on metal. As a consequence, metal now also became accused of being *anti-Christian* and of actively promoting Satanism and outright Devil-worship (e.g. Weinstein 2000: 258–62; Walser 1993: 139–43; Luhr 2009: 46–47)—an accusation that would also develop into a recurring theme in the contemporary 'Satanic panic' writing (e.g. Raschke 1990).

Indeed, the Satanism charge has proven particularly enduring and also assumed a life of its own within wider popular cultural discourse (Wright 2000: 370; Moberg 2009: 121). Considering this, it might seem strange that such a thing as Christian metal ever developed. However, in addition to always having occupied a peculiar position within the wider world of metal music, Christian metal has always occupied quite a precarious position within wider conservative and evangelical Christian circles as well.

As will be discussed in more detail in the following sections, the distinction between 'Christian' and 'secular' metal does not derive from any difference in the 'essence' of the music as such or the way it sounds, is performed or played. Rather, the whole notion of 'Christian' metal needs to be understood as a result of a deliberate attempt on the part of evangelical musicians in the early 1980s to create a more ideologically 'positive' and more 'wholesome' (i.e. 'Christian') alternative form of metal in direct response to the perceived destructive character of 'secular' metal, that is, 'ordinary' metal not characterized by a clear Christian content and an expressed evangelist agenda. However, as I aim to highlight in this chapter, the many controversies that started to surround secular metal in the mid 1980s would come to have a profound and long-lasting effect on the very self-understanding of Christian metal.

As I will suggest, Christian metal can be seen to be characterised for what could be called its 'double controversy'. As metal became singled out as a 'prime symbol' and scapegoat for everything that had supposedly gone awry with contemporary youth culture in the mid 1980s, this served to raise awareness and further reinforce negative attitudes towards metal as a form of music and musical culture *in itself* within many conservative Christian circles (Weinstein 2000: 245). At the same time, many of the accusations levelled at metal during this time gradually also started to become internalized within secular metal culture itself and (often playfully) incorporated into wider discourses about what metal was supposed to be all 'about', making the very idea of 'Christian' metal seem oxymoronic, and therefore controversial, within the wider secular metal community as well.

Thus, in this 'double' sense, within both of these often opposing two camps, Christian metal has been ridden with controversy almost from its very inception for reasons that are different yet inextricably interlinked. Moreover, as I will highlight in this chapter, the doubly controversial character of Christian metal has continued to shape contemporary Christian metal discourse and is thus also key to an adequate understanding of the phenomenon of Christian metal on the whole.

The wider context: evangelical engagements with popular culture

The initial development of Christian metal in the early 1980s needs to be understood in connection to the broader phenomenon of 'Christian' or 'evangelical' popular culture. The establishment in the late 1970s of what has become known as the 'evangelical popular culture industry', firmly rooted in North America and the North American strand of evangelical Protestantism (also called neo-evangelicalism), essentially remains based on the notion of the neutrality and transformability of popular cultural forms in themselves. Whilst this has involved a rejection of the perceived immorality and lack of constructive 'family values' found in the secular popular cultural mainstream on the one hand, it has also involved the creation of a 'morally sound' or 'family friendly' Christian alternative on the other which, in most respects, emulates secular popular culture in outlook and industrial organization (for a detailed account of evangelical popular culture see for example Hendershot 2004; Luhr 2009).

The phenomenon of evangelical popular culture as a whole is intimately connected to the view still held by many evangelicals that the wider contemporary popular cultural environment constitutes an important battleground over the proper (i.e. Christian) socialization of youth (e.g. Clark 2003: 41). As such, evangelical popular culture has typically been represented as an attempt at changing or influencing secular popular culture from *within*. Consequently, mirroring a broader long-standing strategy commonly employed by US conservative and evangelical Christians in their efforts to increase their cultural and societal influence, the tactic preferred by many producers of evangelical popular culture has been that of engagement and *infiltration*. That is, producers of evangelical popular culture tend to hold the view that, in order for them to be able to bring popular culture more into alignment with 'Christian values' and make it more 'moral' and less indecent, the wider contemporary popular cultural environment needs to be actively engaged within its own vernacular and, partly, on its own terms (e.g. Clark 2003: 32; Luhr 2009: 5–8).

However, it is important to point out that the creation of an evangelical popular cultural environment or 'counter-media' (Stout 2001: 7–10) should not merely be understood in terms of evangelical appropriations or borrowings of secular popular cultural forms for purely evangelistic purposes. Rather, it also needs to be understood as mirroring a widespread gradual emergence of increasingly progressive attitudes and 'the remaking of cultural perceptions' among conservative and evangelical Christians towards the wider contemporary cultural/popular cultural environment (Romanowski 2005: 104; cf. Hendershot 2004).

Indeed, one of the clearest examples of such gradual shifts in attitudes actually relates directly to Christian metal. In 1985, the so-called *Sanctuary movement*—a temporary 'rock 'n' roll refuge' for evangelical Christians who were involved in various rock music scenes, but who felt alienated from, bored with and rejected within more conventional and conservative evangelical circles—emerged in Torrance, California. The movement grew fast, became particularly focused on metal and soon established its own congregations. Indeed, the Sanctuary churches not only encouraged their congregants to fully adopt the metal style and look; they also used metal music during church services and, to some extent, even embraced metal concert practices such as headbanging and moshing (Glanzer 2003: 15–38). Sanctuary's congregations would come to function as important breeding grounds and 'centers of socialization' for US Christian metal bands in the mid- and late 1980s (Brown 2005: 125). Sanctuary decided to end its congregational activities in the mid 1990s and transform itself into an international ministry under the name of *Sanctuary International* (Glanzer 2003: 40; Moberg 2009: 131).

Sanctuary thus constituted the first ever 'metal church' movement—a phenomenon that would subsequently inspire the creation of different types of small independent so-called 'metal parish movements' or 'metal ministries' in countries such as Sweden, Germany, Brazil, Mexico and Colombia. As with Sanctuary, through combining Christian worship practices with the musical, aesthetic and bodily practices of metal, these movements are essentially aimed at providing Christians who are fans of metal with an alternative form of religious expression that is fully in line with their cultural sensibilities. While the European variants of these ministries have remained rather loose groupings that organize events only occasionally, their Latin American varieties tend to be more sectarian in character (Moberg 2009: 173–75).

As illustrated by the efforts of Sanctuary, it is important to note that, unlike many other forms of so-called contemporary Christian music, Christian metal not only appropriated metal as a form of music but also wholeheartedly embraced the metal style, general aesthetic conventions, rhetoric, attitude and bodily practices from the very start (Moberg 2009: 134). Musically, Christian and secular metal have always been indistinguishable from one another. Apart from obvious differences regarding the content of lyrics and Christian metal's replacement of satanic or occult imagery with Christian imagery and symbolism, distinguishing between the two often requires attention to detail. However, it is worth noting that although Christian metal usually can be distinguished quite easily from its secular counterpart on the basis of the content of lyrics, Christian metal bands still tend to write lyrics in a rhetorical style typical of metal more generally.

Often verbalized through a 'warrior rhetoric' (Luhr 2009: 117), the tactic of infiltration and the idea of transforming secular metal culture from within constituted a central ideological component of Christian metal of the mid 1980s and early 1990s. It is thus also worth noting that, in contrast to the often overly polite and saccharine lyrical style commonly employed in many other forms of contemporary Christian music, Christian metal bands have always favoured a decidedly more uncompromising and radical type of approach (Moberg 2009: 146).

However, while it is important to point out that the initial development of Christian metal into a distinct Christian musical culture in its own right in the mid 1980s only partly occurred under the auspices of the emerging broader evangelical popular culture industry of the time, it is equally important to recognize that Christian metal nevertheless did develop in close enough connection to that environment in order to become considerably influenced by its main aims and aspirations (Moberg 2009: 135–37, 145–46).

A brief history of Christian metal's 'double controversies'

Throughout the 1980s Christian metal became directly implicated in a series of internal Christian debates on proper and permissible forms of Christian engagement with the broader cultural environment (e.g. Luhr 2009: 124). Indeed, according to Eileen Luhr (2009: 112), Christian metal provides 'an ideal case study for examining the cultural activism of conservative [and evangelical] Christians' during this time.

As noted above, this period of intensified Christian social and cultural activism can also be viewed in connection to the concept of 'culture wars', initially developed to describe a supposedly deepening divide between liberal and conservative sections of the US population since the early 1980s. Although the concept of culture wars has been repeatedly criticized for having exaggerated the nature of such a supposed divide of US society 'into two polarized, warring camps' (Williams 2003: 322), for present purposes, it is nevertheless crucial to note that 'culture wars *rhetoric*' (Williams 2003: 322, my emphasis) has remained a central means through which various religiously and morally motivated social movements alike aim to influence wider public opinion (Williams

2003: 322–27). Indeed, stark culture wars rhetoric, or what Deena Weinstein (2000: 270) terms 'discursive terror', constituted a central component of the 'family values'-centred 'movement culture' (Williams 2003: 317) against popular music's perceived detrimental influence on youth initiated and sustained by the PMRC in collaboration with conservative Christians in the mid 1980s.

As Weinstein (2000: 261) observes, in the conservative Christian perspective, the varied notions of metal fostering suicidal tendencies, encouraging rebellion against parental, social and cultural authority, and promoting sexual promiscuity/perversion and Satanism among its audiences were all understood to be inextricably intertwined and intimately connected to metal *as a form of musical culture in itself* (cf. Wright 2000: 370). Thus, in the conservative Christian rhetoric of the time, these notions (none of which were questioned) were commonly represented as constituting a unitary assault on 'family values' which had to be met with active resistance (cf. Luhr 2009: 7, 52). However, it is important to note that wider debates occurring *within* Christian circles during this time also frequently contained various points of disagreement between progressives and conservatives regarding the long-standing Christian predicament of striving to be 'in but not of the world' (cf. Manza and Wright 2003: 306). Because of its strong affinity to its secular counterpart, it is not surprising that Christian metal developed into one such point of disagreement (cf. Luhr 2009: 143).

One of the debates in which Christian metal became directly implicated was that concerning metal's connection to *rebellion* against traditional and parental authority. Although usually portrayed in deliberately humoristic ways as exemplified in the music videos of bands such as Twisted Sister, youth rebellion against parental and adult authority did indeed constitute a recurring theme in much of the secular metal of the mid 1980s. However, as argued by Luhr (2009: 155), the evangelistic activities of Christian metal bands from the mid 1980s to the mid 1990s 'confirmed the fluidity of oppositional cultural themes such as "rebellion" and "alienation"'. Sharing the widespread contemporary concern among conservative and evangelical Christians that late-modern society and culture were experiencing a progressive erosion in morals and decency—exemplified by the legalization and increasing acceptability of such things as pornography, abortion and gay and women's right movements—Christian metal bands placed themselves at the forefront of progressive evangelical's efforts to reconceptualize and 'redefine "rebellion" as resistance to sin and obedience to parental, church, and divine authority' (Luhr 2009: 118; cf. Manza and Wright 2003: 306).

Moreover, in order to distinguish themselves as 'warriors of Christ' engaged in 'spiritual warfare' in a hostile cultural environment, Christian metal bands also repeatedly strove to demonize their secular counterparts (Luhr 2009: 118). Notably, Christian bands' demonization of secular metal also served as a means to establish and legitimate their own evangelistic mandate—particularly in the face of conservative Christian criticism. This, however, was not something that went unnoticed within the wider secular metal community. Indeed, as a consequence of the untiring evangelistic efforts of many bands, Christian metal increasingly became viewed as a laughing matter and sometimes even met with outright hostility within secular metal settings (Luhr 2009: 123; Moberg 2009: 227–28). Of course, there have always been practicing Christians of various strands among secular metal audiences as well. However, holding a personal Christian conviction and combining one's musical fandom with an expressed evangelistic agenda are two very different things.

Another issue closely related to that of rebellion which also developed into a point of controversy for Christian metal was that of *appearance* and *style*. This particular issue had already been of central concern to the Sanctuary movement discussed above. In particular, Christian metal bands came under attack from conservative Christians for adopting the effeminate and gender-bending style (i.e. of long teased hair, feminine clothes, spandex costumes, makeup etc.) characteristic of 1980s and 1990s glam metal. In the conservative Christian perspective, such appearances posed a direct challenge to traditional gender roles (Luhr 2009: 146–48; Moberg 2009: 293). Christian metal bands, however, emphasized their missiological motivations and argued that styles and appearances constituted 'part of the vernacular of youth culture' and therefore should be regarded as being neutral in themselves (Luhr 2009: 62).

In addition to the issue of style and appearance, various notions found within more radically conservative Christian circles about the music itself or, more precisely, what types of 'inappropriate' and even dangerous *behaviours* the music supposedly encouraged and instilled among its listeners, also developed into a point of controversy for Christian metal. For example, the very idea of such a thing as 'Christian rock' was categorically rejected in the writing of so-called Christian anti-rock critics such as Jimmy Swaggart (1987) and Jeff Godwin (1988). In particular, Christian anti-rock critics had long been arguing that rock music in itself served to bring forth primordial sexual urges among its listeners and therefore also served as a catalyst for sexually promiscuous behaviour—a notion that had become fairly widespread within broader conservative Christian circles in the 1980s. What is more, Christian anti-rock writers (e.g. Godwin 1988) also tended to locate 'the root of rock's power' in the supernatural force of Satan (Luhr 2009: 49–50).

Indeed, the world of secular metal, filled as it was with bands like Mötley Crüe and KISS who never missed an opportunity to flaunt their sexual prowess, seemed to support this notion. Following from this, critics also expressed concern about the bodily practices of the 'dionysian' (Weinstein 2000: 84–85) and intense metal concert setting, in which performers and audiences seemed to behave in uncontrolled and morally questionable ways. Hence, in the conservative Christian view, musical *form* mattered; not every form of music could be 'redeemed' and be used as means for worshipping God. Following on from this, Christian critics of Christian metal thus came to doubt that bands who went out to evangelize among secular audiences would manage to retain their Christian distinctiveness and remain unaffected by the 'immoral', debauchery- and sexual promiscuity-elevating general nature of such environments (Luhr 2009: 115).

Within broader Christian circles, therefore, Christian metal bands became implicated in wider debates ranging from style and appearance to 'proper' and 'suitable' forms of Christian expression and evangelism. Like many other Christian pop and rock musicians of the time, Christian metal bands turned to the Bible (particularly the book of Psalms) in support of their view that *all* forms of music should be regarded as being neutral in themselves; the underlying intentions and motivations for their use being the only important issue. Even so, while 'lighter' forms of contemporary Christian music already had started to develop into an integral component of the worship practices of the emerging mega-church movement as well as many more progressive charismatic and evangelical congregations (e.g. Miller 1999: 173; Romanowski 2005: 110), metal was still widely considered inappropriate to be put to such uses.

In addition, albeit for very different reasons, Christian metal bands encountered quite a lot of criticism on musical grounds within the secular metal community as well. In particular, within the world of secular metal, Christian bands were frequently accused of being musically poor and for only copying and mimicking the sound and style of successful secular metal bands (Moberg 2009: 228; Luhr 2009: 123). This accusation was, however, not totally unfounded since many Christian bands of the 1980s tended to give precedence to evangelism at the expense of musical capability and innovativeness (cf. Glanzer 2003: 28). Even though Christian metal has no doubt become increasingly musically diverse and innovative throughout the years, the view of Christian bands as mere copycats and mimickers has remained widespread throughout the world of secular metal. As a consequence of this, Christian bands continue to be widely discriminated against within the wider secular metal community. For example, secular metal concert- and festival organizers are rarely willing to include Christian bands at their events (Moberg 2009: 227–28).

Finally, as already briefly discussed above, accusations of metal promoting Satanism among its followers have proven particularly enduring in critical debates on metal. It also needs to be noted that the Satanism charge initially developed in connection with the more commercially successful 'classic' heavy metal and glam metal of the mid 1980s. One can only speculate as to the outcome, had conservative Christian critics of metal, or indeed the members of the PMRC, been more aware of the largely underground development of extreme metal subgenres such as thrash- and death metal during largely this same time. In any case, and perhaps somewhat surprisingly, Christian metal bands largely managed to escape this particular charge.

Moreover, as already noted, the Satanism charge also influenced secular metal in a number of ways. For example, one might well argue that, largely due to having become associated with Satanism and the occult in the 1980s and early 1990s, metal's interest in stark religious/spiritual themes has steadily intensified over time (cf. Kahn-Harris 2007: 3–5). In addition to this, *anti-Christian* sentiment also gradually developed into a recurring theme of extreme metal styles such as death- and black metal in particular. This became quite evident in connection with the black metal-related series of church arsons throughout Norway in the early 1990s. Although the reactions to these spectacular events arguably were not as strong as one could perhaps have expected, in the Nordic countries at least, they nevertheless did serve to reinforce conservative Christian views of metal as an inherently 'Satanic', destructive and dangerous form of popular music. Such a description suited contemporary black metal bands and fans well, though, as many of them openly proclaimed to be engaged in a 'war' against Christianity.

These events, however, also spurred the development of Christian black metal, or so-called 'unblack'. The first Christian bands representing this new style, most of which were Swedish and Norwegian, did indeed run into some initial resistance within their own Christian churches. In particular, the controversial issue of style and appearance surfaced anew as some early unblack bands wholeheartedly embraced the black metal aesthetic, including 'corpse paint' makeup. Although Christian resistance to Christian musicians' appropriation of black metal largely appears to have been confined to some isolated cases, the creation of unblack provoked a much stronger negative response within the secular metal community, in which it immediately became widely viewed as a complete contradiction in terms. The case of the 'anti-Admonish' website, set up in the late 1990s by a secular black metal fan who became outraged by the very existence of Swedish unblack band Admonish, provides a case in point (Moberg 2009: 228).

Christian criticism of Christian metal has largely ebbed out as attitudes towards alternative musical practices have become increasingly tolerant. Indeed, these days Christian metal musicians commonly have the expressed support of their own churches. Musicians and fans may still, of course, encounter sporadic resistance from individual members of their own churches but, in general, concentrated Christian criticism of Christian metal has become rare. Within the secular metal community, however, Christian metal appears to remain as contested as ever (Moberg 2009: 226–27).

The 'double controversy' of Christian metal in contemporary transnational scenic discourse

In the late 1980s and early 1990s Christian metal spread to a number of countries outside of the USA, particularly to Northern Europe and Latin America. The early 1990s also witnessed the gradual development of a transnational Christian metal scene and the establishment of a highly independent transnational scenic infrastructure of record labels, promotion- and distribution channels, specialized media and festivals (Moberg 2009: 172–75). Importantly, as Christian metal became embedded in new social, cultural and religious environments it also became considerably more ideologically diverse and increasingly detached from the religious-cultural struggles characteristic of the USA. Even so, as I have argued elsewhere (Moberg 2008, 2009), the development of a highly independent and largely internet-based transnational scenic structure has also enabled the spreading of a set of closely related discursive representations of what Christian metal is supposed to be all 'about'.

In particular, within today's transnational scene, Christian metal is recurrently discursively constructed as constituting an alternative form of *religious expression*, an alternative *means of evangelism*, a fully *legitimate* form of religious expression and evangelism, and a 'positive' *alternative to* secular metal (Moberg 2009: 204–25). Importantly, through these main ways of discursive representation, Christian metal is also rendered an important resource for the forming of an alternative Christian identity. Representing Christian metal in these ways also clearly illustrates how its 'doubly' controversial character has continued to constitute an integral part of its very self-understanding. In the following, I shall take a closer look at the discursive construction of contemporary Christian metal through examples from various (mostly internet-based) types of Christian metal media (grammar has been left unchanged in all quoted excerpts. For a discussion of how these discursive representations surface in the accounts of individual Christian metal musicians see Moberg 2009).

Discursive representations of Christian metal as constituting an alternative form of religious expression are easily found on general Christian metal resource websites, which often contain detailed explanations and arguments on what Christian metal 'is' and what it is supposed to be all 'about'. For example, the extensive *The Metal for Jesus Page* contains a section titled 'Frequently Asked Questions about Christian Metal' in which one can read that Christian metal is 'needed' since 'many Christians love metal music and since we are Christians it's only natural to combine it with our faith' (The Metal for Jesus Page 2010). Moreover, as the argument continues: 'Just because you are Christian that doesn't mean that you have to listen to gospel or pop music! /.../ Great music also deserves a great message, so why not combine them and take the best from both worlds' (The Metal for Jesus Page 2010).

Among many things that could be said about this statement, for our present discussion, the most important point to note is its generally apologetic tone. While there presumably would be no need to explain one's reasons for listening to 'gospel or pop music' as a Christian, when it comes to metal, such an explanation is still necessary. When represented in this way, Christian metal is basically rendered as an alternative and complementary form of religious expression that is more in line with the popular cultural sensibilities and cultural identities of increasing numbers of young Christians today. As such, it is also often represented as serving as an important, albeit unconventional, source of religious inspiration and edification. However, would it not be for secular metal's history of controversy within Christian circles, it is unlikely that this way of representing Christian metal would have remained as central as it has to this day.

Discursive representations of Christian metal as constituting an alternative means of evangelism are also commonly characterized by a similarly apologetic tone. For example, Christian metal is also often represented as a *necessary* and *effective* means of spreading the Christian message to people (i.e. secular metalheads) not easily reached by traditional and conventional modes of evangelistic outreach. The underlying basic line of reasoning remains that, in order to be successful, evangelism among secular metal audiences needs to be done in a way and language that they can relate to and understand. These types of discursive representations frequently appear in 'mission statements' often found on the official websites of Christian metal bands, record labels, fanzines and webzines.

For example, in a 'note from the editor' in issue 3 (Danne 2001: 27) of the Swedish Christian metal fanzine *Devotion Hardmusic Magazine* it is stated that the 'magazine started with a purpose to show that there is a living music culture with a positive message /.../ Its important that christian bands are in the secular market...to be a light in the darkness and let jesus be known... Jesus is the main reason why we do this and try to reach those who is lost...'. Another example, and one which is much more uncompromising in tone, can be found in the editorial of the first English-language issue of the Brazilian Christian metal fanzine *Extreme Brutal Death* (2005: 4). Among other things, the editor proclaims that earlier Portuguese-language issues of the fanzine 'provoked a huge damage in the satanic black metal scene in South America' and that the primary future goal of the fanzine is to 'enlarge this damage'. This defiant statement also provides a clear contemporary example of how secular metal continues to be demonized in Christian metal discourse in order to ascertain Christian metal's evangelistic mandate. Again, however, were it not for widespread views within conservative Christian circles (as well as within conservative sections of more liberal churches and congregations) of secular metal culture as a breeding ground for 'destructive' behaviours and an interest in Satanism and the occult, it would be more difficult to argue for the urgency of a Christian metal ministry.

As has already been touched upon above, representations of Christian metal as constituting an alternative means of religious expression and evangelism frequently also argue for Christian metal's *legitimacy* in both of these respects. This regards not only the music itself but also its associated styles and aesthetics. Notably, the principal purpose of such representations (sometimes called 'Christian metal apologetics') is to provide an argumentative bulwark against potential *Christian* detractors. For example, *The Metal for Jesus Page* mentioned above contains a section titled 'Christian Rock—Friend Or Foe?' in which visitors can ponder '7 Reasons Why It's OK To ROCK FOR JESUS!' (The Metal for Jesus Page 2010). Ever since the 1980s, such legitimating arguments have typically continued to draw on biblical passages which emphasize purity of heart over appearance and encourage the use of music as a means of praise and worship.

It might seem rather strange, however, that representations of Christian metal as constituting a fully legitimate means of Christian expression and evangelism have remained as common as they have in transnational scenic discourse even though attitudes towards alternative musical forms have become increasingly accepting within wider Christian circles. In part, such representations can be understood as a discursive remnant from earlier times when Christian criticism of Christian metal was both more commonplace and concentrated. But, as I have argued elsewhere, such representations also continue to function as a way for today's transnational Christian metal scene to legitimate *itself for itself* (Moberg 2009: 218–22). But, once again, were it not for metal's history of controversy *as a form of music in itself* within Christian circles, such legitimating discursive representations would probably not have been able to retain their rhetorical edge.

Finally, Christian metal has also become commonly represented as constituting a 'positive' and 'uplifting' alternative to the potentially 'destructive' character of secular metal music and culture. One can find a clear example of this on the general Christian metal recourse website *JesusMetal* which contains the following introductory statement: 'Here at JesusMetal we will introduce you to the Extreme Side of Christianity, or the safe side of Metal, it's both really /.../ We try to keep the site 100% Christian' (JesusMetal 2010). Representing Christian metal as providing its followers with a 'positive' or 'safe' alternative to secular metal serves as yet another way of justifying the existence of a Christian metal scene in the first place.

However, this ideology of deliberate separation has long been a much debated issue within today's wider transnational scene. For one thing, it is evident that separating the two categorically seems quite incompatible with Christian metal's evangelistic aims and general ideology of engagement and infiltration. The views of Christian metal musicians and fans remain divided on this issue as increasing numbers of bands have begun to actively distance themselves from the label 'Christian' and to downplay their religious messages in order to better their chances of wider success and acceptance within the secular metal community on purely musical grounds (Moberg 2009: 141–46).

Concluding remarks

In this chapter I have aimed to illustrate how the interrelated criticism levelled at Christian metal both within conservative Christian circles as well as within the wider secular metal community can be understood in relation to a certain broad trajectory. The increasing controversy and criticism concerning metal music and culture in general in the mid 1980s triggered considerable concern and resistance within many conservative and evangelical Christian circles, making the very idea of 'Christian' metal problematical. At the same time, because of its pronounced and often blatantly evangelistic agenda, and its re-working of central metal themes through a Christian frame, the very idea of 'Christian' metal simultaneously also became highly contested within the wider secular metal community. Thus, almost as soon as it first emerged, Christian metal became caught up in struggles over appropriate forms of religious expression and evangelism in many Christian contexts, and struggles over genre-specific notions about musical authenticity and ideology in wider secular metal contexts.

Christian metal's precarious and often contested position within both of these contexts could therefore also be understood in terms of a 'dual' controversy. However, I have chosen the word 'double' as it better captures the sense in which Christian metal at once has had to endure a *double dose* of criticism and resistance from two directions during its now nearly three-decade long balancing act between the often opposing camps of conservative Christianity and secular metal culture. The reasons for Christian metal's controversiality within Christian circles are quite easily traced as they have been closely linked to a set of more particular internal Christian debates on popular culture. The reasons for Christian metal's controversiality within secular metal settings, however, have essentially revolved around the notion that Christian metal falls short on musical authenticity as it combines the music with an evangelist agenda.

As discussed in the latter part of this chapter, Christian metal's 'doubly' controversial character continues to affect the ways in which it is discursively constructed and understood within today's transnational Christian metal scene. However, as I also hope to have been able to illustrate, Christian metal has not only suffered from its double controversy; it has internalized it and managed to thrive on it as well.

Bibliography

Brown, Charles M. 2005. 'Apocalyptic Unbound: An Interpretation of Christian Speed/Thrash Metal Music'. In *Religious Innovation in a Global Age: Essays on the Construction of Spirituality*, ed. George N. Lundskow, 117–37. Jefferson, NY: McFarland & Company, Inc.

Clark, Lynn Schofield. 2003. *From Angels to Aliens: Teenagers, the Media, and the Supernatural.* New York: Oxford University Press.

Danne. 2001. 'Note from the Editor'. *Devotion Hardmusic Magazine* 3.

'Editorial'. 2005. *Extreme Brutal Death* 1: 4.

Glanzer, Perry L. 2003. 'Christ and the Heavy Metal Subculture: Applying Qualitative Analysis to the Contemporary Debate about H. Richard Niebuhr's *Christ and Culture*'. *Journal of Religion & Society* 5. http://moses.creighton.edu/JRS/2003/2003-7.pdf

Godwin, Jeff. 1988. *Dancing with Demons: The Music's Real Master.* Chino, CA: Chick Publications.

Hendershot, Heather. 2004. *Shaking the World for Jesus: Media and Conservative Evangelical Culture.* Chicago: University of Chicago Press.

Hunter, James D. 1991. *Culture Wars: The Struggle to Define America.* New York: Basic Books.

JesusMetal. 'Welcome to the Extreme Side of Christianity', http://members.ziggo.nl/kemman/homer.htm (accessed 28 June 2010).

Kahn-Harris, Keith. 2007. *Extreme Metal: Music and Culture on the Edge.* Oxford: Berg.

Luhr, Eileen. 2009. *Witnessing Suburbia: Conservatives and Christian Youth Culture.* Berkeley: University of California Press.

Manza, Jeff, and Nathan Wright. 2003. 'Religion and Political Behavior'. In *Handbook of the Sociology of Religion*, ed. Michele Dillon, 297–314. Cambridge: Cambridge University Press.

The Metal for Jesus Page. 'Christian Rock—Friend Or Foe?' and 'Frequently Asked Questions about Christian Metal'. http://www.metalforjesus.org/friorfoe.html (accessed 28 June 2010).

Miller, Donald E. 1999. *Reinventing American Protestantism: Christianity in the New Millennium.* Berkeley: University of California Press.

Moberg, Marcus. 2008. 'The Internet and the Construction of a Transnational Christian Metal Music Scene'. *Culture and Religion* 9: 81–99. http://dx.doi.org/10.1080/14755610801963269

—2009. 'Faster for the Master! Exploring Issues of Religious Expression and Alternative Christian Identity within the Finnish Christian Metal Music Scene'. ThD dissertation. Åbo: Åbo Akademi University Press.

Raschke, Carl A. 1990. *Painted Black: From Drug Killings to Heavy Metal: The Alarming True Story of how Satanism is Terrorizing our Communities.* San Francisco: Harper & Row.

Romanowski, William D. 2005: 'Evangelicals and Popular Music: The Contemporary Christian Music Industry'. In *Religion and Popular Culture in America*, 2nd edn, ed. Bruce D. Forbes and Jeffrey H. Mahan, 103–122. Berkeley: University of California Press.

Stout, Daniel A. 2001. 'Beyond Culture Wars: An Introduction to the Study of Religion and Popular Culture'. In *Religion and Popular Culture: Studies on the Interaction of Worldviews*, ed. Daniel A. Stout and Judith M. Buddenbaum, 3–17. Ames: Iowa State University Press.

Swaggart, Jimmy. 1987. *Religious Rock 'n' Roll: A Wolf in Sheep's Clothing.* Baton Rouge, LA: Swaggart Ministries.

Walser, Robert. 1993. *Running with the Devil: Power, Gender, and Madness in Heavy Metal Music.* Hanover, MD: Wesleyan University Press.

Weinstein, Deena. 2000. *Heavy Metal: The Music and its Culture.* New York: Da Capo Press.

Williams, Rhys H. 2003. 'Religious Social Movements in the Public Sphere: Organization, Ideology, and Activism'. In *Handbook of the Sociology of Religion*, ed. Michele Dillon, 315–30. Cambridge: Cambridge University Press.

Wright, Robert. 2000. '"I'd Sell You Suicide": Pop Music and Moral Panic in the Age of Marilyn Manson'. *Popular Music* 19: 365–85. http://dx.doi.org/10.1017/S0261143000000222

Hellfest: The thing that should not be?

Local perceptions and Catholic discourses on metal culture in France

Gérôme Guibert* and Jedediah Sklower**

*University Paris III (La Sorbonne Nouvelle), France
**Editor, *VOLUME!*, France

> 'You mustn't imagine The Good Lord's children just dropped out of trees'.
>   'Cercle des Trois Provinces', anonymous letter to G. Guibert (2008)

> 'Let me ask you a quick question—which by the way failed to come up at the trial which they had: What performer wants his fucking audience dead?'
>
>   Bill Hicks, *Relentless* (1992)[1]

Based on the number of performers, audience and budget, Hellfest is the most important metal music festival in France. It has been held every year since 2006, for three days around 20 June, in Clisson, a small town of 7,000 inhabitants, in the county of Loire-Atlantique in the West of France. It has not stopped growing since its birth: The first time, 62 groups played on two stages for 20,000 people, with a budget amounting to about 800,000 euros. In 2010, 114 groups played on four stages, 72,000 metalheads came, and the budget reached 3,500,000 euros.

The festival takes place in a region where metal music events have been rare. In general, metal in France remains an underground and little-known subculture. Compared to the other festivals in the region of Les Pays de la Loire, the Hellfest's economy is unique, as it is self-financed (subsidies only account for 2% of the budget) and based on an individual, private initiative. Its growth is thus all the more impressive when one considers that subsidies represent on average a quarter of the budget of regional popular music festivals (Guibert 2008). This success also relies on the large number of foreigners who attend the shows (35% of the audience, a national record). Finally, the Hellfest's instigator is a 'local boy': Benjamin Barbaud, now 29 years old, who grew up, played soccer and learned his catechism in Clisson. Obviously, his personal history makes it easier to understand how it was possible to organize the festival there. He gathered a team of mainly local residents to put everything in place. A fast learner, he basically learned by doing, having first created a hardcore punk event, the Fury Fest (2002–2005), before deciding to create one dedicated to metal, with Korn top of the bill in 2006, and KISS the lead billing of 2010. Looking back to the early years, he says:

> We had fun programming GBH and the Dead Kennedys, but it didn't work out that well, which is why we turned to metal. Metalheads spend more money, while punks will have a hard time paying 100 euros for a seat. It's not their state of mind, it's tough explaining to them that we don't get subsidies like general public festivals... We always wanted to bring bands from the eighties, but in the beginning we just didn't have the money... People made unpleasant comments about Kiss, who aren't extreme, but we just thought that there should be a space for that type of band in France. We did great with Manowar last year... Since I've been organizing the Hellfest, I've rediscovered metal (Chelley and Manœuvre 2010: 9).

Barbaud is a pragmatist: he responds to an unsatisfied demand, and that is how he justifies his choices of acts, before considering aesthetic or social reasons. This explains why he invites black metal bands—which are, however, a minority in the festival's program.

Birth of Ignorance: The ambivalent 2006–2007 reactions

The establishment of the Hellfest immediately sparked off important debates. Clisson inhabitants were nervous at the possibility of being disturbed by a rock festival (huge crowd, noise, safety issues). Yet in 2006, the city council, which had a right-wing majority, emphasized its economic benefits.

The outcome of the first festival in 2006 was positive. Clisson storekeepers were quite satisfied with the economic impact of the event (lodging, catering, transportation, tourism). Although some of them complained of the nuisances (traffic, noise, etc.), there weren't any incidents. The police noted that the law was universally respected. Considering the festival's size, problems of violence or offences were barely visible, and the local population, although sometimes shocked by what they perceived as aggressiveness in the dress codes and the music itself, was surprised by the festival-goers' polite behaviour:

> 20,000 festival-goers with their strange way of dressing and their 'shrieking' music: the locals expected the worst. But finally, the Hellfest got almost unanimous support. The various Cassandras got

> nothing for their pains... The attitude, the costume, the music may seem provoking. The attitude isn't. 'They are extremely polite and respectful...' This is what all those who were in contact with them—the mayor and his deputies, municipal counselors, the police, rescue workers, shopkeepers and the population—said (Anon 2006: 6).

Concerns about public safety or 'morality' remained low-level, largely because the festival's team adopted a proactive attitude, overcoming the problems of organization, improving the reception conditions for festival-goers and being open to requests from Clisson inhabitants. Local economic agents also insisted that the festival keep on going, and by the fall of 2006, the second installment (Hellfest 2007) was authorized by the city council. Collaborations with the local civil society developed during the preparations for the following installments (volunteer work, animations, set-building, cleaning-up and a 'green-friendly' festival).

At Hellfest 2007, the organizers encountered management problems due to the terrible weather and the unrelenting rain—they nicknamed it 'Woodstock installment' for that reason. However, these climatic hazards ended up being beneficial, as many 'Clissonnais' helped the festival-goers out, welcoming them into their homes or garages. Generally speaking, links between both populations grew stronger.[2]

By Demons Be Driven: the 2008 turning point

While the festival was taking root in Clisson, the year 2008 was also a polemical turning point. Violently hostile reactions surfaced sporadically during the months preceding the event, followed by a growth in arguments against the festival. The growth of the internet, and in particular of lobbyist blogs, accompanied the debates.

Municipal elections took place in early 2008, and in Clisson the outgoing mayor was defeated by his left-wing Catholic opponent. The latter had an ambiguous position vis-à-vis the Hellfest, which enabled him to gather opponents into his camp without alienating his supporters. He insisted upon the festival's economic and tourist importance, and acknowledged the right for any musical expression to have a platform. But at the same time, he denounced the attacks against Christians in the lyrics of some of the groups invited. The opponents' rhetoric gained in precision, following the visit, early 2008, of father Benoît Domergue, a priest with a PhD in theology, who studied gothic and metal culture, and who offered several meetings on the topic in Clisson. One of them was public, and was attended by about 300 people; another was organized behind closed doors for the city council. Domergue also met both of Clisson's priests.

There is something odd about Father Domergue's strategy. During the festival, he appeared as a moderate. He acknowledged the legitimacy of heavy metal as a culture, while condemning its anti-Christian excesses. He wanted a say in the festival's programming, but only in order to separate the wheat from the chaff, and set aside the bands that were too extreme (he mentioned Belphegor, Dimmu Borgir and Impaled Nazarene). Yet, one can only be surprised by the huge gap between what he would say in public and what he wrote in his book on extreme music (Domergue 2000). In the latter, he proposes a description of Satanist metal, listing dozens of bands, translating the most shocking lyrics—which, undeniably, are easy to find. However, he makes a naïve interpretation of them, as he does for example with bands such as Slipknot or Slayer, one of the apparently most vehemently anti-Christian bands, whose lead singer, Tom Araya, nonetheless sincerely adopts the Christian faith. As Deena Weinstein (2000) or Fabien Hein (2006) put it, taking the calls for the eradication of Christianity literally is problematic, to say the least. Domergue establishes this list as if there were a systematic homogeneity between the musicians' intent and the forms taken by their music. That is to say that sound forms are always perfectly adapted and coherent with lyrics and vice versa, that they are the smoothest, the most faithful vehicle of the explicit message that they are supposed to promote in unison. This fallacious faith in the flat coherence of the musical sign as a whole makes Domergue incapable of conceiving that musicians and audiences can play with meaning and its degrees of seriousness/literalness. The myths (Barthes 1957) they constitute combine intentions, texts, musical forms, gestures, attitudes and styles in such a heterogeneous way that their meaning cannot be assigned to any monolithical interpretation (see also Weinstein 2009: 17). The presence of several 'Christian core' (see Moberg in this volume) bands at each installment of the festival—or, for that matter, of a great majority of non-Satanist bands playing the same type of music—could have given him some sort of clue pointing to the possibility of ambivalence or polysemy, if not voluntary 'misappropriations'.

The second stage of Domergue's reasoning was that formally Satanic music, produced by a Satanist intention, can only have, in an appropriate context (the 'collective trance' created in metal concerts as he puts it), Satanic effects. These effects are, first, *moral*, as the music creates despair, depression, and morbid fascination. Second, they are *proselytic*: music is a technique of converting people to Satanism, based on the conjunction of the mesmerizing show—he mentions 'bewitchment'—and this moral weakness. For example, Domergue writes:

> If one considers Black or Death Metal, one can easily see that there
> is an automatic and mechanical relationship between the tones,
> the rhythms and the sonorities of this type of music and those who
> listen to it...which also results from magic (Domergue 2000: 84).

So, to seal up this harmonious chain of meaning, the corruptive power of the music is not enough; the listener also has to be 'helpless to resist' it, as Robert Walser puts it (1993: 141). During his 2008 conference, Domergue said that 'most young people I meet are lost lambs, but not wolves. For example, some Gothics [sic] came to see me so that I could hear their confessions. These young people swallow the words of a band like Slayer, and their latest anti-Christian album.'[3] Comments such as this that deny any form of agency to the metal listener who presents symptoms of psychological or moral fragility, are legion in the book and his meetings, as well as being present in the discourse of all Catholic opponents to the Hellfest. As Robert Wright puts it, while examining the controversies around Marilyn Manson in the United States: 'the very act of listening becomes symptomatic of antisocial behaviour and even suicidal tendencies' (Wright 2000: 373). Listening is the location where this type of discourse finds its most fertile point of entry, where the Satanist threat can contemplate its ravages, within the intimacy of the not-quite-innocent and dangerously alienable soul it lives to musically deprave. This alleged corruption of course justifies all types of inquisitions wished for by moral authorities: assertion of norms, detection of symptoms and proposal of therapeutics (including, in this case, exorcism[4]). To sum things up, there is a perfect similarity between intentions, forms and effects, which is only possible provided that the meaning is petrified, and that the intentions and the musical form have a direct power on the listener, who is deprived of any autonomous will or sensibility.

While he highlights a certain form of magic and the corrupting psychological potency within the substance of metal, Domergue's discursive strategy carries out a certain moral technique of power that, by mobilizing a whole set of eclectic rhetorical tactics, aims at producing a representation of the metal world that could hook up with vague anxieties within the French Catholic milieu, if not state authorities. The cultural and demographic context of Catholicism in France is one of decline and reaction to different real or perceived 'assaults': loss of flock, influence and authority, multiple recent scandals, failure to impose the idea of a 'Christian origin' of Europe in its Constitution, fear of Islam, and, beyond that, the French anticlerical tradition (Schlegel 2009: 7–16). Thus, finding/inventing heinous and dangerous enemies enables the Church to present itself as 'victim' and exclusive 'scapegoat' of rampant 'cathophobia', and can be an efficient way to mobilize troops. Taking inspiration from Foucault (2004: 68–69), we could call this strategy a *government of the senses* (Sklower 2008: 211): discursive techniques aimed at producing, with the cooperation of the receptive subject, representations and sensorial (in this case, listening) practices that take root in pre-existing fears, in order to unite a community in the rejection of a subculture. In this case, the existence and popularity of metal is not only a peripheral 'excess', but maybe a central revelator of recent evolutions within society. This strategy is ambiguous, as it tries to bind a community together in a fantasmatic fear while still debating with the opponents. The goal is to have some legitimacy within both worlds, a position from which negotiating censorship is possible.

Clisson's town hall wasn't insensitive to the more presentable and relatively consensual aspects of Father Domergue's discourse. As representatives of many of the town's believers, the local authorities kept in mind the idea that metal could promote an insidious and dangerous message. They found further confirmation of their suspicions in the conclusions of the 'Interministerial Mission of Vigilance and Fight against Sectarian Excesses' (Miviludes). This is a state organism in charge of informing the authorities and the public about various sectarian dangers. For example, their 2009 annual report dealt with the influence of 'New Age' movements. At the same time (spring 2008) that the Hellfest was debated in Clisson, Miviludes released its analyses about the 'growing influence' of Satanism. It is important to offer a brief description of these analyses, as they represent the authority of the state, and thus—one would hope[5]—a neutral, scientific and balanced point of view on the reality of Satanism in France. These conclusions were constantly referred to by the festival's opponents, radical or not, including the 'Confédération Nationale des Associations de Familles Catholiques', the association 'Catholiques en Campagne', the 'Cercle des Trois Provinces' quoted at the beginning of this chapter, as well as many Catholic blogs.

What is interesting about this report is that one can find a familiar list of the different 'symptoms' and 'signs' that must 'alert' parents on the risks that their children run when they listen to diabolical music, such as:

- a 'radical change in the dress code and in particular the adoption of black as the only reference'
- forms of 'withdrawal' (rejecting usual activities, family, school etc.)
- 'a total rejection of traditional religions, combined with a growing fascination for pagan emblems, military clothing and relics'
- 'melancholic tendencies'
- 'musical tastes orientated towards the more violent forms of metal'
- 'the excessive consumption of scary and horror movies, as well as of role-playing games or video games that surf on the same morbid themes'

- the viewing of 'Internet websites, forums and blogs' that deal with 'provocation, Satanism, esotericism, pornography (and paedophilia), mind reading and political extremism'
- and, among many others, this poetically elliptical one: 'the attraction to cultural consumer goods forbidden for any younger than age 16' (Miviludes 2006: 79–80).

A short 2004 preliminary report highlighted 'the assiduous frequentation of metal concerts' as 'not without risk (nearly-hypnotic atmospheres that encourage states of trance, subliminal messages calling for acting out and stimulating suicidal drives, etc.)', as well as 'incitement to hatred' and 'anti-Semitic allusions to paganism and nationalism', not to mention the 'sometimes proselyte, fervent Satanists' who haunt the 'nebula of fans of Black Metal idols' (Miviludes 2004: 2)—many elements that one also finds in Domergue's book as well as on various anti-Hellfest blogs and texts.

Adopting these signs can thus indicate a form of 'subjugation' (*mise sous influence*): anything counter-cultural about these practices, anything that can bear a sense of aesthetic identification, that can create values, a sense of community, is immediately rejected as a deleterious manipulation. The Satanist sign, once again, carries a harmful scheme, the threat of dispossession of the self. As Robert Walser puts it, critics of metal 'imagine that fans are passive, unable to resist the pernicious messages of heavy metal, and thus they themselves commit the sort of dehumanization they ascribe to popular culture. They make fans into dupes without agency or subjectivity' (Walser 1993: 144). Of course, the 2006 report clearly says that there is no 'direct causality between listening to Satanist music and acting out', but there still are 'indirect effects' that can constitute a 'favourable terrain for acting out': 'the connection during concerts with practicing and proselytising Satanists; acting out of what is promoted in the songs' lyrics' and 'deep rupture with common family culture' (Miviludes 2006: 94).

The fact is that the Miviludes never discusses the 'sectarian excesses' that can exist in legitimate religions, and that could formally reveal many affinities with the definitions it proposes of this subculture's functioning; nor would it indulge in analysing, for example, the moral weakness, the confusion that can push some to seek refuge within the more respectable belief systems and religious communities, or the examples of charlatanism that exist within some of them. This discourse is proposed in the name of a certain normative—if not religious—order of signs, aimed at the exposure of subcultural forms, as much, if not more, as it is in the name of cultural (freedom of religion, tolerance) and 'biopolitical' (the norms that determine the appearance of moral health, peoples' security) imperatives (Foucault 1976: 184; 2004: 233–37). The insistence on 'influence' and 'acting out'—here, obviously, in a more psychoanalytical register than in Domergue's—reveals the anxiety concerning familial and social stability, which cannot go without cultural (moral, aesthetic) prescriptions. Once again, culture is analysed monosemantically; the listening subject is deprived of any capacity of creating significance through autonomous practices (a subjectivation), that in fact 'undo' this illusory power (De Certeau 1990: 239–42; Rancière 2008: 18–20, 48–49).

Strengthened by this conjuncture, the festival's opponents decided to lead public campaigns against the Hellfest. There was for instance the 'Cercle des Trois Provinces' (Circle of the Three Provinces), a Catholic association politically and ideologically rooted in the extreme-right movement.[6] They mainly used posters and sent letters to the media and festival's supporters. Ben Barbaud received one, in which he was told that he would have to 'answer before God for his deeds'.[7] These messages mixed religious texts, prophecies, prayers, as well as odd articles, for example on AIDS in Africa and the solutions recommended by Pope John Paul II (abstinence). The tracts proposed many elements typical of the rhetoric we analysed above, but in an even more extreme and caricatured way: condemnation of 'anti-Christian racism'; of the authorities' 'criminal' behaviour, in financing an evil festival in the context of a 'multiplication of tomb desecrations in cemeteries'; Satanist proselytism which 'harnesses the weakness of certain young people who go through an identity, mental crisis, lack future perspectives, break with their family, drop out of school' thanks to 'magical', 'sexual' and 'destructive rituals' and their attraction to anything 'morbid' or 'esoteric', and so on.

A right-wing association of Clisson inhabitants wanted the festival to disappear, demanding the 'protection of public order and of youth' (H. P. 2008: 3). In this case, the evocation of humanist and republican or traditional principles, as well of course as the defence of teenagers, constituted a means by which these groups propounded their values within the broader ethical field of civil society and the authorities.

Quite quickly though, the church of Clisson distanced itself from such positions. The festival's third installment dispelled all doubts, as it took place under a bright sky, and without any major incidents. The exchanges between festival-goers and local inhabitants had by then become part of the 'folklore'. The local library presented books on the subject, inviting the authors to present their work; the festival showed films on metal culture in Clisson's movie theatre. More and more people also provided shelter for the metal fans.

God Gave Rock'n'Roll To Everyone: the 2009–2010 confrontation

The Hellfest came out strengthened by the 2008 installment, even though the most conservative Catholics kept on protesting about the Satanist factory it was supposed to be.[8] The festival's organizers feared a big assault because of Marilyn Manson's top billing on 20 June, but no such thing happened. In the Clisson parish bulletin, the priest called for serenity and opened permanent prayer services during the entire festival (Anon 2009a).

But a broader attack coming from national right-wing political parties and traditionalist Catholic blogs took shape shortly before the beginning of the festival, in the form of questioning the (scarce) public subsidies granted by the General Council of the Loire Atlantique county and the Regional Council of the Pays de la Loire. A small right-wing party close to the government's UMP party (Union for a Popular Movement), the CNI (National Independents Centre) opened the assault, declaring that 'the limits of the unbearable have been crossed... Our taxes serve the diffusion of extremely violent messages' (Anon 2009b: 2). The local representatives of the UNI (the main UMP-affiliated students association) and Catholic associations pursued the same agenda.[9] These different organizations wanted to put pressure on the Hellfest by email and phone messages sent to the festival's public or private (Kronenbourg, Coca-Cola) sponsors, and their servers and telephone switchboards were overwhelmed for several days. Coca-Cola, who supported the festival with its Monster Energy Drink, declared in early July that it would withdraw from the festival (however, it agreed to come back in 2010).

Various 'interest groups' reacted to these attacks. First, those who supported the Hellfest, or more globally, metal. Specialized blogs and websites (Metallorgy, spirit-of-metal, Metal Impact, etc.) relayed the information and criticized it. Fans created a specific website in defence of the festival (pro-Hellfest.fr), which gathered the many initiatives, such as Facebook groups.[10] Professionals of the cultural field mobilized by proposing a petition: '*Appel à soutien au Hellfest: pour la diversité artistique*' (Call for the support of the Hellfest: for artistic diversity).[11] As with the year before, it was only days before the festival that the polemic developed, losing force only days after. It was scarcely touched on by the media, as once again there were no incidents in 2009. Security companies even said it was their favourite event in the West of France because of its peaceful nature (Anon 2009c: 11). Besides, the programming of bands such as Europe and Mötley Crüe broadened its appeal within the metal community.

Robert Culat, priest of the Carpentras parish and an active supporter of metal, intervened during the May 2009 debate in Clisson. His perception of the metal milieu opposes that of Father Domergue's in many ways, as well as, *a fortiori*, that of the more fundamentalist Catholic groups. He loves metal (Opeth being his favourite), listens to many anti-Christian bands (like Emperor), and even wrote a book on his experience and encounter with this world (Culat 2008), in which he interviewed dozens of fans about their relationship to this music. In a post on his myspace (28 June 2009), 'Padre Bob' delivered a digest of his thoughts on metal, in which he criticized the caricatured vision proposed by extremist Catholics. He used many biblical references, Church texts, such as the Catholic social teaching, or various encyclicals, in order to dispel the accusation of Satanism and reverse it against 'true Satanism', i.e. hedonistic individualism in contemporary capitalism.

Culat finds positive, and even Christian values within the metal world, such as solidarity (he mentions the grass-root fundraising that was organized to help Chuck Schuldiner[12]). What the anti-Hellfest Catholics consider as perversion or dangerous passivity becomes the sign of a praiseworthy spiritual craving for him: one mustn't judge 'those who seem to refuse God', because 'certain oppositions can be closer to a true religious attitude than soulless conformism' and 'sometimes, "blasphemous" words uttered by Atheists can be the expression of a more or less conscious spiritual research'. Thus, rather than condemning without knowing, one must follow Paul VI's precepts (the 'bête noire' of Catholic fundamentalists), that is to 'get closer to the profane society' and try to 'evangelize the culture, the milieus and the mentalities so that the reference to God find its right place'. Thus, the adoption of signs and even of a specific liturgy by metal fans should not be considered as a threat to Christianity anymore, but as a godsend in disguise for a new evangelization.

In opposition to moral fundamentalism, he proposes a rationale of pastoral efficiency: 'Is asking for censorship or banning the solution to promote the cause of the Gospel and of faith among the young people that are generally very far from Christianity?'[13] he asks. His discourse is not one of universal tolerance,[14] but one of subcultural sympathy. He believes in the spiritual power of the metal community, in its capacity to recognize the true meaning of its practices. The desires that underpin the adherence to metal signs reveal virtues that are absolutely compatible with the Christian faith and way of life: love, understanding and evangelization vs. hatred, stereotypes and inquisition.

The year 2010 was one of national controversies. Adopted by the locals, the Hellfest had become much-loved, and 72,000 fans came to hear the Deftones, Fear Factory, Infectious Grooves, Sepultura, Slayer, Carcass, Alice Cooper and KISS, as well as the 108 other bands. Nonetheless, the polemics resumed, starting earlier than in previous years and reaching an unprecedented scale. Once again, the political context was responsible for making the argument an issue, as regional elections took place in March 2010. On 11 March, during a meeting of the right-wing regional opposition, Catholic and xenophobic politician Philippe de Villiers stated that 'our values aren't the ones that push the actual Regional Council to finance a Satanist festival!' In the heat of the electoral campaign, Christine Boutin, former minister and president of the Christian Democrat party (also in the region's political opposition) disclosed on her website a letter sent to brewer Kronenbourg, asking the company if it was 'relevant to associate [their] image to a festival that promotes and encourages a culture of death?'[15] An idiom that carries all the ex-minister's struggles against other faces of this 'culture'—abortion, homosexuality etc. Against this literal and monosemic interpretation of the sign 'death', one could quote the testimony of death metal musician Dan Saladin, gathered by Harris Berger: 'The energy of a death metal performance, and the attendant subcultural community-building that these musicians so enthusiastically participated in, is pursued as a pro-active response to the apathy, a way of overcoming hopelessness' (Berger 1999: 173). A similar idea can be found in Marilyn Manson's answer to such accusations (Wright 2000: 375). The apparent morbidity of the metal milieu is in fact often the sign of a struggle against the threat of insensibility or spiritlessness: a conjuration of melancholy, an aspiration for energy, a research of community.

On 30 March, socialist deputy Patrick Roy reacted by interrogating Minister of Culture Frédéric Mitterrand, during parliamentary questions. The latter played down the controversy while emphasizing that the state didn't subsidize the festival. The left won the elections, and the controversy disappeared during the month of April. Two elements must be noted here. First, this exposure of the Hellfest proved a lucrative one for the Hellfest's organizers, as the number of tickets sold grew again in 2010. Secondly, the national media globally defended the Hellfest. Even TF1, the most popular French private television channel—although it did show in its reportage[16] a 'shocking' backstage Satanist ritual where the members of Scandinavian band Watain covered their faces with animal blood before their performance—insisted predominantly on the 'friendly atmosphere' that reigned during the whole event.

Conclusion

From this brief review of the controversies surrounding the Hellfest, one can identify two fundamental tendencies. First, on a local level, the perception of the festival—and through it, of metal—evolved from questions and incomprehension to enthusiasm and support. One could consider these debates a Habermasian public sphere (Habermas 1997) in the sense that practical reason and consensus prevailed. During public debates, the various parties were invited to have their say, and organizers tried to deal with some of the critics. But on the national level, it is a public sphere according to Nancy Fraser's definition (Fraser 1992): antagonistic, impassioned, and animated by subaltern counter-publics. The public dominant in previous eras (Catholics opposed to blasphemy and symbolic attacks) has progressively become a minority, as the influence of the Church has declined in French society. Rock's partisans now promote potent norms.

Any strategy of cultural and moral struggle summons a various set of discourses and rhetorical strategies. Specifically in this case, Catholic opponents to the festival proposed on the one hand a moral and aesthetic one, on the value and power of a given cultural sign, and the means by which authorities should fight against it. On the other hand, they used various cultural strategies of struggle that followed an axis going from total ideological intransigence to a set of flexible tactics of negotiation with opponents or other institutions' values. Among the extremists—in this case, Catholic fundamentalists—there was the antagonistic and closed assertion of a conservative value and belief system, and among the pragmatists, the search for some sort of 'settlement' between the ideological systems supported by the different agents of the polemic. This meant, for the anti-Hellfest Catholics, convincing the authorities to put limits on freedom of speech in the name of tolerance (a Republican, secular value), and thus accept the censorship of violently anti-Christian bands (their political goal). These strategies reveal different perceptions of each agent's capacity to defend its values at the moment of the struggle as well as (and thus choose confrontation or negotiation), eventually, interpretations of the state or 'origin' of the loss of influence ('what does the existence of a Satanist festival in this "Catholic" country say about the evolution of our authority?').

The question of the limit imposed on what metal bands can express cannot be judged independently from this context of broader relationships in which the targeted authorities (in this case, the Church, but also eventually others such as the state, the family, the workplace etc.) are entangled. Indeed, the argument according to which similar attacks on Judaism or Islam wouldn't be tolerated is quite right, if considered *in abstracto*. But the difference in this case is that the Catholic Church, despite its long-term decline in influence symbolically, remains a *dominant* moral figure, historically and geographically rooted (especially in Western France), benefiting from traditional privileges (state-funded private schools, for example) as well as recent reactionary presidential endorsements.[17] This is where the French context is different from that of the United States, although the comparison with the Tipper Gore/PMRC debates shows many strong similarities (Walser 1993: 138–42)—notably when it comes to 'preserving' the moral health of the youth. In France, Christianity is a weakening yet symbolically potent figure of moral order and repression. All of this makes it a purely metaphoric—thus caricatured—target of counter-cultural rebellious desires within the vast majority of metal fandom. On the other hand, the stereotypical depiction of metal fans as 'cathophobic' Satanists by certain Catholic groups serves as a pretext to galvanize outrage at Catholicism's specific 'victimization'. What is interesting here is, simultaneously, the recourse to typically secular, 'multiculturalist' rhetorics (denouncing intolerance and lack of respect for freedom of religion) which subtend this strategy.

The question of the limits of freedom of expression is however a problematic one for the metal world. When can one identify the objective signification of a song and its concrete dangers (Kahn-Harris 2003)? If we draw these limits, do we not risk reifying signification when we previously set ourselves up as champions of its collective construction? This same confidence in the 'hijacking' of signification operated by the listener represents a chance or a threat depending on the circumstances, the intentions, the interactions, and the needs of those who preside over the 'choices' guiding such practices. A Western band virulently criticizing Islam offers little doubt about its xenophobia, whereas the wearing of T-shirts with the logo of explicit anti-Semitic bands by Israeli metal fans—although quite meaningful—obviously does not point to a literal identification (Kahn-Harris 2002: 126).

Indeed, metal maintains a counter-cultural aura as long as it keeps sparking off such polemics and remains a subculture that feeds on provocation and excess. From this point of view, the strategy of the Hellfest's organizers, consisting in successfully portraying metalheads as sweet and harmless boys and girls, can be problematic: could these ultra-virile and hyper-mean musical assaults only be a farce, a sort of musical translation of wrestling kitsch? Specific provocative images promoted by bands can only be considered as counter-cultural in context: multiple scales must be taken into consideration, as everything depends on what one considers as the dominant culture targeted by a particular genre, band or song, and the criteria chosen to define its main signification. To insist on the multiplicity of signifying practices (De Certeau 1990: 239–42), on the spectator's activity, against the types of 'distribution of the sensible' (Rancière 2000: 12) that the idea of passivity contains, is to accept the frailty and ideological and political relativity of any 'counter'-culture. Its identity or boundaries are then to be negotiated in a power struggle involving the agents of a cultural polemic (or 'culture war'), the values chosen to judge these forms, the authority of the methods assessing their danger and the right to freedom of speech.

Notes

1. Bill Hicks refers to the 1990 James Vance vs. Judas Priest trial.
2. As can be seen in accounts by the local press (*Ouest France, Hebdo Sèvre et Maine, Presse Océan*).
3. The album *Christ Illusion* 2006. American Recordings. B003CSCHUS.
4. Talking about metal or techno music concerts, he says, elsewhere: 'The human

intelligence and will are not directly concerned by these stimuli, but a true "hyper-saturation" of the senses and an exacerbated imagination are practically capable of isolating them. This conditioning and this oppression...are such, that cases of infestations or possessions can be imagined in such circumstances'. See Le Subliminal, Interview du Père Domergue, http://www.lesubliminal.fr/interview_du_pere_domergue_193.htm.

5. The Miviludes' method and conclusions were severely criticized by one of the members of the commission working on Satanism, sociologist Olivier Bobineau (Bobineau 2008), who led a collective counter-survey on the question, concluding there was barely any Satanist sectarian risk in France.

6. They are an emanation of Jean Ousset's 'Cité catholique', a 'national-catholic', former member of Charles Maurras's 'Action Française' (the inglorious royalist and anti-Semitic league created at the end of the nineteenth century), and member of the 'Jeune légion', an armed wing of the Vichy regime.

7. See Kaosguards. Ben Barbaud, Organisateur du Hellfest, http://www.kaosguards.com/content/view/699/35/.

8. For a synthesis of conservative Catholic blogs and websites about the 2009 installment, see: Christ Roi blog, Synthèse des mobilisations contre le Hellfest et ses soutiens, http://christroi.over-blog.com/article-32838939.html.

9. Among the latter is the site e-deo.typepad.fr, which explicitly refers to the 'real country' (*pays réel*), a concept that refers once again to the ideology of Charles Maurras; see n. 8 above. The site's tone is constantly xenophobic and islamophobic.

10. Soutenons le Hellfest!!! http://www.facebook.com/group.php?gid=92490879863. Support group: Hellfest! http://www.facebook.com/group.php?gid=95531469014 *'Je suis chrétien et j'écoute du metal. Et ce n'est pas contradictoire'*. http://fr-fr.facebook.com/group.php?gid=22098979270.

11. The petition can be accessed here: www.lepole.asso.fr/fichiers/file/petition%20hellfest(3).pdf

12. The leader of very influential death metal band Death, who died in December 2001 of collateral damage from his cancer treatment (pneumonia). During the years 2000 and 2001, metal bands gave charity concerts, and fans sent money to pay for his first surgery.

13. See Padre Bob blog, Qui sont les vrais satanistes? http://www.myspace.com/agedumetal/blog.

14. One can find on his myspace blog the copy of a post in favour of the Swiss 'anti-minaret' November 2009 vote. See *ibid.*, Le Benditisme a encore frappé.

15. The letter can be downloaded here: http://tinyurl.com/clq77em.

16. The link to the video: http://videos.tf1.fr/sept-a-huit/la-guerre-des-mondes-5898258.html.

17. In his 20 December 2007 speech at the Lateran, Nicolas Sarkozy created quite a scandal back in France, for saying that 'teachers will never be able to replace the priest or the pastor' in the moral education of our children. The speech can be accessed here: http://www.elysee.fr/president/les-actualites/discours/2007/allocution-de-m-le-president-de-la-republique.7012.html?search=Latran.

Bibliography

Anonymous. 2006. 'Hellfest. Une organisation exemplaire'. *Ouest France*, 27 June: 6.

—2009a. 'L'Eglise veut rester vigilante vis-à-vis du Hellfest'. *Ouest France*, 20 June: 8.

—2009b. 'Le CNI pas rock'n'roll'. *Presse Océan*, 20 June: 2.

—2009c. 'Secours, la tranquillité en alerte maximale'. *Hebdo Sèvre et Maine*, 25 June: 11.

Barthes, Roland, 1957. *Mythologies*. Paris: Seuil.

Berger, Harris. 1999. 'Death Metal Tonality and the Act of Listening'. *Popular Music* 18(2): 161–78. http://dx.doi.org/10.1017/S0261143000009028

Bobineau, Olivier, ed. 2008. *Le satanisme. Quel danger pour la société?* Paris: Flammarion-Pygmalion.

Chelley, Isabelle, and Philippe Manœuvre. 2010. 'L'inconscience de la jeunesse. Interview de Ben Barbaud'. *Rock & Folk* 514: 16–19. Paris: Éditions Larivière.

Culat, Robert. 2007. *L'Âge du metal*. Rosières-en-Haye: Camion Blanc.

De Certeau, Michel. 1990. *L'Invention du quotidien*, vol. 1, *Arts de faire*. Paris: Gallimard.

Domergue, Benoît. 2000. *Culture barock et Gothic flamboyant. La musique extrême: un écho surgi des abîmes*. Paris: François Xavier de Guibert.

Foucault, Michel. 1976. *Histoire de la Sexualité*, vol. 1, *La Volonté de savoir*. Paris: Gallimard.

—2004. *Sécurité, Territoire, Population: Cours au Collège de France (1977–78)*. Paris: Seuil.

Fraser, Nancy. 1992. 'Rethinking the Public Sphere: A Contribution to a Critique of Actually Existing Democracy'. In *Habermas and the Public Sphere*, ed. Craig Calhoun, 109–42. Cambridge: MIT Press.

Guibert, Gérôme. 2008. 'Les festivals musiques actuelles en Pays de la Loire. Entre logiques d'implantations locales et reconfigurations nationales'. *Le Pôle, Enquête Flash* 1: 1–12.

Habermas, Jürgen. 1997. *L'Espace public: archéologie de la publicité comme dimension constitutive de la société bourgeoise*. Paris: Payot.

Hein, Fabien. 2006. *Rock and Religion: Dieu(x) et la musique du diable*. Boulogne Billancourt: Autour du Livre.

H.P. 2008. 'Un collectif clissonnais veut la mort du Hellfest'. *Hebdo Sèvres et Maine*, 8 May: 3.

Kahn-Harris, Keith. 2002. '"I Hate this Fucking Country": Dealing with the Global and the Local in the Israeli Extreme Metal Scene'. In *Music, Popular Culture, Identities*, ed. Richard Young, 119–36. Amsterdam: Rodopi.

—2003. 'Death Metal and the Limits of Musical Expression'. In *Policing Pop*, ed. Martin Cloonan and Reebee Garofalo, 81–99. Philadelphia: Temple University Press.

Miviludes. 2004. Report 'Satanisme et dérive sectaire. Quels sont les risques, comment les prévenir?'. Paris.

—2006. *Le satanisme. Un risque de dérive sectaire*. Paris: La Documentation française.

Rancière, Jacques. 2000. *Le Partage du sensible. Esthétique et politique*. Paris: La Fabrique.

—2008. *Le Spectateur émancipé*. Paris: La Fabrique.

Schlegel, Jean-Louis. 2009. 'Benoît XVI et les intégristes: tempête sur l'Église'. *Esprit* 353: 7–16. Paris: Esprit.

Sklower, Jedediah. 2008. 'Rebel with the Wrong Cause: Albert Ayler et la signification du free jazz en France (1959–1971)'. In *Volume!* 6-1/2: 193–219. Bordeaux: Mélanie Seteun.

Walser, Robert. 1993. *Running with the Devil: Power, Gender, and Madness in Heavy Metal Music*. Middletown, CT: Wesleyan University Press.

Weinstein, Deena. 2000. *Heavy Metal: The Music and its Culture*. New York: Da Capo Press.

—2009. 'The Empowering Masculinity of British Heavy Metal'. In Gerd Bayer, *Heavy Metal Music in Britain*, 17–31. London. Ashgate.

Wright, Robert. 2000. '"I'd Sell You Suicide": Pop Music and Moral Panic in the Age of Marilyn Manson'. *Popular Music* 19(3): 365–85. http://dx.doi.org/10.1017/S0261 143000000222

Part II: Countercultures

'I want *you* to support local metal'

A theory of metal scene formation

Jeremy Wallach* and Alexandra Levine**

*Bowling Green State University, Ohio, USA
**Graduate of Bowling Green State University, Ohio, USA

Much of the existing literature in metal studies contains an implicit theory of scene formation. The following chapter aims to articulate an explicit theory that can be applied to metal scenes across the planet. Such a theory must go beyond synchronic conceptions and instead account for the emergence, development, and continually fluctuating fortunes of local heavy metal scenes, including considerations such as generational succession, relations with neighbouring scenes, and the role of musical amateurism. We argue in the pages that follow that while specific, widely divergent details do matter profoundly in every scenic context, so do the larger features of the picture, and that these latter are likely to strike the metal scholar as every bit as familiar as the amplified sounds of the music. In this essay we draw on ethnographic research both in Indonesia (conducted by Wallach in 1997, 1999–2000 and 2011) and the US (carried out by Levine in 2009).[1] Data will be drawn from the metal scenes in Jakarta, the sprawling capital city of Indonesia, with roughly nine million inhabitants and growing, and Toledo, Ohio, a postindustrial city in the Midwestern United States with a population of around 300,000 and shrinking.[2] Our intention in presenting material from these two very different field sites is neither to engage in ethnographic thick description nor to offer an intricate theoretical discussion of the utility of the scene concept in cross-cultural analysis. Rather, in this brief essay we wish merely to propose in a highly schematic fashion a practical guide to researchers conducting empirical research on metal scenes anywhere in the world. For this reason the material is organized around four functions served by metal scenes and six generalizations about them that we have identified. While these functions and generalizations may not be applicable to every single case, we believe they are useful nonetheless for the initial framing of empirical inquiry.

It turns out that the metal scenes in Toledo and Jakarta have much in common despite their considerable cultural, demographic and geographic distance. Moreover, we suggest in this essay that these commonalities in scenic dynamics and institutions may in fact derive from metal's unique cultural characteristics and, furthermore, that it is these same characteristics that have allowed metal to encircle the globe and become one of the best-known musical styles on the planet, attracting legions of serious and dedicated fans on every inhabited continent (cf. Weinstein 1991; Kahn-Harris 2007; Dunn and McFadyen 2005, 2008; Wallach, Berger and Greene 2011).[3] Our hope, then, is that this essay will provide material on which worldwide metal researchers can draw instead of having to reinvent the wheel.

The term 'scene' is used to refer to local, national and global entities in both everyday parlance and in scholarly discourse. This lack of precision— using the same term to refer to vastly different scales of organization—is, we believe, highly unfortunate for scholarship, but we also believe it is quixotic at this point to expect to stamp it out. Therefore, rather than propose alternate terminology here, we will try to qualify what we mean as best we can by using the usual modifiers. Folklorist Ruth Finnegan is often credited as the scholar to first call analytical attention to the grassroots, non-commercially-oriented performance of popular music far away from the centers of the entertainment industry (1989), while Will Straw (1991) first introduced the concept of the scene as a category of analysis for popular music scholarship as an interface between local music-making and the larger musical universe.[4] The scholar who has been most vocal in calling for the application of scene analysis to metal is Keith Kahn-Harris (Harris 2000; Kahn-Harris 2002, 2004a, 2004b, 2007, 2011). Kahn-Harris employs a Bourdieuan framework, viewing scenes as networks where participants seek to maximize the accumulation of particular forms of capital. This is an exceedingly useful approach, but as French sociologist and metal scholar Gérôme Guibert has recently argued (2011), the Bourdieuian paradigm has unavoidable limitations when discussing the collective actions of musical communities rather than individuals' strategies within them. This essay is an attempt to promote a more holistic understanding of metal scenes as social formations open to specific discursive pathways and conforming to specific cultural logics.

What, exactly, is a scene? Definitions may strike one as a throwback to antiquated twentieth-century social science, but in this case they're helpful. We contend that local metal scenes should be seen as more than rhetorical tropes strategically deployed in discourses characterizing small-scale amateur and semiprofessional metal music-making. We regard metal scenes as *loosely bounded functional units* containing a finite number of participants at any one time. We contend that metal scenes perform four crucial functions in the following order of chronology and priority:

1. They act as *conduits* to the global circulation of metal sounds and styles.
2. They provide gathering places for the *collective consumption* of metal artifacts and the display of metal-related fashion and expertise.[5]
3. They provide *sites for local performance and artifactual production*. At this point some interaction with the larger economic order of society becomes unavoidable, and *scenic institutions* become vital.
4. They *promote local artists* to the larger network of scenes. These promotional aims are not usually oriented towards commercial interests and are rarely focused on one single, exceptional band.

Thus we define scenes as social formations that perform at least two of the above functions and conform to at least one of the following generalizations.

Six generalizations about metal scenes

Metal is unique. Throughout the following discussion, although some of the claims we make could apply to scenes dedicated to other global popular music genres (punk, gothic, rave, hip hop, and so forth), others are definitely metal-specific. The available research to date indicates that metal's global spread, from Ohio to Indonesia and beyond, has been characterized by cultural dynamics rarely encountered in other music cultures. To cite an important example, commentators are constantly proclaiming punk and hardcore 'dead' while fans and detractors alike appear to agree that metal is 'the beast that refuses to die'.[6] The following generalizations therefore primarily apply to metal scenes.

First generalization: All metal scenes begin with sites for the collective consumption of extralocal artifacts
This is obviously related to the first two functions of scenes (acting as conduits and gathering places), which we listed as the two most important. This step constitutes, as it were, phase one, preceding the formation of and concerts by cover bands (phase two), and the live performance and recording of bands' original material (three). Anthropologist Greg Urban (2001) argues that in contemporary mass-mediated societies culture primarily moves through the world in the form of disseminated cultural objects. It is far less common for culture to circulate through *replication* rather than *dissemination*. This is a feature more commonly found in societies that Urban defines as operating with a 'metaculture of tradition'. Although metal scenes are always found in a metacultural context of modernity, some of the consumers of disseminated metal recordings choose to develop performative competence to replicate collaboratively the sounds on the recordings in cover bands and even compose new

songs within the genre conventions of metal (which Urban also defines as a type of cultural replication). Recordings of these original songs can then be disseminated themselves, circulating through the social pathways formed by networks of interconnected local scenes spanning the globe.

Arian13, former singer of Indonesian underground legends Puppen and current singer of metal super-group Seringai, relates that at first people sent him lots of free stuff because they were amazed that a poor, faraway country like Indonesia even *had* a metal scene. But now, 25 years later, 'everybody knows about Indonesia' and the free merchandise is less forthcoming. Indonesia's enormous metal scene has long been in the third phase of cultural replication, producing new variations of the metal genre, and the channels for circulating cultural artifacts between the Indonesian and the global scene are now wide and robust and known to 'everybody'. Arian13 is not mistaken regarding this: one day in the spring of 2011, Wallach and Esther Clinton found seven Indonesian extreme metal CDs for sale at RamaLama Records in Toledo, Ohio, USA—an unexpected point of contact between the two very different scenes described in this chapter.

Perhaps the most dramatic example of all of the importance of extralocal artifacts in scene formation can be found in a metal scene that we are otherwise not discussing in this essay. China's underground rock scene, in which metal has played a prominent role (as it has in almost all national underground rock scenes—but more on that later), is about ten years younger than the scene in Indonesia and has faced a more hostile social and political climate. Ivanova (2009) vividly describes how *dakudai*, international-repertoire albums withdrawn from circulation in the West and marked for destruction that instead ended up being sold on the black market in Beijing and other Chinese cities, became the seeds of an underground rock scene that defiantly celebrated freedom, self-expression, and rebellion in the shadow of an authoritarian state that sought total control of its citizens. By the late 1990s, the Beijing scene was thriving and Chinese heavy metal bands like Black Panther and Tang Dynasty enjoyed huge nationwide followings (Wong 2005, 2011).

I have argued previously (Wallach 2003a) that scholars studying rock music have overemphasized the role of live performance in rock culture and therefore paid inadequate attention to recordings. Observers who overemphasized the role of imported recordings in the formation of the Indonesian scene, on the other hand, ran the opposite risk. Particularly in the early to mid 1990s, when the underground metal scene was composed mostly of teenagers performing covers and singing in English, observers accused the scene of cultural inauthenticity, of trying to imitate Americans, of being uncreative, derivative. What these criticisms overlook is that *all* scenes begin with cover bands—Toledo was no different, except that metal albums were easier to obtain and accessed earlier. By the late 90s, most veteran Indonesian metal bands were singing in Indonesian, not English, and a number had developed highly distinctive styles of their own (Wallach 2003b). If given the resources and time to mature, it is almost a certainty that every metal scene will give rise to bands writing original material and experimenting with new sounds and singing in local vernaculars. Heavy metal, a musical style that valorizes freedom and self-expression, does not inspire mere mimicry as the endpoint.

Second generalization: Metal scenes are dependent on institutions for their survival
It is worth remembering that there are many peer groups for whom metal music is crucial, but who lack the material and institutional resources for scene building. Gaines's masterful ethnography of a circle of suburban New Jersey metalheads in the 1980s (1991) is a poignant account of one such group, one of the few available in the ethnographic literature. For 'scenic consciousness' to be achieved, a minimum number of scenic institutions must first exist: a record store, a hangout (which could be the record store), and at least one *all-ages venue* (i.e., not a bar that prevents minors from entering) that can be used on a regular basis by local bands.

In Toledo, record stores often act as all-ages venues, and, as in many US scenes, record stores are important scene anchors because they tend to last much longer than all-ages venues. Founded in 1973, Boogie Records became a focal point for the Toledo metal and punk scenes until it closed in 2004 and two new stores, Culture Clash and RamaLama Records, emerged to take its place. The former establishment, opened by Pat O'Connor, one of the founders of Boogie Records (the other original founder went on to start the CD reissue company Rykodisc) specializes in indie rock, while the latter, run by scene veteran Rob Kimple, is primarily devoted to metal. Metal makes up a full one-third of RamaLama's CD shelves and many of the groups stocked in the 'Popular' section that claims most of the rest of the store's CD racks are from closely allied genres, from hard rock (AC/DC, Ted Nugent, Blue Öyster Cult) to hardcore punk (MDC, Nomeansno). Both of the new record stores are in large spaces and host bands with full sound systems, amplifiers and drum kits, causing at least one neighboring store to move out of RamaLama's building due to the resultant noise bothering its customers.

Jakarta's metal scene relies on *distros*, specialized retail outlets that supply the scene with hangouts as well as T-shirts, CDs, zines, stickers, patches, buttons, and other accessories from sweatshirts to skull-festooned flip flops. Most distros are too small for a band to play in and are owned by musicians active in the scene. For example, Howling Wolf Rock 'n' Roll Merchant is owned by

Arian13 of Seringai, and Ishka-Bible Sick Freak Outfits Shop was run by the late Robin Hutagoal of Brain the Machine. Employees of distros are also usually scene members. Distros usually carry both international and domestic metal bands' products, with a great deal more of the latter, particularly bands from Jakarta who are friends with or include the owner(s).

A scene from Terror Merch, a distro in South Jakarta, January 2011. Photo by Jeremy Wallach. Used with permission

Despite the unquestionable importance of record stores, distros, practice spaces, independent and college radio stations, youth centres, and other establishments, live performance venues (especially the few that manage to survive more than a few years) tend to be the most celebrated scenic institutions. In Toledo, the most beloved venue is Frankie's Inner City. The following excerpts from Levine's field notes give a sense of this venerable rock club, which hosts bands of a variety of genres, metal prominently among them.

> Frankie's Inner City is located at 148 Main Street, Toledo, Ohio. The club is a black building that almost disappears at night. You have to be looking for it to find it. The front of the club has a small overhang right above the main entrance; it's almost too small to stand under.

> Inside Frankie's Inner City there are two rooms and a basement. The first room is only occupied by a few tables and chairs. There is also a desk and cash register used for cover charges. In order to enter the performance area you need to turn right towards the cash register; it is a good way of making sure everyone pays the cover charge. The main room is huge. There is a main stage and a bar area. Along the back wall there is a long glass case. Inside is a collage filled with flyers of past bands that have played at Frankie's. A large metal sign above the case announces it is 'Frankie's Wall of Fame'. Underneath is the legend, 'a history of shows that have played make Frankie's one of the nation's great venues for emerging bands'. There is a light above the sign to make it readable in a dark bar. Underneath the collage there is a small black ledge covered with drinking glasses and empty beer bottles...

With a smallish stage but a large, well-stocked bar, Frankie's has been an important fixture in the metal scene for many years.[7] Like all such venues, it must balance blatantly aggrandizing self-promotion ('one of the nation's great venues'), economic self-interest (including expensive drinks), and attractiveness to outsiders with insider exclusivity (you have to be looking for it to find it) and commitment to unpopular genres (like metal) in order to maintain its reputation in the scene and ensure its economic survival.

Third generalization: Metal scenes are populated by musical 'amateurs'
Colin Helb's valuable study (2009) reveals the importance of musical amateurs for the continued vitality of music scenes. That is, in order for scenes to survive, there must be a critical mass of musicians willing to remain for long periods in a liminal state, never really crossing over into the realm of the professional musician due to the amount of actual earnings obtained from playing in a band—even a touring band—that plays its own songs instead of covering popular hits that appeal to a bar-going crowd. These semiprofessional ensembles are the lifeblood of any rock scene, and metal is no exception.

In some regions, such as the US and Indonesia (though not Western Europe), the fact that vibrant underground metal scenes are often found in college towns can be attributed to non-profit college radio stations becoming key scenic institutions (their ability to fulfil three of the four functions listed above is obvious; moreover the station facility itself often becomes an important scene hangout [see Baulch 2007: 53–55]). Additional salient factors include the cultural vitality and tolerance generally found in college towns (especially compared to surrounding areas) and their relatively low cost of living.

In addition there is a factor that is perhaps more important than all the rest: in patriarchal societies (that is to say, Indonesia, the US, and everywhere else we know about), men (and every metal scene we know of is male-dominated) are expected to make enough money to support themselves and, if they have them, their families. This is why careers in the arts, including popular music, are viewed as disreputable, since in most countries they often fail to provide a man with a living wage. The one partial exception to this expectation is if the man in question is a 'student'. Students are even allowed to be unable to support their families through their incomes, as this is thought to be a temporary state pending graduation and a dramatically increased earning potential. This category can be expanded as necessary to include guys who live in a college town who enrolled at university but flunked out six years ago. Such people are essential for scenic integrity—they provide continuity and often become the owners and chief employees of central scenic institutions.

Metal, of course, is considered the very antithesis of 'college rock' in the West. Nonetheless, metal scenes still benefit immensely from the presence of local post-secondary educational institutions, particularly the promotional opportunities afforded by college radio. Metal is often associated with the middle and even upper-middle classes in non-western milieus and the connection between metal music and university life is therefore much less problematized in those places.

Fourth generalization: Metal scenes often make a show of patrolling their boundaries, but differ from other scenes in the intensity and function of this patrolling
Metal scenes generally do not emphasize ideological purity, as do punk and hardcore scenes, and they do not contain the same overt and covert elitist class prejudices of rave and indie rock scenes[8] (as metal valorizes working-class 'realness', one could almost argue class bias moves in the opposite direction, but such an argument would fail to take into account the political, cultural and economic realities of class stratification in the larger society). While there is certainly concern about 'poseurs' (usually spelled without the 'u') 'infiltrating' the scene, this is not as intense as in other scenes that aspire to an exclusive hipness that metalheads for the most part tend to shun and be shunned by. That said, there are certain things metalheads cannot abide. The following is from Levine's field notes from a metal show in Bowling Green, Ohio, a small college town just south of Toledo.

> What is 'legit' metal? What qualifies as metal? Fans do not consider Love Hate Hero, the band that performed with Four Letter Lie [a concert Levine had attended previously], a legit metal band. Two

audience members called it 'pussy music'. Legit for metal music is similar to 'indie credibility' for independent music. I learned the hard way, though, that if you compare it to 'indie cred' metalheads look at you funny. You become legit based on how many different metal bands you know and have seen. You also become a legit band if you and your bandmates know how to perform obscure styles of metal.

'Posers!' The two men I am talking to point out posers in the crowd. They tell me it is because of their shirts. They are pointing out two people wearing Metallica's *Ride the Lightning* shirts. I've started calling it 'the ride the lightning poser' because this is not the first time I have heard someone say, 'Go to Spencer's or Hot Topic [US retail chains] and you'll find those shirts for under twenty dollars.' To test this theory I went to Spencer's Gifts in the mall and sure enough, *Ride the Lightning* shirts were sitting right there. It is a taboo to wear this shirt at a metal concert. Anyone wearing it automatically receives the label of 'poser' from fellow audience members.

This passage not only illustrates intolerant attitudes towards what is perceived as a superficial commitment to the music, but also certain unexamined attitudes about gender and class. Musical weakness is likened to female genitalia and superficial commitment is conflated with lower financial investment, as if the ability to pay exorbitant sums for a T-shirt demonstrated one's level of commitment to the music instead of economic status—an ironic stance considering metal's core 'blue collar ethos' (Weinstein 1991), but less so when considering the shift in the fanbase for metal as the music has evolved in more extreme and esoteric directions and the mainstream audience has increasingly embraced non-rock popular musics.[9]

Indeed, the emergence of thrash metal, a seismic event that Gaines (1991: 203) terms The Great Crossover, while salutary in innumerable ways, also introduced punk-style elements of exclusivity to an inclusive 'proud pariah' (again, the term is Weinstein's) music culture whose main criteria, above all else, were knowledge of and enthusiastic appreciation for the music (Hickam and Wallach 2011). Metal struggles with this mottled legacy to this day—Levine's interlocutors may have refused to recognize that their criteria for metal legitimacy had any relation to snobbish 'indie cred' (even though these are both direct offshoots of punk) but they also are no more likely than Jakartan metalheads to welcome a 'poser' (like *distro*, a key English loan word in Indonesian underground parlance) at their gigs.

As for the perennial, complex issue of sexism in the metal scene, Levine's informant's remark is on one side of a core conflict between metal's inclusive ethos and history of intense female involvement in scenic activities (cf. Hickam and Wallach 2011) and the pervasive sexism and misogyny not only of the dominant culture but of male-dominated rock club/gig culture in particular (Donze 2010).

Fifth generalization: In order for a scene to have coherence through time, there must be a 'generation gap': there must be an older generation aging out of and younger members entering the scene

Thus there are always two groups of scenesters: old-timers who run the institutions (that generally fail after a while due to the hostile climate of the outside world in which they have to operate) and the youngsters entering the scene who constitute the main customer base and form the new crop of bands. Without oldsters, it's hard for a scene to survive, or even to exist in the first place (incidentally, both *survive* and *exist* are also English loan words in Indonesian that are used frequently when discussing the fluctuating fortunes of underground metal scenes). Metal has the advantage of being a subculture that does not cast out its elders (Weinstein 1991: 110), which is quite possibly the main reason why predictions of its demise are much less common than they are for punk, hardcore and hip hop. (Not that they've ever been accurate in those cases, either.)

Nonetheless, the generation gap is *always* an object of perception, and is often felt to be a challenge, even a threat, as it is always an open question whether the knowledge and wisdom held by the former group can be successfully conveyed to the latter, since the latter group's willingness to listen and the former's ability to convey said knowledge in an understandable manner are often in doubt. This problem of generational continuity, familiar to any social group, leads to the senior members of the scene attempting to document its history. These accounts can be used by scholars to understand scenic histories, although of course they contain their own blind spots. For one thing, official histories of the scene rarely begin with the stage, previously discussed, of listening to recordings. Instead, scene beginnings usually are recorded not at the beginning, but at the emergence of local bands that play their own songs, a stage that we have seen occurs rather late in scenic development. Nonetheless, this is usually the part of the scene's history that is deemed worth documenting, and the original bands in the scene are celebrated along with a handful of original scenic institutions. As stated previously, live venues, usually long since defunct, are almost always the most celebrated of these scenic institutions. Here is a typical scene narrative:

> The Great Barbecue Gods later recorded...our original songs such as 'The Witness', '1-900-909-Fool', 'Barbecue Power', 'Thieves of Time'

and a few others...we also did our own renditions of songs by Black Sabbath, Living Colour, the Bad Brains, the Red Hot Chili Peppers, Thin Lizzy, Motörhead. We intended to release the original material, but by then it was too late, with Scott Shriner moving out to LA and the band disbanded... Brad Coffin formed Five Horse Johnson and Tim Gahagan and I formed 'Head with Steve Szirotniyak on guitar and Miguel Oria on bass... 'Head basically did our own versions of Motörhead and Thin Lizzy tunes...and once again were one of the biggest draws in town...our first show was with Babes in Toyland, a riot grrl group from Minneapolis...it was at Frankie's Inner City and was classic as folks were curious about what my new band was about...and we had been rehearsing all the time and I was on a strict athletic regimen at this time in preparation for the show... and hundreds and hundreds of people showed up.....we rocked out and ruled the stage...and after we played pretty much everyone left and the Babes in Toyland girls [*sic*] were bummed...we did some other classic shows with many bands who were on tour, most notably Urge Overkill... 'Head was really only to be a one-off show and ended up lasting a bit longer than that... One of our infamous events was a festival that I organized called the 'Pop Goes the Weasel Festival' which was held at Frankie's. This was a venue that was meant to feature a variety of creative forms including visual art, poetry and music...the event was a fundraiser for David's House which was a home for terminally ill patients...

The two authors of this chapter represent the two age groups under discussion. Dr Donahue is a true scene elder, and we hope that he will one day help to produce a history of the Toledo scene, as none currently exists. As for the Jakarta metal scene, Wendi Putranto, an executive editor at *Rolling Stone Indonesia*, is currently writing a scene history based on a sequence of performance venues going back to the mid 1990s (Wendi Putranto, personal communication, 21 January 2011).

Sixth generalization: All metal scenes are defined not just by their relationship to the global metal scene but by their relationship to other neighbouring scenes and to overlapping scenes dedicated to other genres
Metal seems to always be first. Even though metal is more complex musically and harder to play than punk, for example, metal scenes tend to emerge in non-Western locales before punk scenes.[10] Matt Donahue's narrative illustrates the coming together of punk and metal in the US in the 1980s:

Great Barbecue Gods Matt Donahue and drummer Tim Gahagan onstage in Toledo ca. 1990. Photo by Gerald Grindstaff. Collection of Dr Matthew Donahue. Used with permission.

> Later Guitar Heroes morphed into St. Jude Travel Club...we added a second guitarist Brian Haney, an amazing guitar player, and John Tolmes was on bass, by this time we were morphing punk and metal as we were all fans of both styles...metal groups that we were influenced by were Motörhead, Iron Maiden, Judas Priest, Black Sabbath, Metallica, Accept, Tank, and many others...particularly groups who were influenced by or were part of the New Wave of British Heavy Metal...as far as punk groups we were into, the Misfits, Minor Threat, Black Flag, the Circle Jerks, D.O.A., the Cro-Mags, Agent Orange, the Adolescents, the Meatmen and the Necros.

In Indonesia bands also developed sounds influenced by bands from both camps, part of the long distinguished history of crossovers between the two genres (see Waksman 2009).

Flyer for a 4 June 1991 concert featuring 'Head at Frankie's Inner City in East Toledo. Collection of Dr Matthew Donahue. Used with permission.

But the inevitable sharing of space and mutual influencing between genres is not the only important extrascenic contact. The vast majority of scenes define themselves vis-à-vis another relatively nearby scene dedicated to the same genre. The metal scene in Jakarta was constantly comparing itself to the scene in the West Javanese provincial capital of Bandung, a smaller city that was once over three hours away but now, after the recent completion of a superhighway, is much closer. Bandung is seen not only as smaller and cooler, but as more relaxed, friendlier and more creative. The rivalry is a lot like the famous rivalry between the metal scenes in Los Angeles and San Francisco in California; Jakarta would be analogous to LA, Bandung to San Francisco. Toledo's metal scene, on the other hand, is forever in the shadow of Detroit's, and thought to be a less creative, miniature version of the latter. Their relationship is more like Malang and Surabaya (respectively) in Indonesia, both East Javanese cities that boast active metal scenes. A striking feature of these relationships is that they tend to be dyadic. That is, they don't tend to involve more than two players. Although there are active scenes in Cleveland, Ohio and Yogyakarta, Central Java, for instance, one doesn't hear much about them in Toledo or Jakarta (respectively).

The libidinal economy of scenes and the sonic materiality of metal: some inflammatory closing remarks

This essay has mostly been concerned with the functions and historical trajectory of metal scenes which, we have suggested, are similar around the world. It seems appropriate to end with some guidelines on how to conduct the all-important empirical investigation into the subjective *meanings* of metal for scenic participants in particular local scenes, meanings which tend to be, in contrast, rather diverse.

We maintain that theoretical models of the apprehension of the social world are fundamentally incomplete if they rely exclusively on semiological, textualist theories of cultural meaning based on the abstract Saussurean model of signifier and signified. Wallach has argued elsewhere (2008a) that Peircean semiotics provides a more grounded approach to the meaning of popular musics in local contexts. Hence the materiality of the particularities of social life (including scenic contexts) in specific places has important implications for analyses of global metal scenes. Moreover, the materiality of the *musical sounds themselves* limits the horizon of possible interpretations of metal music in those places. While musical sounds can be resignified in different cultural contexts, these new meanings are not infinite. This may seem a reasonable proposition, but in fact it is a dangerous claim to make. To posit that the material form of musical sounds or any other cultural object can circumscribe the range of possible interpretations only makes sense if we posit the existence of universal properties of sensory experience. Naturally this is not an easy claim for an ethnomusicologist to make. Yet we would argue certain sonic elements, including the preponderance of bass or treble frequencies, tempo, and the iconic relationships these attributes form with environmental sounds and human vocalizations (crying, screaming, laughing, etc.) are not subject to random variation depending on cultural context. We also think that understanding the cross-cultural aesthetic properties of popular musics and their iconic, non-arbitrary relationships to the experiential condition of modernization is necessary to fully assess popular music as a global cultural phenomenon. In particular, we think this seems a compelling avenue towards understanding the remarkable global expansion of heavy metal music and culture.

By way of a conclusion, we want to suggest that the framework outlined in this chapter, by addressing the formation of scenes as social networks of circulation dependent on a relatively stable institutional infrastructure capable of maintaining durable links to external sources of cultural production, leaves the most interesting and essential questions unanswered, as these can only be addressed after detailed and careful empirical research. For the sociology, economics and politics (whether in the form of the petty rivalries between bands and among scene members or the life-and-death struggles for survival scenes wage against the outside world) of a scene ultimately cannot tell us why they form in the first place. They only begin to address what we might call the libidinal economy of scenes, the forces of longing and desire that cause scenes to coalesce and cohere. Barry Shank's Lacanian analysis of the 1980s postpunk scene in Austin, Texas (1994) would be an interesting model for metal scholars to emulate in this respect, as well as Harris Berger's ethnographically grounded phenomenology (1999). In any case, the answers are located at too great a depth for a cursory treatment to succeed when dealing with metal fans and their attachments to their music. In his essay on the Slovenian metal scene, Rajko Muršič puts it well: '[H]eavy metal may be too complex to deal with without extensive ethnographic and phenomenological methodologies... It is almost impossible to say anything reasonable about metal without detailed ethnography. Otherwise, silence and ignorance...are unavoidable' (2011: 299).

Indeed, frequently the *worst* way to understand the meanings of metal in the lives of metalheads in the scene is to ask them directly about it point blank, though at times the responses thus elicited are revealing, in an oblique sort of way. We end with a final excerpt from Levine's field notes.

> When I ask people why they listen to metal, I usually either get laughed at or a snarky answer like 'Why not?'
>
> I've also gotten:
>
> 'It's got a great bass'.
>
> 'It's powerful and epic'.
>
> 'It's really creative'.
>
> 'The lyrics are hilarious, have you ever listened to death metal...it makes me laugh every time'.
>
> 'It is a combination of different styles of music'.

'It rocks'.

'That's a stupid question'.

'It helps you deal with pressure'.

'It's not all about violence, death, and creepy vocals; it actually takes a lot of talent to play heavy metal'.

'It's a way of life'.

'You should try it!'

Acknowledgements

The authors wish to thank Matthew A. Donahue for sharing his knowledge and memories of the Toledo scene, Esther A. Clinton for extensive, constructive feedback and editorial assistance on multiple drafts, and all the metalheads of Indonesia and America who helped us in this endeavour, especially Brian Hickam, Rob Kimple, Arian13, and Wendi Putranto. The title of the chapter, 'I Want *You* to Support Local Metal', is taken from a flyer advertising a Toledo metal concert that depicts a rotting, zombified Uncle Sam pointing at the viewer in a parody of the vintage US Army recruitment poster.

Notes

1. For background on the Indonesian metal scene and the underground music movement of which it is a part, see Baulch 2007; LeVine 2009; Wallach 2003b, 2005, 2008b, 2010, 2011. Berger 1999 contains an account of the metal scene in North-eastern Ohio, USA (about two hours from Toledo).

2. While the following focuses primarily on these two case studies (plus a brief detour into China), the functions and generalizations also apply to the descriptions of other metal scenes in the recent *Metal Rules the Globe* edited volume (Wallach, Berger and Greene 2011). This multiply-authored work (sixteen contributors in all) contains information about metal scenes in Brazil, Canada, Israel, Japan, Malaysia, Malta, Nepal, Norway, Rapanui (Easter Island), Singapore, and Slovenia in addition to China, Indonesia and the United States. Judging from the information provided in this collection, scenes in all these locales share fundamental features with the two main scenes analysed in the present essay.

3. There have been numerous changes in the production, consumption and mediation of heavy metal music in the 42 years since the debut release by 'a blues band that had decided to write some scary music' (Osbourne 2009: 83) named Black Sabbath. This chapter concentrates on the last 25 years of the genre's development. Straw famously characterized 1970s metal fandom as a taste public dependent on the mainstream recording industry (1990), an interpretation he maintains was valid

for the time (personal communication, 16 June 2011). Kahn-Harris describes the early 1980s as 'the days when the extreme metal scene consisted of a few hundred scattered, letter-writing, tape-trading pioneers' (2011: 223). This network consisted of often solitary individuals and was of limited geographical scope compared to the global metal scene of today. There is thus reason to believe that metal scene dynamics differed significantly prior to the late 1980s, though more research is required.

4. The most thorough treatment of the scene concept applied to popular music in general is Bennett and Peterson 2004.

5. In Kahn-Harris's formulation, these would be prime opportunities to accrue 'subcultural capital' (2007, 2011; see Thornton 1997 for the term's origin).

6. A typical example from a US music journalist: 'But the fact of the matter is that as a national musical movement with the power to attract new partisans and to fortify the old ones, hardcore is dead and has been for almost a year' (Brown 2010: 266). This was originally published in 1983! A year later in another column, Brown, no fan of metal, marvels at how heavy metal was 'probably more popular now than it's ever been, a fact doubly remarkable for the tenuous state of the record industry's recovery from the "depression" which lasted from 1979 to 1982' (163). 'The Beast that Refuses to Die' is the subtitle of chapter 2 of Weinstein's seminal 1991 monograph.

7. Frankie's may now have less to worry about than most rock venues regarding economic survival. In an odd twist of fate, its owner, Robert Croak, became a wildly successful entrepreneur when one of his creations, Silly Bandz, became a fashion craze among American children in 2010.

8. See Thornton 1997 for the former; for the latter see Fonarow 2006.

9. Namely country, pop and hip hop in the US—a gradual process that began in the late 1970s but has accelerated since the mid 1990s. In Indonesia, *dangdut* is the most popular style of music by far, with a vast largely poor and working-class audience. Metal bands also have large followings there; in fact extreme metal is probably more popular in Indonesia than in the US.

10. In contrast, the DIY ethos that is the prerequisite for full-blown scene activity unquestionably originated in the punk scene in the West in the late 1970s.

Bibliography

Baulch, Emma. 2007. *Making Scenes: Reggae, Punk, and Death Metal in 1990s Bali*. Durham, NC: Duke University Press.

Bennett, Andy, and Richard A. Peterson, eds. 2004. *Music Scenes: Local, Translocal, and Virtual*. Nashville, TN: Vanderbilt University Press.

Berger, Harris M. 1999. *Metal, Rock, and Jazz: Perception and the Phenomenology of Musical Experience*. Middletown, CT: Wesleyan University Press.

Brown, Bill. 2010. *You Should've Heard Just What I Seen: Collected Newspaper Articles 1981–1984*. Cincinnati: Colossal Books.

Donze, Patti Lynne. 2010. 'Heterosexuality Is Totally Metal: Ritualized Community and Separation at a Local Music Club'. *Journal of Popular Music Studies* 22(3): 259–82. http://dx.doi.org/10.1111/j.1533-1598.2010.01241.x

Dunn, Sam, and Scot McFadyen, dirs. 2005. *Metal: A Headbanger's Journey*. Seville Pictures.

—2008. *Global Metal*. Seville Pictures.

Finnegan, Ruth. 1989. *The Hidden Musicians*. Cambridge: Cambridge University Press.

Fonarow, Wendy. 2006. *Empire of Dirt: The Aesthetics and Rituals of British Indie Music*. Middletown, CT: Wesleyan University Press.

Gaines, Donna. 1991. *Teenage Wasteland: Suburbia's Dead End Kids*. New York: Pantheon.

Guibert, Gérôme. 2011. 'Espace et lieu dans l'étude des musiques populaires, les paradoxes de la sociologie française'. Paper presented at 'Music and Environment'. The Annual Meeting of the International Association for the Study of Popular Music—Canada, Montreal, Quebec, 18 June 2011.

Harris, Keith. 2000. 'Roots? The Relationship between the Global and the Local within the Extreme Metal Scene'. *Popular Music* 19(1): 13–30. http://dx.doi.org/10.1017/S0261143000000052

Helb, Colin. 2009. 'Use and Influence of Amateur Musician Narratives in Film, 1981–2001'. PhD dissertation, American Culture Studies Program, Bowling Green State University.

Hickam, Brian, and Jeremy Wallach. 2011. 'Female Authority and Dominion: Discourse and Distinctions of Heavy Metal Scholarship'. *Journal for Cultural Research* 12(3): 255–77. http://dx.doi.org/10.1080/14797585.2011.594583

Ivanova, Maranatha. 2009. 'Limning the *Jianghu*: Spaces of Appearance and the Performative Politics of the Chinese Cultural Underground'. PhD dissertation. Department of Political Science. Berkeley: University of California.

Kahn-Harris, Keith. 2002. '"I Hate This Fucking Country": Dealing with the Global and the Local in the Israeli Extreme Metal Scene'. In *Music, Popular Culture, Identities*, ed. R. Young, 133–51. Amsterdam: Editions Rodopi.

—2004a. 'The Failure of Youth Culture: Reflexivity, Music and Politics in the Black Metal Scene'. *European Journal of Cultural Studies* 7(1): 95–111. http://dx.doi.org/10.1177/1367549404039862

—2004b. 'Unspectacular Subculture? Transgression and Mundanity in the Global Extreme Metal Scene'. In *After Subculture*, ed. Andy Bennett and Keith Kahn-Harris. New York: Palgrave Macmillan.

—2007. *Extreme Metal: Music and Culture on the Edge*. New York: Berg.

—2011. '"You Are from Israel and That Is Enough to Hate You Forever": Racism, Globalization, and Play within the Global Extreme Metal Scene'. In *Metal Rules the Globe: Heavy Metal Music around the World*, ed. Jeremy Wallach, Harris M. Berger and Paul D. Greene, 200–223. Durham, NC: Duke University Press.

LeVine, Mark. 2009. *Headbanging against Repressive Regimes: Censorship of Heavy Metal in the Middle East, North Africa, Southeast Asia and China*. Copenhagen: Freemuse.

Muršič, Rajko, 2011. 'Noisy Crossroads: Metal Scenes in Slovenia'. In *Metal Rules the Globe: Heavy Metal Music around the World*, ed. Jeremy Wallach, Harris M. Berger and Paul D. Greene, 294–312. Durham, NC: Duke University Press.

Osbourne, Ozzy, with Chris Ayres. 2009. *I Am Ozzy*. New York: Hachette Book Group.

Shank, Barry. 1994. *Dissonant Identities: The Rock 'n' Roll Scene in Austin, Texas*. Hanover, NH: Wesleyan University Press.

Straw, Will. 1990. 'Characterizing Rock Music Culture: The Case of Heavy Metal'. In *On Record: Rock, Pop, and the Written Word*, ed. Simon Frith and Andrew Goodwin, 97–110. New York: Pantheon.

—1991. 'Systems of Articulation, Logics of Change: Communities and Scenes in Popular Music'. *Cultural Studies* (5)1: 368–88. http://dx.doi.org/10.1080/0950238910049 0311

Thornton, Sarah. 1997. *Club Cultures: Music, Media, and Subcultural Capital.* Middletown, CT: Wesleyan University Press.

Urban, Greg. 2001. *Metaculture: How Culture Moves Through the World.* Minneapolis: University of Minnesota Press.

Waksman, Steve. 2009. *This Ain't the Summer of Love: Conflict and Crossover in Heavy Metal and Punk.* Berkeley: University of California Press.

Wallach, Jeremy. 2003a. 'The Poetics of Electrosonic Presence: Recorded Music and the Materiality of Sound'. *Journal of Popular Music Studies* 15(1): 34–64.

—2003b. '"Goodbye My Blind Majesty": Music, Language, and Politics in the Indonesian Underground'. In *Global Pop, Local Language*, ed. Harris M. Berger and Michael T. Carroll, 53–86. Jackson, MS: University Press of Mississippi.

—2005. 'Underground Rock Music and Democratization in Indonesia'. *World Literature Today* 79(3-4): 16–20. http://dx.doi.org/10.2307/40158922

—2008a. 'Living the Punk Lifestyle in Jakarta'. *Ethnomusicology* 52(1): 97–115.

—2008b. *Modern Noise, Fluid Genres: Popular Music in Indonesia, 1997–2001.* Madison, WI: University of Wisconsin Press.

—2010. 'Distortion-Drenched Dystopias: Metal and Modernity in Southeast Asia'. In *The Metal Void: First Gatherings*, ed. Niall W. R. Scott, 357–66. Oxford: Inter-Disciplinary Press.

—2011. 'Unleashed in the East: Metal Music, Masculinity, and "Malayness" in Indonesia, Malaysia and Singapore'. In *Metal Rules the Globe: Heavy Metal Music around the World*, ed. Jeremy Wallach, Harris M. Berger and Paul D. Greene, 86–105. Durham, NC: Duke University Press.

Wallach, Jeremy, Harris M. Berger and Paul D. Greene, eds. 2011. *Metal Rules the Globe: Heavy Metal Music around the World.* Durham, NC: Duke University Press.

Weinstein, Deena. 1991. *Heavy Metal: A Cultural Sociology.* New York: Lexington Books.

Wong, Cynthia P. 2005. '"Lost Lambs": Rock, Gender, Authenticity, and a Generational Response to Modernity in the People's Republic of China'. PhD dissertation, Department of Music, Columbia University.

—2011. '"A Dream Return to Tang Dynasty": Masculinity, Male Camaraderie, and Chinese Heavy Metal in the 1990s'. In *Metal Rules the Globe: Heavy Metal Music around the World*, ed. Jeremy Wallach, Harris M. Berger and Paul D. Greene, 63–85. Durham, NC: Duke University Press.

Voice of our blood

National Socialist discourses in black metal

Benjamin Hedge Olson

University of Hawai'i, Manoa, USA

> 'Some people are larger than life. Hitler is larger than death' (Don DeLillo, *White Noise*).

National Socialist Black Metal (NSBM) has been highly influential throughout the international black metal scene since the millennium (Gardell 2003: 285). While NSBM is in no small part influenced by Varg Vikernes and his transformation into an Old Norse pagan neo-Nazi after his incarceration, the NSBM movement is far more than the result of younger black metalers mimicking a figure with proven extremist credentials. Black metal defines itself to a large degree through transgression, alienation and provocation, and in western culture, few things are more transgressive, alienating and provocative than neo-Nazism.

As Keith Kahn-Harris writes in his analysis of extreme metal: 'In many ways Nazis are *the* preeminent transgressive symbol in the modern world' (Kahn-Harris 2007: 41). National Socialist discourses also speak to notions of place, history, identity and traditional culture that are endemic to black metal of all persuasions (Moynihan and Söderlind 2003: 33–43). In this chapter, I describe the ways that NSBM utilizes discourses concerning race, nation and culture, as well as the ways that those discourses are contested by non-racist black metalers. Racism and neo-Nazism force black metalers to confront the ambiguity of hatred and define the limits of transgression in a globalized black metal scene.

Neo-Nazism is nothing new to transgressive music-based youth culture; neo-Nazi punk, or 'white noise', has been widely distributed throughout the far-right underground for nearly three decades (Gardell 2003: 69–70). Black metal is unique in the world of racist rock in that it has been endowed with a militant, fanatic quality carried over from the Norwegian church-burning days. It is also decidedly anti-Christian, which gives it a hyper-transgressive quality to participants sympathetic to neo-Nazi ideology, but bored with the rhetoric of Christian identity and other racist Christian groups (Lee 2000:

338). NSBM is also indelibly linked with Asá Trú (a reconstructed version of old Norse paganism) and dismissive of Satanism, which gives it a 'blood and soil' attraction to many young neo-Nazis looking for identity in their distant, ancestral past. Satanic black metalers are usually dismissive of NSBM, and vice versa. Many Asá Trúers also take great offense at their religion being used as justification for racist ideology. With that in mind, the majority of NSBM articulates a neo-pagan, usually Old Norse perspective.

What is perhaps even more significant than why some black metalers accept neo-Nazi ideology is why most black metalers reject it. Many black metalers whole-heartedly accept National Socialism, while others vitriolically condemn it, and many others look upon it with vague scepticism and indifference (Moynihan and Söderlind 2003: 347–56). Black metal brings basic questions of morality, identity and 'goodness' into question; why, then, balk at racist and genocidal ideologies? Most black metalers have no problem speaking about their hatred of Christians and Christianity, but many are uncomfortable adding Judaism and discourses of race into this equation. Black metal prides itself on being hyper-transgressive and iconoclastic, but the majority of black metalers are unwilling to cross the threshold of the radical-right. In this chapter, I will explain how and why this unwillingness occurs.

Even 'mainstream' neo-Nazis often express confusion, disgust and fear when confronted with the bizarre sight of a corpse-painted, orc-like creature vomiting blood in front of a swastika (Gardell 2003: 304-307). This radical departure from humanity, modernity and rationality is a major aspect of black metal's appeal. In some cases this is all NSBM is: one more transgressive signifier among many others. For others, notions of ultra-nationalism and militant racism take on deeply meaningful connotations when placed within a black metal context. Black metal, in all of its forms, glorifies the distant past and seeks to annihilate the mundane present. Neo-Nazism makes this assertion very simple by imposing notions of otherness onto virtually everyone unlike oneself and elevating the angry, megalomaniacal back metaler to the status of a God among sheep. Notions of modernity and civilization seem vague and intellectual to many black metalers; race, nation and tradition are less so (Kahn-Harris 2007: 41). NSBM utilizes logic very similar to that of non-racist black metal: the present is sick and degraded; the past was glorious and vital; the present must be destroyed and/or escaped in order to attain a meaningful existence. The primary difference for NSBM is the polarization of the them/us dichotomy into strictly racial and national categories. This dichotomy, like much of the cultural activity evident in black metal, attempts to reconcile the paradox of hyper-individuality and empowerment through group identity.

Norsk Arisk black metal

Like all of black metal culture, NSBM began in the Nordic countries. Many of the early Norwegian bands flirted with neo-Nazi imagery and ideology, but prior to Varg Vikernes' murder conviction, swastikas and racism were largely provocations; one example of misanthropy among many. In the infamous 1993 *Kerrang!* article, Vikernes exclaims: 'I support all dictatorships—Stalin, Hitler, Ceaucescu—and I will become the dictator to Scandinavia myself'(Moynihan and Söderlind 2003: 101)! During the early days of the scene, misanthropy, not politics, was the order of the day. Euronymous himself was an avowed Stalinist, believing that brutal totalitarian communism was the perfect expression of his misanthropy and the will of Satan (*Close-Up* 1992). Politics was a method of taboo transgression in the early 90s, one of the less important methods compared to religion, violence and general misanthropy.

During his imprisonment Vikernes fully embraced his role as a far-right ideologue (Burzum.org). He has, however, become a hero and a martyr to the international NSBM movement, a role he has not declined. Upon his release from prison in 2009 Vikernes once again took up the black metal banner, releasing a new album and gracing the covers of both *Decibel* and *Terrorizer* (Bennett 2010; Minton 2010). The combination of Asá Trŭ and racism that Vikernes espouses has been embraced by a large section of the Asá Trŭ groups in the world, usually identifying themselves as Odinists as opposed to more neutral terms like Asá Trŭ or Heathen (Durham 2007: 72–73). Vikernes explains the relationship between his attacks on Christianity and his anti-Semitism:

> There was a t-shirt that Øystein printed that said 'Kill the Christians!' I think that is ridiculous. What's the logic in that? Why should we kill our brothers? They're just temporarily asleep, entranced. We have to say, 'Hey, wake up!' That's what we have to do, wake them up from the Jewish trance. We don't have to kill them because that would be killing ourselves, because they are part of us (Moynihan and Söderlind 2003: 163).

Here we see a radical departure from the earlier rhetoric of Norwegian black metal: Vikernes asserts that Christians are the victims of an anti-human other, and they must be 'awakened' and mobilized. This is a significant shift away from the generalized misanthropy and denial of humanity, goodness, and progress that characterized the ranting of Euronymous and the early declarations of Vikernes himself. During this period Vikernes may have concluded that Satanism had only limited value as a transgressive signifier and that Satanists would inevitably be viewed as children playing dress-up by the larger culture. In a very real sense, these kinds of statements mark the end of Vikernes' career as a black metal ideologue, and the beginning of his career as a neo-Nazi ideologue whose rhetoric is not very divergent from hundreds of far-right ideologues all over the world.

Although various Norwegian scene members flirted with neo-Nazi imagery prior to Vikernes' conversion in prison, the Norwegian scene was relatively apolitical during the early 90s. Ihsahn and Samoth from Emperor explain their feelings regarding racism and far-right politics in an interview with *Terrorizer*:

> Samoth: 'Well that's something Vikernes started'.
>
> Ihsahn: 'As I have said before, I feel black metal should have nothing to do with politics. It's not a political thing, it's something more spiritual. I realize that many people think that fascism, Satanism and black metal are one and the same, probably because they are all extreme ideologies.'
>
> *Terrorizer*: Plus it's not such a great leap from the strong over the weak philosophy, which is an integral part of Satanism, to fascism.
>
> Samoth: 'That's something I can identify with, but that doesn't mean I wear a swastika and worship Adolf Hitler or whatever.'
>
> Ihsahn: 'If we look down on anything, then it is humanity as a whole. It's rather naïve to think that your intelligence is based on the colour of your skin. Of course, there are cultures which are hard to understand for people in different countries, but I think that's positive as well. Like in the States, everything gets mixed together. They have no old culture at all. I think it's important to keep different cultures as they are, because so many cultures have been lost because of the Christian religion. Like you have Christian missions going into the jungle and forcing their religion upon tribes that have been living on a very primitive basis for thousands of years. What do they need Christianity for?' (Whalen 1997).

This quote reiterates black metal's reverence for the 'primitive'. For Ihsahn, and many other black metalers, their hatred for modernity trumps the transgressive qualities of National Socialism. In this interview, Emperor reference pre-industrial cultures as being closer to the medieval golden age that they aspire to than the mediocrity and cultural pluralism of the United States or contemporary Western Europe. The racism inherent in National Socialism excludes those pre-industrial peoples who remain untouched by Christianity and is therefore contraindicated for the black metal worldview.

The Satanism and individualism of much of the Norwegian scene is often in conflict with National Socialist ideology. King, formerly of Gorgoroth and currently working under the moniker Ov Hell, asserts:

> NSBM as a movement is more or less made up. It's only kids using words to spread some kind of fear to be shocking in a way. Nazism to me is a flock ideology. Black metal, or at least Gorgoroth, is about the individual and creating your own moral out of chaos, and be your own God more or less (Zebub, dir. 2006).

King's contention that Satanism and National Socialism are ideologically incompatible is repeatedly echoed by anti-Nazi Satanists, most notably Gavin Baddeley (Baddeley 1999: 148–59). Satanic black metalers place a great deal of emphasis on individualism and self-creation, aspects that National Socialism is awkwardly adapted to. The attempt to adapt neo-Nazi ideology to an arch-individualist credo is yet another attempt to reconcile the contradiction between the self and the group that runs throughout black metal culture. It is far less successful in doing so than other methods, and NSBM tends to place less emphasis on individualism than do other types of black metal.

USNSBM

North America, the United States in particular, has become one of the most prolific producers of NSBM in the last ten years. This is partially due to the longstanding racist underground and existent infrastructure to produce and distribute racist and neo-Nazi material, as well as constitutional protections for free speech that do not exist in countries like Germany (Durham 2007: 31–32). Resistance Records has been particularly important in promoting 'pro-white' music and has in recent years begun to distribute NSBM bands. NSBM is a contentious issue within the militant racist counter-culture, as black metal in all of its forms is fairly anti-Christian and continues to carry connotations of Satanism with it, although very few NSBM bands identify with Satanism. NSBM in the United States, more so than in other parts of the world, works in conjunction with the larger National Socialist and militant racist counter-culture, garnering little respect or audience outside of that circle as a result.

Vinland Winds records was an independent label dedicated primarily to NSBM and was run by Richard P. Mills, a.k.a. Grimnir Wotansvolk, a.k.a. G. Heretik, front-man for NSBM stalwarts Grand Belial's Key until his mysterious death in 2006 (vinlandwinds.com). In a 2005 interview with the zine *Nihilistic*, Mills pontificates about his lyrical motivations:

The lyrics deal with religious topics that go deeper than the early days of Christianity. The true roots of this pestilence are explored, exploring pre-Christian Judaism and its gross culture. Disgust in others and pride in ourselves inspire us to express our bigotry through music. I think that our latest release, and songs like *Vultures Of Misfortune*, paint a great picture of the horrific ways of ancient Jewish culture and their customs. I am offended by the poor quality of music that my peers are recording. Musically, I hope to bring something unique to the table. All our lyrics express an enmity for Juden-Christianity, and endless sadistic cynicism which mocks and ridicules the religion with a twisted sense of sarcasm (*Nihilistic* 2005).

We see in this quotation a common tactic among NSBM ideologues, particularly in the US: the extension of hostility towards Christianity to hostility towards Judaism. NSBM bands attempt to make their anti-Semitism more palatable to people outside of the scene by equating anti-Semitism with anti-Christian sentiments that are far more accepted within extreme metal. NSBM tries to achieve an ideological bait-and-switch; equating enmity towards a powerful majority, with enmity towards a marginalized minority.

Antiracist watchdog groups in the US like the Southern Poverty Law Center (SPLC), while taking notice of NSBM, have represented it with varying degrees of accuracy. In a 1999 report titled *Sounds of Violence* the SPLC describe their perceptions of USNSBM: 'Today's new generation of metal bands, known as the black metal underground, is so extreme it makes Marilyn Manson look square. For those who want to turn teenage angst into hatred, this metal scene is a natural target' (Ward, Lunsford and Massa 1999). *Sounds of Violence* contextualizes itself within the long-standing tradition of parent-directed hysteria that has been taken to an extreme by people like Carl A. Raschke in his fanciful 1990 scree *Painted Black*, which asserts that heavy metal is but one part of a wide-ranging Satanic conspiracy (Raschke 1990). Moral panics and contemporary legends concerning Satanic conspiracies attempting to infiltrate American culture have been well documented by scholars of conspiracy theory and American folklore. Jeffrey S. Victor's *Satanic Panic: The Creation of a Contemporary Legend*, Bill Ellis' *Raising the Devil: Satanism, New Religions and the Media*, as well as Gary Alan Fine and Patricia A. Turner's *Whispers on the Color Line: Rumor and Race in America* all chart in fascinating detail the construction and proliferation of contemporary legends concerning Satanic conspiracies and their unholy designs for America's children (Victor 1993; Ellis 2000; Fine and Turner 2001). Unfortunately, in *Sounds of Violence*, the SPLC place themselves within this tradition of feverish hysteria, making neo-Nazism and Satanism synonymous terms while ignoring the complicated cultural and ideological politics involved.

Sounds of Violence asserts that all Satanic, racist, or vaguely suspicious-seeming bands can be branded as National Socialist black metal. The report does seems less interested in delineating musical or aesthetic qualities that might contribute to a definition of black metal; if a band or artist uses both Satanic and far-right symbolism, that apparently constitutes NSBM as far as the authors are concerned. As we have seen, Satanism and neo-Nazism rarely go hand-in-hand in the black metal world. *Sounds of Violence* claims that the industrial bands Electric Hellfire Club and Blood Axis are both black metal bands, which they are not. The report goes on to describe Boyd Rice and his band NON as being, 'often referred to as the vanguard of the American black metal scene' (Ward, Lunsford and Massa 1999). Although Rice has connections to the far-right, he has never produced black metal of any kind. Although there have been strains of Satanism that have allied themselves with neo-Nazism, Satanic NSBM is quite rare. *Sounds of Violence* goes on to argue: 'Among others, Dylan Klebold and Eric Harris—who murdered 12 of their classmates and a teacher at Columbine High School in Colorado last April—were said to have been influenced by this kind of music' (Ward, Lunsford and Massa 1999). This claim is repeated in Nicholas Goodrick-Clarke's book *Black Sun: Aryan Cults, Esoteric Nazism and the Politics of Identity* (Goodrick-Clark 2003: 209–10). There is no hard evidence of any sort to suggest that the Columbine tragedy was even tenuously associated with black metal. These distortions point to a general misunderstanding of youth culture, an impulse towards moral panic, and a climate of religious hysteria within many factions of American culture. Specificity dissolves in frantic attempts to sensationalize aberrations of teenage ideology.

Black metal, and NSBM in particular, are certainly ripe for sensationalism, but attempts to brand every form of teenage racism or violence as manifestations of neo-Nazi black metal are misguided. In the decade since *Sounds of Violence's* publication, neo-Nazi websites have gleefully posted some of the report's more inaccurate claims as evidence of the SPLC's dishonesty (www.nsbm.org/media/splc_report.html). In failing to sufficiently research and accurately represent the youth cultures they discuss, the SPLC undermine their worthwhile project and give ammunition to the potentially dangerous hate groups that they target. One year after the publication of *Sounds of Violence*, the SPLC released a more sober and accurate assessment of NSBM entitled *Darker than Black* (Potok 2000).

Resistance Records, the most prominent white power record label in North America, was purchased in 1999 by William Pierce, head of the National Alliance, one of the largest militant racist groups in the US, prior to his death in 2002 (Gardell 2003: 135). Resistance subsequently acquired the independent label *Unholy* which is dedicated almost exclusively to NSBM (Bennett 2006). In researching this section, I was given the opportunity to interview Pierce's successor, Erich Gliebe, current head of both Resistance Records and the National Alliance, who has been largely responsible for the popularity of NSBM in North America. Gliebe explained the steady rise of NSBM in North America since the late 90s and its ability to create inroads into groups of young people that other types of racist music have been unable to reach. Part of NSBM's popularity, Gliebe explained, was due to its pro-pagan and anti-Satanic attitude:

> We have no part in that Satanic stuff, that's exactly what we are against. We are totally against that Satanic nonsense. There are many people in the NSBM scene that would like to see the whole scene cleaned out of all the Satanic stuff... We consider Satanism to be a Jewish creation. The people, of course, in the NSBM scene don't believe in the bible, we basically see it as Hebrew mythology. So that is where the figure of Satan comes from, and when somebody is talking about Satan, we consider it to be just a character in the bible (interview with Erich Gliebe, 8 February 2008).

NSBM, particularly in North America, tends to characterize Christianity as being some type of sinister Jewish trick to subvert the minds of Euro-Americans. Gliebe is emphatic in his insistence that NSBM has no connection with Satanism and draws its strength from the culture and heritage of pre-Christian Europe. NSBM takes its cultural paradigms straight from the apolitical Norwegian scene, but modifies them slightly to fit a racist/neo-Nazi political agenda.

Visually most NSBM eschews the corpse-paint, spikes and other fantastical aesthetics that characterize other forms of black metal. Artists often present themselves visually as primordial Vikings returned from some pure, uncorrupted past to save the present from multiculturalism. Equally common is the tactic to remain faceless and anonymous; artists can represent themselves with nothing more than an unspoiled landscape on an album cover. This tactic allows NSBM artists to convey a sense of underground mystery; an anonymity that connotes the avoidance of governmental agencies or other perceived racial enemies.

Some of Gliebe's most fascinating insights were in reference to NSBM's approach to the group/individual paradox that is so central to black metal culture. Gliebe explained to me the NSBM fan's tendency towards isolation:

> I have noticed with a lot of NSBM types, a lot of them don't associate in cliques. They do their own thing. I would say they are more creative and more spiritual than someone into your more typical pro-

> white music... A lot of white kids, they don't want to be told what to do. They don't want to get their hair cut. I don't think that a lot of the NSBM people out there are really into any kind of clique, they may have friends on the internet and they might go to concerts, but there are not big groups of them like there are big groups of skinheads (interview with Erich Gliebe, 8 February 2008).

Gliebe attempts to characterize NSBM fans as more intellectual and less gang-like; if skinheads are the new storm-troopers, then NSBMers are the new intellectual elite, propagandists, ideologues and mystics. Gliebe articulates the tendency within North American black metal to reject group identities in the traditional subcultural sense in favor of virtual groups and temporary groups like those found at concerts. Black metal constantly negotiates the paradox between singular and group identities, but rarely with any long-term success.

Gliebe would have us believe that notions of race allow black metalers to identify with their 'true identity' while also maintaining individual autonomy:

> I don't see BM as being part of some anarchist scene where everyone just does their own thing. I think it binds people together. In a way they do want to get away from the herd mentality, it's true because they tend to not belong to any organization. They don't have patches on their jackets that say "such and such a place black metal," like skinheads do. A lots of black metalers, whether they admit it or not, are part of a larger group: the race. Black metalers would freak out if one day they went to a concert and half the audience was black and had dreadlocks (8 February 2008).

Gliebe attempts to impose a specific, unavoidable notion of group on black metal; that of race. The fact that black metal is wildly popular in Latin America and other 'non-white' regions of the world, and that non-racist black metalers tour in those regions with the greatest enthusiasm, seems to have escaped Gliebe (Kahn-Harris 2007: 70–71). The fact that many black metalers often do wear patches endorsing region-specific black metal may indicate Gliebe's relative inexperience with black metal beyond the NSBM he is familiar with. When I read to Gliebe the quote from King denouncing NSBM, quoted earlier in this chapter, Gliebe responded:

> King might say those things, but I think he has a racial consciousness whether he admits it or not, and that he would prefer to live in a white neighborhood. We do have room for individualism. We encourage people to pursue their own interest and their own occupations and hobbies without causing any detriment to the race (8 February 2008).

It is very unlikely that King's hyper-individualism would sit well with Gliebe or any other NSBMer; it's certain that King's Satanism would not. NSBM attempts to unite black metalers under the banner of race. For the vast majority of black metalers, in the US as well as elsewhere, the homogenizing effects inherent in National Socialism and its de-emphasis of individuality and free-will are simply incompatible with black metal culture.

Far-right propaganda aside, the majority of US black metalers have little interest in National Socialism or racist ideology. As we have seen in the Norwegian scene, most US black metalers approach NSBM ideology with ambivalence and a certain degree of skepticism, but rarely open condemnation. Xasthur, a highly respected one-man black metal band from California, explains his feelings on the subject of NSBM:

> I don't mind it, they have their reasons for their beliefs, who's really to say who are the real one's [*sic*] behind it and who isn't? I am not in any way affiliated with National Socialism, yet in layman's terms I see it, or they may see it as a fist in the face of a liberal society. When humans are given too much freedom, they often abuse it, being free to overpopulate and let everything go to shit. But then again, if National Socialism came into power, into effect in their own countries, I think there would end up being a lot of details to it that they wouldn't like about it. I would say I'm a fan of some of these bands like Gontyna Kry, Veles, Kataxu etc.... as they play some dark, grim and hateful black metal (*Maelstrom* 2004).

Xasthur's comments are fairly typical of most black metalers' feelings towards neo-Nazism: distrust mixed with a hesitancy to condemn an ideology with such intense transgressive power. While unwilling to overtly reject an ideology that instills fear and outrage in all corners of mainstream culture, an ideology that is often proffered as the definition of evil, the majority of black metalers understand that National Socialism is anathema to their project and that they would be the first against the wall if neo-Nazis ever got their way.

Wolves in the Throne Room (WITTR) are one of the US black metal bands who vigorously oppose racism and neo-Nazism. In a statement on their Myspace page, WITTR assert their opposition to NSBM:

> In scores of interviews we have expressed our deep philosophical and spiritual opposition to racism, anti-Semitism, authoritarianism and the glorification of war. We have specifically condemned National Socialism and the bands who explicitly or implicitly endorse these simple-minded and weak ideas (Myspace.com 2008).

In black metal terminology, 'simple-minded', and 'weak' are two of the most condemnatory adjectives at their disposal. Anti-racist black metalers attack NSBMers for following a collective, herd mentality and denying the pure, pre-Christian character of pre-industrial 'non-white' people. NSBMers accuse anti-racist black metalers of denying the voice of their blood and ancestry. The disagreement comes back to the conflict between those who emphasize a resonant ancestral culture, accessible through the blood and psychological archetypes, and those who emphasize individualism, self-creation and the rejection of modernity, regardless of its political manifestation.

NSBM in the United States has a lot going for it: relatively free speech, entrenched racism and large, well-funded groups like the National Alliance to give them support, financially and otherwise. The majority of black metal enthusiasts in the United States offer NSBM little beyond sarcasm, as the May 2006 feature on NSBM in *Decibel* illustrates:

> As if acting out some bizarre atavistic saga—half comedy, half high drama—our protagonists assume their marks in the theatre of the absurd. Somewhere not-so-deep in the sub-underground, the forces of National Socialist Black Metal—henceforth known as NSBM—are circling their Panzer tanks (or at very least their amplifiers) against the evil forces of Jewry, Niggerdom and Fagitude. No, wait—the NSBM dudes are the evil ones (Evil is, after all, a requirement of all black metal) and they're aligning themselves against the Zionist Occupation Government, jungle fever and same-sex marriage. Or is it Israel, multiculturalism and gay bars? Point is, if it ain't white—and straight, and pagan—it ain't right (Bennett 2006).

As the thinly veiled mockery of Bennett's article illustrates, NSBM is not likely to gain much political support outside of its already established base of skinheads and neo-Nazis. For the majority of American black metalers, racism has only limited transgressive value.

Ukrainian insurgent army

Eastern Europe has one of the most vibrant, fanatic and racist black metal scenes in the world. Poland has a fairly rich tradition of extreme metal, with bands like Vader and Behemoth gaining international popularity since the early 90s, as well as a flourishing racist and far-right movement (Hockenos 1996: 193–296). Russia and Ukraine have seen an explosion of fascist, racist and ultra-nationalist activity since the fall of the Soviet Union, with metal, and more recently black metal, playing an important role in the now thriving far-right movement (Shenfield 2001, chapter 3). Black metal in Eastern

Europe has taken on a fanatic, genocidal tone that is reminiscent of the bombastic proclamations of the early Norwegian scene, but with decidedly neo-Nazi overtones. The political chaos, poverty, corruption, and organized crime of the former Soviet Union has created a volatile and fanatic NSBM underground across Eastern Europe (Hockenos 1996: 193).

With the exception of Burzum, Poland's Graveland are perhaps the most revered NSBM band in the world. Regarding his band's origins, Graveland's only permanent member Darken explains to *Pit* magazine:

> Graveland was born at the beginning. Time did not exist then; there was only darkness. Graveland was born from hate dreaming in our lands. We take revenge for our dying ancestors who protected our pagan lands from our foes who wanted to destroy the harmony of nature. Christianity brought false goodness... Graveland knew this. Our souls burn with fire of hate and retribution! Aryan race wake up! The new era of paganism and darkness is coming. Graveland will show you the way. Start the holocaust again, kill Jews and Christians. Destroy the false god of Jesus Christ! I, Darken, the Black Druid of Darkness, Karcharoth of Infernum and Capricornus are the spirits of war. We come from the land of everlasting funerals; from the unholy winter. We are three angels of retribution. War! (*Pit*, issue 15)

Rhetoric of this type is rare among NSBM in North America. Graveland asserts that it is a spiritual entity, some type of mystical force outside of time. Darken's statements are genocidal, apocalyptic and very much in reference to the early Norwegian scene's interest in 'darkness' and 'evil'. Although Darken is an outspoken pagan, his rhetoric is clearly inspired by Satanic Nordic black metalers like Euronymous and It. Graveland's pontifications are partially designed to establish cultural capital; in the 90s black metal, particularly outside of Norway, had to be as uncompromising as possible to be taken seriously. However, shock and transgression are not the only reason for this type of extreme oratory. As we have seen, black metal combines hyper-transgression with mystical religious ideas that offer participants a method for transcending the mundane, escaping modernity and the creation of highly empowering identities. Although blasphemy is illegal in Poland, some Polish bands seem to have concluded that Satanism and anti-Christianity lack the connection to a romantic past that they desire. In the former Soviet bloc, modernity has taken a particularly grim and unappealing form, causing eastern European black metalers to be particularly keen to escape it.

Ukraine has produced some of the most internationally respected black metal of the new millennium, and almost all of it is NSBM. The Ukrainian scene is close-knit, incestuous in terms of band make-up, and fanatic. The Ukrainian NSBM band Hate Forest's website proclaims:

> Hate Forest's first songs were created in the year 1995 in the Ukraine. Hate Forest's art is based upon the Aryan/Slavonic mythology, Nietzschean philosophy, and the ideology of elitism. Now Hate Forest includes four persons. Every subhuman buying Hate Forest releases buys a weapon against himself (www.supernalmusic.com/labels/supernal/hate_forest.htm, no longer available).

Ukrainian NSBMers are fond of terms like 'subhuman', which are often spurned by 'pro-white' activists in the West who seek mainstream legitimacy. Hate Forest is famously secretive, the quote above being one of the few press statements available in English, which adds to their aura and cultural capital in the international black metal scene. The equation of the terms 'Aryan' and 'Slavonic' in Hate Forest's lexicon speaks to the instability of both terms; racial and cultural terminology can be redefined at will to suit ideological purposes. Hate Forest incorporates Ukrainian folk music and traditional vocals into their music in a highly effective way, a tactic which adds both to their nationalist credentials at home and their exotic appeal abroad. NSBM attempts to create a sense that European cultures all over the world are 'waking-up' and realizing their national/racial identity. Ukrainian NSBM asserts a distinct nationalist, pagan, racist perspective that is specific to a place and a culture, while suggesting that other European traditions could be applied to the same framework by NSBMers in their respective cultures.

The organized racist movement in the West is very keen to capitalize on the intensity, fanaticism and quality of eastern European NSBM. Erich Gliebe explained to me during our interview:

> We have pretty good communication with bands from Eastern Europe. Poland, Russia, Ukraine. We have put out over here CDs or albums from Graveland, of course, Nokturnal Mortum, Aryan Terrorism, and we carry a lot of NSBM and Pagan type music from Russia... These Europeans don't have the finances to travel around the world the way that Western Europeans do. So they are a bit limited, perhaps they come from a harsher environment and they are more concerned with things on a local level (8 February 2008).

Organizations like Gliebe's National Alliance are opposed to Judaism, Christianity, and Satanism. Bands from distant European cultures and traditions espousing their pre-Christian national/cultural identity lend themselves effectively to their worldview. Eastern European NSBM provides a very specific model for identity creation, a model that can be adapted to any Euro-centric culture in the world.

Conclusion

Satanic black metalers have widely condemned NSBM, and vice versa. Although neo-Nazi strains of Satanism gained a fair amount of popularity during the 1980s, Satanic black metal has largely dismissed these trends, particularly in the post-church burning era. Satanic French black metalers Arkhon Infaustus assert:

> Racism and politics are so far away from our vision of black metal. Politics is nothing but the science of man to rule over other men. And to be interested in all of that just means that you are someone locked to these natural and social society [*sic*]...and we are really different from that. We respect this kind of racism, like all these kinds of racism in the world because they breed war...they breed hate... they breed killing...they breed rape and all of that kind of thing. So, we can kind of understand this, but they are too low life of hate [*sic*] to be performed by any of ours. Your spirit is much more important than the country where you were born (Zebub, dir. 2006).

As this quote illustrates, Satanic black metalers' rejection of racism and neo-Nazism has nothing to do with notions of a universal humanity or a rejection of hate. Arkhon Infaustus dismiss racism because its hatred is too specific and exclusive. Satanic black metalers often perceive the war, death and anguish that result from racism and Nazism as happy accidents caused by a misguided and contemptible herd mentality.

NSBM, like Nazi punk, will continue to be marginalized from the main body of black metal culture until it is a separate scene altogether. Its intolerance of Satanism, unwillingness to embrace non-European audiences and inability to do business with mainstream record labels like Nuclear Blast or Earache will continue to isolate NSBM and alienate the majority of black metal scene members. Black metal's generalized fascination with an imagined past and its hatred of modern secular culture will always lend itself to appropriation by far-right racist groups and individuals, but its inherent contradictions and incompatibility with many of black metal's most cherished ideas will prevent it from gaining widespread popularity within the scene. Whatever transgressive power National Socialism might contain is outweighed by its unavoidable connection with modernity and herd mentality in ways that are very similar to black metal's critique of Christianity. National Socialism's attempt to reconcile the individual with the group is awkward and, to the vast majority of black metalers, unsatisfying. Black metal seeks to create transgressive identities removed from both the modern world and constrictive notions of self and other. NSBM does not achieve this complex cultural and theological feat, usually falling back on tired notions of race and tradition that reassert the problematic aspects of modernity rather than reconciling them.

Bibliography

Interviews
Gliebe, Erich. 8 February 2008.

Books
Baddeley, Gavin. 1999. *Lucifer Rising: Sin, Devil Worship and Rock'n'Roll*. London: Plexis.
DeLillo, Don. 1985. *White Noise*. New York: Viking Penguin.
Durham, Martin. 2007. *White Rage*. New York: Routledge.
Ellis, Bill. 2000. *Raising the Devil: Satanism, New Religions and the Media*. Lexington: University Press of Kentucky.
Fine, Gary Allen, and Patricia A. Turner. 2001. *Whispers on the Color Line: Rumor and Race in America*. London: University of California Press.
Gardell, Mattias. 2003. *Gods of the Blood: The Pagan Revival and White Separatism*. Durham, NC and London: Duke University Press.
Goodrick-Clarke, Nicholas. 2003. *Black Sun: Aryan Cults, Esoteric Nazism and the Politics of Identity*. New York and London: New York University Press.
Hockenos, Paul. 1996. *Free to Hate: The Rise of the Right in Post Communist Eastern Europe*. New York: Routledge.
Kahn-Harris, Keith. 2007. *Extreme Metal: Music and Culture on the Edge*. Oxford and New York: Berg.
Lee, Martin A. 2000. *The Beast Reawakens*. New York: Routledge.
Moynihan, Michael, and Didrik Söderlind. 2003. *Lords of Chaos: The Bloody Rise of the Satanic Metal Underground*. Los Angeles: Feral House.
Raschke, Carl A. 1990. *Painted Black: From Drug Killings to Heavy Metal—the Alarming Story of How Satanism is Terrorizing Our Communities*. San Francisco: Harper & Row.
Shenfield, Stephen. D. 2001. *Russian Fascism: Traditions, Tendencies, Movements*. London: M. E. Sharp Inc.
Victor, Jeffrey S. 1993. *Satanic Panic: The Creation of a Contemporary Legend*. Chicago: Open Court.

Magazines, fanzines, websites and documentaries
Bennett, J. 2006. 'And Out Come the Wolves'. *Decibel* (May).
—2010. 'The Wolf is Loose'. *Decibel* (May).
Burzum.org. 2010. *The Burzum Story*. http://www.burzum.org/eng/biography.shtml.
Close Up. 1992. http://true.mayhem.free.fr/interviews/interview6.htm.
Hate Forest. www.supernalmusic.com/labels/supernal/hate_forest.htm (accessed March 2008, no longer available).
Maelstrom. Issue 11. http://www.maelstrom.nu/ezine/interview_iss11_130.php.

Minton, James. 2010. 'The Man Behind the Myth'. *Terrorizer* (May).

Myspace.com. 2008. Wolves in the Throne Room. http://www.myspace.com/wolvesin-thethroneroom (accessed March 2008, no longer available).

National Socialist Black Metal. www.nsbm.org/media/splc_report.html (accessed 12 December 2010, no longer available).

Nihilistic. 2005. http://nihilistic.darkbb.com/skull-fucking-metal-worship-satan-f8/inter-view-with-gbk-hordes-final-one-before-suicide-for-wsz-t636.htm.

Pit. Issue 15. http://www.angelfire.com/nh/carpathianwolves/graveland2.html.

Potok, Mark. 2000. *Darker Than Black*. SPLC Intelligence Report, Fall 2000, Issue 100. http://www.splcenter.org/get-informed/intelligence-report/browse-all-issues/2000/fall/darker-than-black.

Ward, Eric K., John Lunsford and Justin Massa. 1999. *Sounds of Violence*. SPLC Intelligence Report, Fall 1999, Issue 96. www.splcenter.org/get-informed/intelligence-report/browse-all-issues/1999/fall/sounds-of-violence.

Whalen, Gregory. 1997. 'Emperor: Their Satanic Majesties Request...' *Terrorizer* (May).

Zebub, Bill, director. 2006. *Black Metal: A Documentary*.

Extreme music for extreme people?

Norwegian black metal and transcendent violence

Michelle Phillipov

University of Tasmania, Australia

Concerns that heavy and extreme metal music promotes or glorifies violence have been circulating for much of the past four decades. Sustained campaigns by the Parents' Music Resource Center (PMRC) and criminal actions taken against Ozzy Osbourne, Judas Priest and their record labels in the 1980s, civil proceedings brought against the record labels of Cannibal Corpse, Deicide and Slayer in the 1990s, and metal's implication in the Columbine High School massacre in 1999, have each been premised on the notion that music can cause or contribute to violent actions, either against the self or against others (Moynihan and Søderlind 1998: 290–91; Walser 1993; Weinstein 2000; Wright 2000). Such concerns have resurfaced more recently in fears that Deicide's album *Once Upon the Cross* could incite 'violence, hatred and the killing of Christians' ('"Anti-Christian" CD Faces Ban' 2003: 9), and in the claim that a German trainee teacher's performances with his death metal band Debauchery constituted 'a form of mental instability that made him unsafe to be around children' ('Death Metal Teacher Sacked' 2010).

Perhaps because 'metal studies' as a field of scholarship emerged shortly after the height of metal's moral panic in the 1980s, studies of heavy and extreme metal have often focused on debunking such claims of connections between metal, violence and other problematic behaviours. Controversies in which metal music is implicated as a contributor to violence are typically understood by scholars as being fabricated by conservative groups seeking to impose their own moral agendas on those with different values, tastes and cultural practices (see Richardson 1991; Rosenbaum and Prinsky 1991; Walser 1993; Weinstein 2000; Wright 2000).

Much of this work persuasively demonstrates that lyrics or music do not 'cause' violence in any straightforward way, and that metal is rarely as extreme as its critics suggest, but critics' insistent distancing of metal from claims of violence misses an important opportunity to explore more complex connections between music and violence in the metal scene. This chapter focuses on the events of the Norwegian black metal scene in the early 1990s, a period in which violent aesthetics in metal music became explicitly and deliberately articulated to real acts of violence. Concentrating on the musical and criminal activities of the band Emperor, I suggest that the group's success was, at least in part, the result of members' simultaneous promotion and disavowal of their involvement in violent crime.

The case highlights not only how not all claims of a link between music and violence are entirely fabricated, but also the necessity of rethinking conventional approaches to music, violence and controversy, given the ongoing legacy of the events of the early 1990s within the contemporary black metal scene.

Metal and violence

Since the emergence of metal studies, critics have generally sought to distance metal from claims of a connection between music and violence. Walser (1993) and Weinstein (2000), focusing on the high-profile controversies of the 1980s, present criticisms of the genre as part of a moral crusade to neutralize challenges to parental and other authority, rather than as an indication of any real connection between metal and violence. Pettman describes the Australian response to death metal as a 'moral panic' in which media reports were 'distorted through both ignorance and the consistent need to find a scapegoat' for problematic behaviours (1995: 217). Roccor argues that metal's 'negative public image' has developed because the music has been interpreted without 'detailed knowledge of its historical development and current stylistic diversity' (2000: 84–85).

Similarly, Kahn-Harris argues that extreme metal musicians and fans might play with violent imagery, but apart from a few anomalous instances of violent crime, activities in the extreme metal scene are generally oriented not towards transgression and violence, but towards what he calls a 'logic of mundanity' (2007: 59). Musicians and fans might play with the *imagery* of violence, but their *actions* within the scene mostly revolve around the more 'ordinary' activities of listening to music, writing to other fans, and collecting and exchanging recordings (Kahn-Harris 2007: 56–57). For Kahn-Harris, the logic of mundanity is what enables scene members to explore transgressive themes textually without their own behaviour or the scene itself ever becoming unequivocally transgressive (2007: 156). Indeed, a commitment to overly transgressive practice threatens the very survival of the extreme metal scene as it inevitably leads to the death or imprisonment of scene members—something undesirable for most extreme metal aficionados (Kahn-Harris 2004: 116).

While such studies convincingly demonstrate the frequency with which both heavy and extreme metal are mischaracterized and its transgressiveness overstated, not all controversies surrounding metal are simply moral panics fabricated by conservative interest groups. Although real acts of violence are rare, the unusual cases in which metal musicians and fans have deliberately attempted to articulate music to violence provide productive case studies for understanding the more complex functions of violence and controversy within the metal scene. As Thornton has argued, academic criticism so often views youth cultures as innocent victims of negative stigmatization and moral panic, yet conservative condemnation is welcomed—even desired—by music fans who see such criticism as a certification of their scene's transgressive impulses (1995: 135–36).

If controversy alone can extend the life of otherwise ephemeral musical moments (Thornton 1995: 122), the Norwegian black metal scene is an example of how evidence of 'real' acts of transgression can be even more powerful in ensuring longevity. Such cases should not simply be explained away as unrepresentative of the majority of extreme metal practice; rather they offer valuable insight into one way that metal scenes can be popularized and sustained.

'True' Norwegian black metal

The Norwegian black metal scene in the early 1990s is perhaps metal's most famous example of the prestige and status that can be gleaned from connecting music to real acts of transgression. This is one case in which violent imagery was employed not simply as part of a 'performance' of transgression, but as a serious attempt to construct music as a springboard from which violent actions could logically emerge. In the case of the Norwegian black metal scene, such actions included arson and murder. Indeed, the notion that those who engaged in such activities were authentically 'living out' the sentiments of the music has been crucial to the meaning and significance attributed to the black metal genre, and to the sustained interest that this movement has enjoyed for the past two decades.

Black metal as a genre traces its roots to the early 1980s, with the formation of bands like Venom and Bathory, which combined raw, aggressive metal with theatrical styles of performance, and lyrics employing Satanic and Norse pagan themes. Venom's influence on black metal is especially clear, with the group's outrageous blasphemy an important precursor to the Satanic inclinations of some bands in the Norwegian scene (although the playfulness of Venom's 'Satanism' was largely lost in the work of black metal bands whose music it influenced).

Contemporary black metal now encompasses a diverse range of styles, ranging from commercially popular symphonic black metal to drone and noise, but it is the genre's incarnation in the early 1990s that is still the most well known. The status and authenticity attributed to the music of this period are evident by the label that this movement is sometimes given: 'true' Norwegian black metal.

In the late 1980s, a group of young Oslo bands—among them Mayhem, Burzum, Emperor, Darkthrone and Immortal—sought to turn what they saw as the fake theatricality of earlier metal acts into a more authentic commitment to the sentiments of the music. The music was initially quite primitive, characterized by poor production values, fast tempos, and 'rapid flat-pick reiterations of massive, muddy triads' (Bogue 2004: 106). Some bands later adopted more polished styles of production, and incorporated melodic and symphonic elements into the music, but this early style of black metal is characterized overall by an aesthetics of 'evilness' or 'grimness' that is expressed in both sonic and ideological terms. For example, bands such as Immortal have described the harshness of the Norwegian winter landscape as a natural inspiration for the coldness and brutality of black metal music. Others have suggested that aggressive musical forms are the most appropriate conduit for the expression of nihilistic, anti-Christian, Satanic and (later) Norse pagan ideologies.

Black metal band members adopted demonic stage personae, painted their faces with sinister black-and-white make-up known as 'corpse paint', and employed aestheticized images of war, battle and violence, donning stage costumes that included bullet belts and arm spikes and adopting medieval weaponry as stage props. In contrast to Venom's playful theatricality, members of the Norwegian scene stressed that their music and personae were genuinely evil, rather than something contrived only for the purposes of performance.

For example, Deathlike Silence Productions label founder and Mayhem guitarist, Euronymous, explained in interviews his desire to make and release only 'truly evil' music (quoted in Moynihan and Søderlind 1998: 66). Burzum's Varg Vikernes has claimed that the purpose of black metal is to 'spread fear and evil' (quoted in Moynihan and Søderlind 1998: 93). Other figures in the scene have criticized music that employs only aestheticized (i.e. not 'real') representations of death and destruction, arguing that metal music should function as a springboard for action. For instance, in the *Kerrang!* article that first brought Norwegian black metal to the attention of the international metal community, Emperor drummer Faust said: 'The old bands just sang about it [i.e. death and violence]—today's bands do it!' (quoted in Arnopp 1993: 43).

In contrast to other extreme metal musicians who generally reject the idea that music is or should be linked to real acts of violence (see Kahn-Harris 2007), between 1992 and 1993, key figures in the black metal scene sought to prove the seriousness of the music by undertaking criminal acts. Within the space of only a few years, 15 members of the scene were arrested for crimes including arson, grave desecration, burglary, assault, rape and murder. Most famously, members of the black metal scene were involved in arson attacks on somewhere between 15 and 20 of Norway's historic wooden stave churches (the exact number has never been officially established). No longer confining anti-Christian sentiments to song lyrics, key figures in the scene claimed that these attacks constituted retaliation against Christianity and a reclaiming of a pagan heritage that the Christian religion was thought to have destroyed (see Moynihan and Søderlind 1998). There were 11 arrests for the church arsons, including: Varg Vikernes, who was convicted for his involvement in arson attacks on Holmenkollen Chapel, Skjold Church and Åsane Church; Bård 'Faust' Eithun, who was involved in the arson of Holmenkollen Chapel; and Samoth (guitarist of Emperor) who served a 16-month sentence for the burning of Skjold Church. These acts were constructed as natural (and inevitable) expressions of the music's blasphemy and anti-Christianity. For example, Vikernes described one of Burzum's recordings as a 'hymn to church burning' (quoted in Arnopp 1993: 43). He told *Kerrang!* magazine that 'it's saying, "Do this. You can do this too"' (quoted in Arnopp 1993: 43).

The black metal scene's criminal activities were not merely confined to the destruction of property. Faust received a 14-year sentence for the 1992 murder of Magne Andreassen, a homosexual stranger who approached him in a Lillehammer park that was well known for cruising. Andreassen died from blood loss following 37 stab wounds with a pen knife. Faust was released from jail in 2003, after serving approximately 10 years of his sentence; he has never expressed any remorse for his crime. Vikernes was also convicted of the murder of his former friend, Euronymous. In August 1993, Euronymous's body was found in the stairwell leading to his apartment; he had sustained 25 stab wounds to his face, back and chest. Vikernes' motive for the murder is still subject to much speculation. Some have speculated that the murder resulted from a conflict between the two men over money; others have suggested that Vikernes was seeking to outdo Faust with an even more outrageous murder (Moynihan and Søderlind 1998: 116; Baddeley 1999: 196). For his part, Vikernes testified in court that he killed Euronymous in self-defence—somewhat speciously, given the number of stab wounds that Euronymous sustained to the back as he was being chased by Vikernes down the stairs of his apartment block. Vikernes was sentenced to 21 years in prison, Norway's maximum prison sentence. He was released in 2009, after having served nearly 16 years—including the additional 14 months served for an attempted escape in 2003. Snorre Ruch, the Thorns guitarist who drove Vikernes to and from Euronymous's house and witnessed the stabbing, received an eight-year sentence as an accessory to murder.

While the events of the early 1990s signalled the height of black metal's violence, occasional violent incidents have occurred since. For example, in 1998, Dissection's Jon Nödtveit was sentenced to seven years in prison for being an accessory to the murder of gay man Josef Ben Maddaour; Nödtveit committed suicide in 2006 following his release from prison. In 2005, Gaahl, frontman for Gorgoroth, was sentenced to 14 months in prison for beating a 41-year-old man and threatening to drink his blood.

Such incidents have now become an important part of the identity of black metal; they have received a level of interest in both the metal and non-metal media that can only be described as disproportionate to their 'objective' significance. This is especially true of the events of the early 1990s: after all, this was a small group of young men from what was, at the time, a peripheral metal scene, who engaged in acts that were (and are) entirely unrepresentative of those of the rest of the international metal community. Yet the activities of this small handful of bands have been subject to a book-length exposé, in the form of Moynihan and Søderlind's salacious *Lords of Chaos: The Bloody Rise of the Satanic Metal Underground* (1998, revised in 2003), several documentaries, including the feature-length *Until the Light Takes Us* (2008), and a forthcoming fictional film based on Moynihan and Søderlind's book, also called *Lords of Chaos*. Long-running extreme metal magazine, *Terrorizer*, has released a *Secret History of Black Metal* (2009), which compiles previous articles from the magazine's archives and devotes a significant proportion to stories on the Norwegian bands.

Even Peter Beste's coffee-table book, *True Norwegian Black Metal* (2008), which otherwise focuses on the ordinariness of black metal musicians and on the constructed theatricality of black metal performance, still reiterates a narrative of crime and violence as being central to the emergence of the black metal scene. The fact that this is a narrative that is continually repeated—and repeated even in recent texts—highlights the extent to which violence has become a lynchpin in the mythology and meaning of the genre. While it is precisely the anomalousness of this violence that has contributed to its ongoing interest, this interest has bestowed the Norwegian black metal scene with a level of importance that would have been unlikely had this scene been governed by the 'logic of mundanity' characteristic of most other extreme metal scenes.

Black metal's links to violent crime, and the bestowal of those involved with 'transgressive subcultural capital' (Kahn-Harris 2007: 128), has contributed to the endurance of what might otherwise have been a transitory moment in extreme metal's musical history. However, it is important to avoid any overly simplistic understanding of black metal's relationship to violence. While at certain times, some bands in the Norwegian black metal scene have engaged in deliberate attempts to articulate the music to violence, at other times, bands have also sought to disengage their music from any such connections. This produces an ongoing tension between transgression and mundanity in the black metal scene (see Kahn-Harris 2007: 133).

Exploring how this tension works in relation to the music of Emperor helps to better understand the scene's articulations and disarticulations of music and violence. While the media coverage of early 1990s black metal focused primarily on Euronymous, Vikernes and their bands Mayhem and Burzum, Baddeley has argued in his history of the movement that it is Emperor, more than any of the other Norwegian groups, that was most active in black metal's 'brief, blasphemous rampage' (1999: 195). Emperor has also been among the most commercially successful of the early Norwegian groups, particularly in the period after members' involvement in criminal activities had ceased. As a result, Emperor highlights both the complexity and malleability of black metal's articulation to violence. By engaging in both transgressive and mundane practices, the group has been a key beneficiary of the status and prestige associated with criminal activity *and* of the protections afforded by the logic of mundanity.

Transcendent violence

Emperor was formed in 1991 by guitarist Samoth and vocalist/guitarist Ihsahn. The group officially disbanded in 2001, but have since reformed several times for one-off appearances and live performances. Three of Emperor's founding members have served jail time in the early- to mid-1990s for crimes associated with the black metal scene: drummer Faust for murder, guitarist Samoth for arson, and bass player Tchort for burglary, assault and grave desecration. Of the original membership, only Ihsahn has no criminal convictions. Between 1994 and 2001, the group released four studio albums.

The band's debut, *In the Nightside Eclipse*, was recorded in 1993, and was released during Samoth's imprisonment in 1994. The music and performance strategies associated with this album offer clear examples of the textual conventions through which black metal music was articulated to violence in the early 1990s. In contrast, its follow-up *Anthems to the Welkin at Dusk* (1997) was written, recorded and released following Samoth's parole in 1996; it represents a concerted attempt by Emperor's members to style themselves as serious musicians who no longer wished to perpetuate their criminal past.

The fact that Emperor was able to do so without a substantial shift in musical direction was in part due to the music's sonic and lyrical complexity. Rather than a simple springboard from which violent acts must (or must not) emerge, Emperor's music employs conventions that, under some conditions, can become a springboard for real acts of violence; under others, it can lead to the construction of powerful, but ultimately benign, sonic affects.

In Emperor's work, violence is conceived primarily as a source and signifier of transcendence: something that invites the listener (and performer) to step outside of their everyday identities and become something 'other'. While this changed somewhat as the band's career progressed, in the case of the early releases—*In the Nightside Eclipse* in particular—the 'otherness' that the band sought to create was one associated with 'evilness'. For example, live performances and promotional materials from this time employed the kind of violent imagery that was generally viewed as an authentic merging of music and practice. Live performances saw the members don full corpse paint and regalia signifying war and battle (e.g. spiked arm bands, bullet belts, and weaponry). Emperor, like other black metal bands, has claimed that such performance styles assist in leaving the conventional self behind and more completely embodying the sentiments and atmospheres of the music. On the subject of corpse paint, Faust has said:

> When we, under a gig or during a photo session, are using corpse-paint [*sic*], we are usually in a state of mind that makes us feel like we are getting nearer darkness (and maybe even one with darkness)... At such events, I look at myself as one of the creatures of the night...child of darkness (quoted in Metalion 1994: 5).

The idea of becoming something 'other' is also conveyed through the band's promotional photos. One of the promotional photos for *In the Nightside Eclipse* shows members in corpse paint, black band T-shirts and bullet belts, wielding various weapons, including a sword and a double-headed axe. Among other images on the back cover of the album is a corpse-painted Faust ready to attack with a machete.

As Faust indicates in his discussion of corpse paint, these performance styles are employed as a source of transcendence of the ordinary and everyday, but it is a transcendence explicitly centred around iconographies of violence. Significantly, such performance styles are not used to construct purely fictional personae, but are presented as an embodiment of real values, desires and actions. For Faust, there is a particularly obvious synchronicity between the imagery employed in performance and his real actions, but the connections between music and practice have also been asserted by other band members.

For instance, while Ihsahn has never been implicated in the criminal activities of his bandmates, he has nonetheless sought to connect the imagery represented in the music to his real beliefs and values. Particularly early in the band's career, he was outspoken about his commitment to Satanism: in interviews, he explicitly identified himself as a Satanist, which was presented as a nihilistic, hyper-individualistic and anti-Christian philosophy that was also reflected in the band's music.

Conforming to the dominant view in the black metal scene at the time that the music should inspire 'hate and fear' in the listener, lyrics on *In the Nightside Eclipse* represent a straightforward embrace of Satan, evil and other forces of darkness as both desirable and all-powerful. 'Inno a Satana', for example, is an invocation and pledge of allegiance to Satan. 'Into the Infinity of Thoughts' endorses fear, hatred and suffering in the name of Satan. Unlike other popular forms of Satanism, Ihsahn's lyrics do not seek to challenge or re-evaluate Christian understandings of evil but rather employ the image of Satan as symbol of the misanthropy, misery and extreme individualism that the band members claim to embrace in their 'real' lives. For example, in an interview with *EsoTerra Magazine*, Ihsahn declared that, 'It is the law of nature. The strong survive. That is basically the mentality behind my Satanism—the individual. Strong, intelligent, and powerful' (quoted in Hensley 1995). These values of dominance, power and social hierarchy, then, find ideological compatibility with the iconography of weaponry and battle—other such symbols of these values.

Sonically, Emperor's music invites the listener to view this embrace of evil and cruelty as noble and awesomely powerful. On 'Into the Infinity of Thoughts', a section of the song which depicts brutal slaughter in the name of Satan is preceded by a stirring keyboard section. This section resolves the dissonance of the previous riff, and connotes a sense of majesty and splendour by contrasting the tension of the riff (which employs the interval of the tritone) with a consonant harmony (B^{min}-$F^{\#7}$) and I-V movement. On 'Cosmic Keys to my Creation', lyrics that describe the cosmos as holding 'unlimited wisdom and power for the Emperor to obtain' are paralleled with a repeated, ascending keyboard pattern (A^{min}-B^{min}-C^{maj}) that sonically conveys the enormity and magnificence of this power.

While Emperor's debut album is characterized by a greater melodic sensibility than many of its contemporaries, it can ultimately be seen as a product of the values that typified the early 1990s Norwegian scene. Violence and oppression are positively evaluated on *In the Nightside Eclipse* and in the promotional interviews that accompanied it. However, following Samoth's parole in 1996 and the release of *Anthems to the Welkin at Dusk* in 1997, Emperor's members began to style themselves as more 'serious' musicians. The band was very explicit in this, and included in the liner notes of *Anthems to the Welkin at Dusk* the statement: 'Emperor performs Sophisticated Black Metal Art exclusively!'

One of the key departures from *In the Nightside Eclipse* was the eschewal of much of the obvious imagery of weaponry and battle. While the album's back cover shows Samoth holding a sword and several of the other members wearing forms of armour (such as a chest plate and a chain-mail vest), the overall sensibility of these images is one of solemnity and majesty: none of the members is wearing corpse paint, but sit proudly and regally on thrones. The most frequently reprinted promotional photo from this period features a shot of the four band members, heads bowed and solemnly looking downward. Although Trym (Faust's replacement as drummer) is wearing a chain-mail vest, there is little other evidence of the paraphernalia of weaponry that characterized earlier band photos.

The lyrics are still characterized by the misanthropic Satanism of the debut album, but they are tempered by atmospheres of questioning, yearning and longing that are largely absent on *In the Nightside Eclipse* (and, indeed, on many of the early black metal releases). When hate is described, it is increasingly self- rather than other-directed, as is the case in 'With Strength I Burn': 'I hate my flesh... It made me question the essence of the <I>'. Such lyrics express a desire to transcend the corporeality of the body and to become the true 'I' with no reliance on the weakness and mortality of human 'flesh'. The song expresses desires that were previously expressed through the wearing of corpse paint and adoption of the regalia of weaponry and battle: to leave the ordinary self behind and to become something stronger and more powerful than one's existence in everyday life. At the same time, however, this power is not absolute and suggests a greater acknowledgement of individual weakness.

Meanwhile, while hatred might be expressed lyrically in 'With Strength I Burn', it is not reflected musically. The vocals in this section are sung, rather than growled or rasped, and this singing is melodic, full-throated and expansive—a significant contrast with the more aggressive style of 'grim' vocals that otherwise dominates Emperor's music (and which may have signified hatred and disgust in a more straightforward way). Hatred is described in this song, but it is also—sonically—transcended. Similarly, on 'Thus Spake the Nightspirit', lyrics suggest a valuing of individual power and control, but the repeated, transcendent vocal line which concludes the song ('Nightspirit... embrace my soul') implies willingness to also relinquish such power and control and be subsumed by a more powerful spirit.

While both *In the Nightside Eclipse* and *Anthems to the Welkin at Dusk* retain many connections generically, sonically and thematically, *Anthems to the*

Welkin at Dusk is, on the whole, less certain in the value it places on violence and evil as desirable and appealing goals. This shift from the signifiers of 'evil' associated with the first album to the more complex emotional palette of the second parallels the band members' decision to no longer participate in the destructive acts of violence that had characterized the early black metal scene. With the release of *Anthems to the Welkin at Dusk*, the change in members' attitudes and practices is reflected in the band's creative outputs, which were no longer focused on violent one-upmanship but on producing 'sophisticated black metal art'. For Kahn-Harris, this would be considered evidence of how the logic of mundanity ultimately 'saved' the black metal scene by redirecting scene members' energies to more 'ordinary' practices of musical production (2004: 116).

However, it was never the case that *In the Nightside Eclipse* straightforwardly signified the 'evil' that was a fitting soundtrack to murder and church burning, and that *Anthems to the Welkin at Dusk* signified a more mature or mundane sensibility that accompanied members' transitions to a more 'respectable' and crime-free life. Although an ideological shift between the two albums was evident in the band's changing performance styles, lyrical themes and iconography, sonic differences between the two albums are less dramatic than they may initially seem. *Anthems to the Welkin at Dusk* is certainly a more polished album characterized by more sophisticated song writing and a more explicit melodic sensibility, but the music's expansive and transcendent impulses, which would seem to complicate its potential to straightforwardly promote evil and violence, are also evident on *In the Nightside Eclipse*. On the band's debut, sounds which lend depictions of violence a sense of majesty and splendour can also offer pleasures disconnected from violent actions. For example, the consonant harmonies and ascending melodies on 'Into the Infinity of Thoughts' and 'Cosmic Keys to my Creation' may be interpreted as sonically conveying the magnificence of unchecked power and domination (as argued above) or simply as connoting *magnificence* and an aesthetics of transcendence not necessarily connected to violence. Both of these songs feature images that suggest the expansiveness and incomprehensibility of the self and the natural world in ways that are similar to those on *Anthems to the Welkin at Dusk*. Repeated motifs of 'infinity' (e.g. 'May the infinity haunt me') also suggest a transcendence of the self, but this transcendence need not be about power or aggression.

In other words, Emperor's aesthetics of transcendence is what constructs violence as appealing and noble, but it is what also provides opportunities for the construction of different kinds of sonic affect. The music's majesty and splendour can be used as a springboard for real acts of violence, but it also offers experiences of listening that do not necessarily require musicians or listeners to connect the music to their real actions or values.

Rhetorically, as well as sonically, Emperor has been careful to leave both possibilities open. While the members of Emperor were no longer engaged in criminal activities following Samoth's imprisonment and release, at no point have they disavowed their own or others' involvement in these crimes. For example, while Samoth claims that he can now see more effective ways of attacking or undermining Christianity, he has described church arson as a 'good symbolic anti-Christian act' and acknowledged that he 'still find[s] the concept of reducing a church to a pile of ashes appealing' (quoted in Moynihan and Søderlind 1998: 100–101). Ihsahn has similarly declined to fully distance himself from the violence of the early black metal scene. Reflecting on the events of the early 1990s, he said:

> That there were burned churches, and people were killed, I didn't react at all. I just thought, 'Excellent!' I never thought, 'Oh, this is getting out of hand', and I still don't (quoted in Moynihan and Søderlind 1998: 99).

Although since the release of *Anthems to the Welkin at Dusk*, Ihsahn and Samoth have claimed to be 'tired of the arson talk' (Whalen 1997), they are also reluctant to fully relinquish the status and prestige that comes with black metal's reputation for violence. The black metal scene from the mid-1990s onwards might well be described as one characterized by a logic of mundanity, but there is still a valuing of 'real' transgression as something that is central to the meaning and importance of black metal music.

With its members no longer involved in criminal pursuits and other acts of violence, Emperor was able to achieve a level of commercial success with *Anthems to the Welkin at Dusk* that was unavailable to many of the other bands in the early 1990s Norwegian scene. In this sense at least, Emperor offers one of the clearest examples of how black metal, and individual bands within the scene, can not only be 'saved' (Kahn-Harris 2004: 116) by the logic of mundanity, but can also prosper as a result of it. The fact that the music never promoted violence in any simple or straightforward way perhaps assisted Emperor to be more successful in this transition than many of their contemporaries, particularly because the shift into a more 'mature' and 'sophisticated' musical sensibility did not require an overly radical sonic or thematic change. But Emperor is also an example of how the logic of mundanity wins out to 'save' the music only because of the 'transgressive subcultural capital' conferred through members' previous association with violence.

Conclusion

The legacy of the black metal scene has perhaps not been its ability to balance tensions between competing impulses of transgression and mundanity, but through its ability to sustain itself through both its logic of mundanity and its reputation for transgression. Apart from a small number of violent incidents that have occurred since the early 1990s, the events of the Norwegian scene are largely aberrant in the context of the global extreme metal scene; however, the value and importance that continues to be placed on them suggests that 'violence' is still an important part of what black metal means. This is indicated by the ongoing interest in books and films about the Norwegian scene, the fact that many of the most commercially popular black metal bands today are the 'survivors' of this early scene (Hinchliffe and Patterson 2009: 71), and the fact that the success of some contemporary black metal bands (such as Gorgoroth) continues to hinge on a notion of black metal as 'authentically evil' music.

Given that academic studies have conventionally viewed claims of a connection between metal and violence as evidence of a moral panic designed to scapegoat metal and/or to serve conservative social and political interests, the events of the early 1990s problematize some of this conventional thinking about heavy and extreme metal. These events show that the relationship between metal and violence is not always one entirely exaggerated or fabricated by conservative critics. Indeed, an understanding of black metal requires that transgression and violence be thought *with*, rather than dismissed as aberrant or unrepresentative of extreme metal practice. Rather than seeking to simply defend metal from attack, critics' attempts to think with metal's violence contribute to a more nuanced understanding of the importance of transgression and controversy for past and current metal scenes.[1]

Note

1. Assistance with the musical analysis was provided by Julius Schwing, supported by NARGS funding from the University of Tasmania.

Bibliography

'"Anti-Christian" CD Faces Ban'. 2003. *Daily Telegraph*, 15 August.
Arnopp, Jason. 1993. 'We are but Slaves of the One with Horns...'. *Kerrang!* 436, 27 March.
Baddeley, Gavin. 1999. *Lucifer Rising: Sin, Devil Worship and Rock'n'roll*. London: Plexus.
Beste, Peter. 2008. *True Norwegian Black Metal*. Brooklyn: Vice Books.
Bogue, Ronald. 2004. 'Violence in Three Shades of Metal: Death, Doom and Black'. In *Deleuze and Music*, ed. Ian Buchanan and Marcel Swiboda, 95–117. Edinburgh: Edinburgh University Press.

'Death Metal Teacher Sacked'. 2010. *Orange*, 6 May. http://web.orange.co.uk/article/quirkies/Death_metal_teacher_sacked.

Hensley, Chad. 1995. 'Legion of the Night: An Interview with Emperor'. *EsoTerra Magazine* 6. http://www.esoterra.org/empor.htm.

Hinchliffe, James, and Dayal Patterson. 2009. 'Soaring on Blackened Wings'. In *Terrorizer's Secret History of Black Metal*, ed. Louise Brown, September (Special issue of *Terrorizer* magazine).

Kahn-Harris, Keith. 2004. 'Unspectacular Subculture? Transgression and Mundanity in the Global Extreme Metal Scene'. In *After Subculture: Critical Studies in Contemporary Youth Culture*, ed. Andy Bennett and Keith Kahn-Harris, 107–118. London: Palgrave.

—2007. *Extreme Metal: Music and Culture on the Edge*. Oxford: Berg.

Metalion. 1994. 'Emperor'. *Slayer* 10: 4–5.

Moynihan, Michael, and Didrik Søderlind. 1998. *Lords of Chaos: The Bloody Rise of the Satanic Metal Underground*. Venice, CA: Feral House.

Pettman, Dominic. 1995. '"It'll All Come Out in the Mosh": The Articulations of Death Metal'. *Southern Review* 28: 213–25.

Richardson, James T. 1991. 'Satanism in the Courts: From Murder to Heavy Metal'. In *The Satanism Scare*, ed. James T. Richardson, Joel Best and David G. Bromley, 205–217. New York: Aldine de Gruyter.

Roccor, Bettina. 2000. 'Heavy Metal: Forces of Unification and Fragmentation within a Musical Subculture'. *The World of Music* 42: 83–94.

Rosenbaum, Jill Leslie, and Lorraine Prinsky. 1991. 'The Presumption of Influence: Recent Responses to Popular Music Subcultures'. *Crime & Delinquency* 37: 528–35. http://dx.doi.org/10.1177/0011128791037004007

Thornton, Sarah. 1995. *Club Cultures: Music, Media and Subcultural Capital*. Oxford: Polity Press.

Walser, Robert. 1993. *Running with the Devil: Power, Gender and Madness in Heavy Metal Music*. Hanover: University Press of New England.

Weinstein, Deena. 2000. *Heavy Metal: The Music and its Culture*. Boulder, CO: Da Capo.

Whalen, Gregory. 1997. 'Emperor: Their Satanic Majesties Request...'. *Terrorizer* 39. http://www.users.globalnet.co.uk/~jasen01/warsongs/emperorinterview.htm.

Wright, Robert. 2000. '"I'd Sell You Suicide": Pop Music and Moral Panic in the Age of Marilyn Manson'. *Popular Music* 19: 365–85. http://dx.doi.org/10.1017/S026114300000222

Discography

Emperor. 1994. *In the Nightside Eclipse*. Candlelight MIM7318-2CD.

—1997. *Anthems to the Welkin at Dusk*. Candlelight MIM7327-2CD.

The extreme metal 'connoisseur'

Nicola Allett

Loughborough University, UK

The 'extreme' content of the extreme metal music genre and the transgressive practices of its musicians have placed both the genre and the culture as controversial and at the edge of the acceptable. In the present cultural climate, however, to claim oneself 'extreme' is problematic, due to a notable cultural shift towards extremity. This can be seen in changes in media and its multiplicity of content, and the permeation of extremity into popular culture and popular music genres and artists. Extreme metal's indices of extremity now appear contradictory. On the one hand, extreme metal can be seen as part of this shift towards extremity; on the other hand, the shift has removed some of extreme metal's impact as counterculture.

This chapter draws on my research with extreme metal fans to consider the construction of the extreme metal community in the UK, in the light of controversies and set against a wider culture that is increasingly celebrating the extreme. I consider a discursive strategy by fans to define extreme metal against a mainstream and legitimate their taste by adopting a system of values and distinctions that position themselves as 'connoisseurs'. I demonstrate that my respondents' consumption of extremity contrasts with their presentation of selves as connoisseurs of 'high' art who value knowledge, virtuosity, distance and expert judgement. Such an emphasis upon connoisseur values and 'high culture' characteristics place extreme metal music as art, removing allegations of profanity and distancing extreme metal music and community from the 'low' culture of the popular mainstream. The first part of this chapter briefly considers extreme metal, its extremity, and how extreme metal's character is complicated by the democratization of extremity in wider culture. The second half of this chapter considers the UK extreme metal community, as experienced by my respondents; specifically, the strategies of my respondents to construct the extreme metal community through an examination of their shared values and interactions.

The discussion below is based on an analysis of a small study of extreme metal fans. In 2007, I conducted ten recurring in-depth interviews with a group of extreme metal fans to investigate their collective identifications and their relationships with extreme metal music. The respondents—5 males and

1 female aged 19 to 31—were involved in the UK extreme metal community as fans, and as musicians and event organizers. The semi-structured group interviews were interspersed with the methods of memory work, media elicitation and music elicitation in order to gather rich descriptions of experience and to promote interaction and discussion between my respondents. Additionally, in order to examine my own taken-for-granted identity as an extreme metal fan and community member, I participated in the group tasks and contributed to discussions, which were analysed accordingly.

Extreme metal and 'extremity'

Extreme metal is a collection of music genres (including death metal, black metal, doom metal and grindcore) that are stylistically diverse, but united in the artists' pursuit of extremity, intensity and dissonance in music. Extreme metal has its roots in heavy metal. Indeed, the emergence of the genres involved the repetition, and combination, of existing heavy metal and extreme metal genre styles to achieve new sounds and also to give a literal interpretation of heavy metal. Extreme metal retains the heavy metal genre characteristics of distorted electric guitar and strong bass rhythms, while pushing those genre sounds to 'extremities'. Extreme metal presents the listener with an extremity of sound and content. This can be seen in the genres' utilization of extreme forms of tempo (both slow and fast), unconventional song structures, sound-scapes of amplified distortion and vocal manipulations (i.e. grunts, growls, rasps and screams), and lyrical themes that often include death, violence and the occult. When they emerged, the extreme metal genres functioned outside the corporate structures of the music industry, through being created and distributed via small-scale, non-corporate record labels and global underground scenes. Extreme metal bands, genres and scenes draw upon the notion that extreme metal is an 'underground' musical form and movement situated against the 'mainstream'. Despite being placed against 'the mainstream' by its artists and fans, much of extreme metal music and imagery is no longer hard to access in the UK (it can be legally and illegally downloaded); and its imagery, history and characteristics can be found and consumed (via the music media and the internet).

Extreme metal may provoke negative reactions because of its often misanthropic, misogynist, violent, anti-religious or neo-fascist lyrical content, album artwork and visual effects in live shows. It also appears controversial due to the deviant actions of its musicians (as has been the case for Norwegian black metal) and the 'extreme' politics present in the extreme metal subgenres. For instance, Goodrick-Clarke (2003) has considered the development of a National Socialist following of the black metal genre, and Beckwith (2002) has highlighted the white supremacist politics of prominent black metal musicians and the symbols within the music genre that reinforce them. The genre of grindcore, in contrast, is interspersed with far-left politics, with many bands and artists supporting anti-capitalism, anarchism and animal-rights activism (Purcell 2003; Mudrian 2004). A key feature of the extreme metal genres, and the communities surrounding them, is an acceptance and celebration of extremity of content. Kahn-Harris (2004) argues that a key contradiction within the global black metal scene is the 'reflexive anti-reflexivity' of its musicians and members. There is an acceptance that anything is publicly say-able no matter how offensive. Any conflict with politics is privately worked through and not publicly challenged by those participants. The refusal to challenge and the adoption of a laissez-faire attitude means that racist and sexist discourse is accepted by those participating in the extreme metal community and thus continues to exist. Extreme metal can be regarded as a counterculture due to its extremity. Its extremity separates it from the heavy metal genre and subculture, and places it as a non-normative culture with shared values, and hierarchy.

The 'extreme' character of extreme metal may place it at the edge of the acceptable, but in the past decade there has been a larger 'turn to extremity' that has crossed popular media and music genres. Extremity is becoming a normative factor in popular media and culture. A rise in extremity is visible in the increased exposure of sex and violence in the media, such as in the content of videogames and the graphic content of films. It is also reflected in a wider process of cultural sexualization, that has been described as a 'pornografication of the mainstream' (McNair 2002), in which physical eroticism has become appropriated by consumer culture. Taboo is now celebrated and seen, for example, in the creation of celebrity through sex-tapes and adultery scandals. Furthermore, the availability of the internet and the growth of the posting of self-made videos on the internet, popular with the rise of web-hosts such as YouTube, have increased the diversity, and indeed extremity, of what can be viewed and heard. There is a marketing potential for anything extreme. Seemingly, the more extreme, the more it sells and attracts viewers because it appears to offer something beyond the ordinary. Boothroyd (2006) has identified three areas which show a 'turn to the extreme' in culture today: extreme sports, that emphasize endurance, exposure to danger and pushing limits; extreme leisure, ranging from bungee jumping to recreational drug taking that blur the distinctions between the acceptable and unacceptable; and the extreme on television, with programmes that focus on the 'extreme case scenario' in relation to such things as engineering (i.e. tallest building), medical conditions and natural conditions (i.e. weather);

and also programmes that have intense sado-masochistic emotionality. This 'cruelty realism', 'characterized by gross spectacle and humiliation of and by ordinary people' has become present in reality TV shows such as game shows, talk shows (Epstein and Steinberg 2003: 93) and documentary footage (Epstein and Steinberg 2007). In her exploration of extreme body culture, Kosut (2010) highlights that alongside a mediatized shift to the extreme recently a new set of uniquely distorted body representation has invaded the visual realm: bodies that are interiorized (i.e. reduced to organs) and bodies that are spectacularized (expected to undergo radical transformations). This can be seen in the coverage of activities considered 'extreme', for example 'extreme' makeover via the gory spectacle of cosmetic surgery on television. In certain respects, these representations of the body mirror the aesthetics of extreme metal which depict interiorized bodies reduced to gore, blood and bodily organs and spectacularized bodies that transform through violence and death. The voyeuristic consumption of the violent, gory, and bodily spectacle in popular culture is a way in which extremity has become democratized. As a result, extreme metal's indices of extremity, that position extreme metal as alternative and counter-culture, now appear contradictory. This democratization of extremity threatens to disenfranchise extreme metal's extremity, because extremity does not have the cultural impact it once had.

The cultural shift towards extremity is also visible in popular music. Extremity permeates other (more popular) music genres and artists. This can be seen in the moral panics that surround the offensive content of popular music and the deviant actions of fans, such as the Columbine high school massacre[1] which was linked to Marilyn Manson fans (Wright 2000). In addition, the sonics of extremity are increasingly seen within other popular music genres. For example, popular metal band Slipknot uses musical traits from the extreme metal music genres such as drumming with blast-beats[2] and double-bass pedal,[3] and growling vocals which place the band at the boundary of extreme metal, although remaining unaccepted by the majority of extreme metal musicians and fans (Mudrian 2004: 256–58). Hebdige (1979) has argued that over time a subculture's signifiers face cultural incorporation by the dominant culture, which in effect defuses their signifying power. The 'mainstreaming' of metal subcultural styles and music genres have been linked to wider claims of a movement towards the 'commodification of dissent' and the corporate cultivation of the 'rebel consumer' (Frank and Weiland 1997). This is most visible in the existence of what Halnon (2005) names 'F*** the mainstream music in the mainstream' with the success of bands (such as Slipknot, Marilyn Manson and Eminem) who are popular for their rebellious antics, lyrics and rage that, in effect, commodify the alienation experience. The genre shifts towards extremity, placing the unacceptable as accepted and something associated with underground music within the mainstream. It has thus become harder to claim and justify extreme metal as underground music or as counter-culture, due to the permeation of extremity into other genres. Despite this recent shift in popular music, extreme metal is still distinct in many ways that can be linked to its fan practices and changing aesthetics. Although there are continued attempts to create extremities and dissonance in music by extreme metal musicians, there is also an ongoing celebration of past extreme metal sounds, older artists and genre styles. Many extreme metal bands are, therefore, not chasing extremities in their music but reiterating extreme metal genre traits. In addition, there is a continued emphasis on DIY culture. Extreme metal music is often produced and performed not-for-profit. There are many small scenes of musicians and fans that rely on one another's support to survive. Extreme metal fans are often actively engaged in the scene; they play in bands, write for zines, interact online, trade music, and organize local scene activities. The extreme metal scene is, therefore, a space for cultural production that reinforces its position as counter-culture.

There are many aspects of wider society and popular culture that are celebrating and consuming the extreme. Extremity is now a characteristic of the mainstream that extreme metal situates itself against. This may lead to struggles over definition and authenticity within extreme metal, so that extremity and the pursuit of dissonance becomes a contradictory goal. Extreme metal is unable to remain outside the wider public eye. However, extreme metal does continue to be sustained as both a music genre and culture. Extreme metal has subcultural nuances that continue and defend its existence in changing times. It is the distinctions of authenticity, performances, interactions and alternative discourses within the extreme metal community which I explore in this chapter through a consideration of extreme metal fans' appropriation of connoisseurship.

'High' and 'low' culture and the connoisseur

The connoisseur is an expert of taste who embodies high culture through distanced judgement and a reserved disposition. The connoisseur displays good taste in the cultured domain and draws the lines of cultural distinction through discriminating taste. The figure of the connoisseur is associated with the high-art viewer, who is concerned with aesthetic judgement and enjoyment. In other words, a concern with form over content and sight rather than the other senses (Nead 1996). The connoisseur is a sub-species of the 'flâneur'.

The flâneur is seen as a stance of modernity (Tester 1994). He is immune to the enticements of the commercial and loses himself in the crowd. He uses his distance to gain a form of control in which he observes and does not participate. Whereas the flâneur observes passively, however, the metal fan is active. This is reflected in extreme metal's DIY culture and the active listening practices of the metal fan (Berger 2004: 58). A consideration of connoisseurship exhibited by extreme metal fans places the 'high' culture figure in a 'low' cultural form. There remains an aesthetic hierarchy that places popular music in the realm of 'low' mass culture, while the music of 'high' culture is considered 'serious music' and educated choice. Tastes signify social differences. For instance, the figures of the aficionado and fan appear to be alike, but as Jenson (1992: 21) explains, 'the Opera buff and the Heavy Metal fan are differentiated not only on the basis of the status of their desired object, but also on the supposed nature of their attachment'. The aficionado of 'high' culture (the opera buff) is assumed to have intellectual detachment, while the fan of 'low' culture (heavy metal) is associated with uncontrolled bodies and emotions, being represented as obsessed, unstable, hysterical and isolated. Despite these demarcations based on social difference, high culture aesthetics and judgements have been shown to exist in low cultural forms. Fan cultures have their own practices of distinction and forms of 'popular' or 'subcultural' capitals that serve to communicate social prestige and 'authentic' collective fan and music-centred identities (Fiske 1992; Thornton 1995). Furthermore, as with the horror movie fans in Hills' (2005) study who debated over horror's aesthetics and affect and argued that non-fans watch naïvely, connoisseurship can emerge as a master trope in fan struggles against 'inauthentic' consumers and policing authorities.

The music genres of metal are deemed 'low' culture, despite their similarities with 'high' cultural forms. Heavy metal and extreme metal performatively reference excess, physicality and emotionality all of which are opposite principles to which the connoisseur is devoted. However, Walser (1993: 53) has highlighted the classical influence on heavy metal music, which 'marks a merger of what are generally regarded as the most and least prestigious musical discourses of our time'. Extreme metal shares nuances of 'high' culture with its pre-occupation with musical virtuosity, aesthetics and form over and above what is represented. Walser (1993) demonstrates that the distance that separates classical music and heavy metal is not a gap of musicality; rather the genres are markers of social difference. Heavy metal is frequently associated with 'low' culture and seen as a cultural signifier of white working-class masculinity. It has been shown that heavy metal in Britain had strong associations with the working class, although class politics remained largely absent in the subculture (Moore 2009; Nilsson 2009). Extreme metal is, however, distinct from heavy metal. It may borrow idioms and traits of heavy metal but extreme metal in the UK has a larger middle-class following and, as shown in this chapter, it displays more in common with 'high brow' cultures that can be seen in its celebration of aesthetics, virtuosity and cultivated taste, notwithstanding its obscenities and sound.

The extreme metal connoisseur

The extreme metal fan, as subcultural member, possesses values and dispositions, and makes distinctions that locate him/her as an 'insider'. My respondents had shared practices, values and distinctions that can be associated with 'high' cultural connoisseurship, which characterized their membership of the extreme metal community. This connoisseurship could partly be a reflection of the prevalence of university-educated participants in the research group and the high proportion of middle-class and university-educated fans within the extreme metal community. Yet, my respondents' connoisseurship also appears to be linked to their strategies to define and defend their extreme metal identity.

The connoisseur exhibits knowledge and mastery of a subject. Likewise, my respondents had thorough knowledge and expertise related to extreme metal music and culture. Such knowledge, which included extreme metal music history, genres, underground bands, instruments, music labels, and terminologies, can be interpreted as forms of subcultural capital, which (if acquired) give status and validation to the extreme metal fan. This subcultural capital was also displayed via my respondents' personal music collections, which were regularly added to. Music fans can exhibit their extensive knowledge of music through the ownership of a large and well-chosen music collection (Straw 1997). Kahn-Harris (2007) describes activities such as record collecting as a means to gain 'mundane subcultural capital'. The effort to gain and display knowledge and expertise signifies the fan's work and commitment, which serves to bolster the maintenance of hierarchy within extreme metal subculture. The valuing of knowledge and the expert fan are elements of extreme metal community that can be related to connoisseurship, which further maintain extreme metal community and hierarchy.

The positioning of the extreme metal fan as a connoisseur of 'high' culture contrasts greatly with the imagery, sound and physicality of extreme metal music. According to Bourdieu (1991: 364), the connoisseur of sport has a differing perception from the public: 'The "connoisseur" has schemes of perception and appreciation which enable him to see, to perceive a necessity where the outsider sees only violence and confusion'. If this perception is applied to extreme metal music instead of sport, the extreme metal fan, as connoisseur, can be seen to appreciate the art of music whereas the non-extreme metal fan might only react to what can be described as the violence and confusion of the extreme metal sound. The fan, as connoisseur, values the virtuosity of extreme metal music, as seen in Rob's comments on the importance he placed on musicianship:

> Rob: Musicianship is very important... I'm a guitarist and it is the most boring instrument to play because everybody does it and everybody these days is in a band, but there is a difference between, say, somebody just playing in a band and [somebody] being a musician. It's a big difference. Being a musician is more artistic and music should be an art form.

Rob makes the distinction between 'somebody just being in a band' and the 'musician'. The musician is placed as a producer of 'art' rather than popular music. The musician is given a specific identity amidst the mass of 'anybody' and 'everybody'. Rob's statement also implies that he is placing himself in the role of musician and artist, and avoids being placed as just another 'boring' guitarist. A valuing of art was also reinforced by an emphasis on musical virtuosity. For instance, when evaluating extreme metal music that had been played during a music elicitation task, my respondents placed emphasis on musical technique:

> Ben: I like this drumming on this record. I think it is quite intrusive, which I normally don't like, but it seems to work with this music that is more intricate.
>
> N.A.: Yeah, perhaps because all the instruments are very clear.
>
> Liam: I like the layout style as well.
>
> Ben: That is something that can appear over used but in this instance sounds good.
>
> Rob: It depends how it's done, perhaps because most people do it in a Sabbath style time and time again.

Here, the music track is considered in relation to the successes of the musicians, structure and style. The research group regularly talked about the importance of feelings and the affective experiences of music listening, but when it came to evaluating what made a piece of music particularly good, it was the musical technique, and musicians' talent, rather than the feelings, that they chose to evaluate. Additionally, my respondents celebrated the musical originality and intelligence of extreme metal bands and musicians:

Rob: These guys [Eyehategod] were quite a pioneering band from New Orleans. Sound wise I like the dirty, gritty sound that they have. Really, it is quite sort of aggressive isn't it? In a lazy sort of way.

Ben: I don't particularly identify with their themes of what they're singing about, but I think they do it in an intelligent way—good lyrics.

Rob: Yeah they are clever, and the vocalist was a journalist and he's written a book of poetry. Quite intelligent really.

Ben and Rob emphasize that the intelligence of the lyrics/musicians are important aspects of the band's appeal. They use 'high' culture values to evaluate extreme metal music, which would normally be considered as a 'low' cultural form. My respondents' emphasis on musical virtuosity places extreme metal as a legitimate and serious music genre and places the fan as connoisseur.

A focus on extreme metal music as art was also shown in the research group talk about the music media. My respondents adopted a particular way of critiquing the extreme metal music press. Critique of the magazines centred upon the failure of many of the journalists concerned to demonstrate their passion for music, knowledge and serious review of it. In looking through extreme metal music magazines and fanzines,[4] my respondents commented upon the failure of many of the journalists concerned to demonstrate their intellect and expert knowledge of music. For instance, Ben used such criticisms when he commented upon an extreme metal music festival review featured in the extreme metal magazine *Terrorizer*:[5]

Ben: He's talking about how much he hates festivals, Pot Noodle, you know, he's talking about how festivals are commercialized, which is reasonable enough but, you know, he says about five words about the bands. He talks about how he sneaked some alcohol into the festival. Great. Then he says he can't remember seeing Onslaught. Most of this is about him and it's just bollocks basically. In my opinion, he takes very little time talking about the music and makes stupid comments about lots of the bands.

Ben identifies that the journalist does not make informed comments about the bands' performances at the festival. This is of particular annoyance to Ben because he considers the band Onslaught worthy of attention. Ben also criticizes the journalist's narcissism, which is deemed key to the article's failure ('Most of this is about him and it's just bollocks basically'). It is the journalist's failure to place importance upon music and to write an intelligent review of it that Ben is therefore disapproving of (although while doing so, Ben uses the 'low' cultural language of a swearword to express his distaste). In a previous group discussion, Nathan also expressed a particular expectation of extreme metal journalism to be serious:

Nathan: You get the readers' poll[6] in Terrorizer. It's supposed to be a serious maga-
           zine, and they have 'Most shaggable female' category. Come on; don't dumb
           it [the magazine] down.

Chloe: Yeah, it's making it into Kerrang! doing that.

Nathan wants to distance himself from something he regards as part of low-brow mass media, which he characterizes by its objectification of female celebrities. He is annoyed that a piece of extreme metal media fails to retain an intelligent approach and tone ('Come on, don't dumb it down'). Chloe compares this 'dumbing down' to the weekly metal magazine, *Kerrang!*, which covers more mainstream rock and metal artists. By distinguishing such dislikes, my respondents reinforced their alignment with 'serious' music and separation from the mainstream. Their valuing of reserved, intelligent and serious journalism highlighted a shared identification with the connoisseur of 'high' culture.

Connoisseurship can be seen as a form of distinction work that serves the purpose to exclude through discriminating taste. By defining their fandom in relation to expertise, appreciation of art, originality and musicianship and a serious disposition, my respondents situated extreme metal, and themselves, against other popular music genres and fans. Similar distinctions between the distinguished and the vulgar can be seen in Redhead's (1997) observations of high and low distinctions of taste being made within popular music, privileging rock over pop, and pop over dance. This is additionally reflected in Thornton's (1995) study of club cultures, which demonstrated the ways in which club culture members made a distinction between authentic and mainstream dance music and further distinctions based around authentic versus phoney, hip versus mainstream and underground versus media. By being on the edge of a body of music, extreme metal invokes a similar status to that of the female nude body in art. It is situated between creativity and profanity. Nead (1996: 238) highlights that the female nude in art represents a meeting place between creativity and profanity: 'erotic art takes the viewer to the frontier of legitimate culture, it allows the viewer to be aroused, but within the purified, contemplative mode of high culture'. Extreme metal may appear controversial and extreme, yet its fans situate it as artistic and serious music. Whereas the extreme appears a significant trait of extreme metal music and, increasingly, of popular culture, respondents created distance between extreme metal and wider culture. An emphasis upon distanced judgement of music and intelligence placed extreme metal as culturally legitimate and distanced the extreme metal fan (and subculture) from the perceived 'mainstream' and mass popular culture. This is similar to the activities of 'cult fans', which tend to communicate social and cultural capital defined against the mainstream (Sandvoss 2005). Through the commercial mainstream being defined as conformist, the label 'cult' gives cultural legitimacy to texts ranging from kitsch to graphic violence or hardcore pornography (Jancovich 2002). The separation of tastes from the mainstream was a key distinction made by my respondents. For example, Ben and Liam did so to reinforce their superior sense of taste:

Ben: Do you feel elite when you listen to something extreme do you think? ... Well, because you can find value in something that most people wouldn't be able to find value in.

Liam: Yeah, I think so. [Pauses] Yeah, to bring yourself outside of the herd mentality, isn't it? You are able to see something. If you can find that in something that most people would dismiss as being too, you know, off the radar then, yeah.

The phrase 'herd mentality' (and 'sheep' in other conversations) was used to describe the behaviours of those considered to be part of the 'mainstream', to indicate mass conformity, and a lack of individuality. The description of music's value in the conversation: 'you can find value in something that most people wouldn't be able to find value in' and 'you can find that in something that most people would dismiss as being too, you know, off the radar' highlight the importance of having a different and distinctive taste to others. By being 'off the radar', the extreme metal fan is able to feel 'elite' because s/he has the refined taste of only a select few. The research group's discussions situate their extreme metal fandom against a 'mainstream' and their own activities as counterculture and, therefore, culturally legitimate. As a result, extreme metal music is placed by its fans as separate from other forms of popular culture and positioned as a 'high' cultural form.

The connoisseur has a reserved and unaffected disposition. S/he considers that art should not be judged by the viewer's reaction, but rather his/her evaluation of its execution. Although respondents attempted to take on the language and stance of the connoisseur, it was a managed identity that at times proved a difficult position to inhabit. Nead (1996) draws attention to the connoisseur's body, which 'renders pure aesthetic judgment impossible'. When viewing the nude body in art, the connoisseur's body is seen to get in the way, disabling distanced judgment. If one considers the body's response to music, its response to rhythms and beats whether it is tapping feet, dancing or headbanging, the retaining of reserved distance becomes difficult. Once the connoisseur's body is considered, rather than just what s/he sees or hears, it becomes apparent that true connoisseurship is impossible. Respondents' 'high' culture values clashed with the group's physical practices associated with extreme metal. When Chloe chose to play an Obituary song to the group in a music elicitation task, it was significant that she characterized it as less intelligent than other group member's choices:

Chloe: Right, I'm going to go from the rather intelligent of you lot to something a bit less intelligent, you know...a bit Obituary.

After the music had been played, Chloe explained Obituary's specific appeal in relation to physical practice:

Chloe: Yeah, and you can headbang to it all the way through from beginning to end without really even having to change pace too much. You can just plant yourself on the dance floor and go for it and I've done that.

Chloe's comments establish an association between the physical practices associated with metal music (i.e. headbanging) and unintelligence. The extreme metal gig shares much in common with the heavy metal gig with many audience members taking part in physical expressions such as headbanging. Where it differs from heavy metal is that there is often a refusal to move by some of the live audience taking an 'anti-mosh stance',[7] and in the case of the genre of doom metal, the music's tempo is unnaturally slow to achieve the same levels of physicality. The live event is the coming together of the audial and the performative, both of which make high culture difficult, maybe even impossible, to achieve. Although music (and particularly live music with its emphasis on crowd interaction) creates this inconsistency, my respondents also gave accounts of managing their physical practices. For example, Nathan described avoiding physical practice at extreme metal gigs:

Nathan: I think you go to gigs sometimes and you're perfectly content on standing back and watching, and have your own little personal space and just watch what's going on, and then someone walks past acting like a nutter.

Here, Nathan avoids physical practice because it enables viewing. He views the physical fan as a 'nutter', uncontrolled and absurd. Physical practices had to be approved as appropriate; my respondents had many debates on the values underpinning the 'rules' of the live event. Liam was the most vocal in his dislike of certain behaviours and, in particular, stage diving:

Liam: I hate it [stage diving] with a passion and I think anyone stage diving should be thrown out of the venue. It really, really annoys me. I can't see how, in any way, it is tied in with the music. I think it's just someone who wants to get up on stage and draw some attention to themselves. I just really hate it. People just get up [on stage], fuck about, and it's always the same three or four blokes as well, again and again and again. I think you're not listening to the band, you're just wanting to get up on stage, jump off then get on stage, jump off, 'look at me I'm on stage', jump off.

Liam places stage-divers as self-obsessed, and failing to appreciate the music. He cannot understand the motivation because he 'can't see how in any way it is tied in with the music'. Herein lies the belief that the fan will not be respected if s/he affects others' appreciation of the performance. These accounts highlight that the research group viewed the physical practices associated with extreme metal as something which should be managed, controlled and appropriate, most importantly not affecting one's appreciation of the music. Connoisseurship can, therefore, be interpreted as a managed identity which often conflicts with the affective and physical experiences of music. It involves a significant amount of work in retaining the ideal of intelligence and a distanced disposition in relation to extreme metal music.

Conclusion

In this chapter, I have illuminated the strategies of fans in adopting a 'high' culture position to define a community identity and reinforce a sense of boundaries and membership. My respondents placed importance upon musical virtuosity, intelligence, expert knowledge, and distanced judgement in their discussions with one another and in their evaluations of music, journalism and live performance of music, which mirrored connoisseurship of art. Connoisseurship was a shared system of values that characterized their evaluations and expectations of the extreme metal community. It served to distinguish extreme metal as 'serious' music, distance extreme metal music from the mainstream and justify its extremity and profanity as art. This was struggled over at certain points due to the inevitable clash between 'high' and 'low' culture that extreme metal presented and the physical presence of the feeling fan. This investment in 'high' culture values, the celebration of the music as 'high' art and the adoption of 'high brow' aesthetics also distances extreme metal music and community from the mainstream and 'low' culture stereotypes placed onto heavy metal. Connoisseurship can, therefore, be seen as a form of distinction work that serves the purpose to exclude. Through attempting to place high culture onto extreme metal, my respondents' connoisseurship reinforced a collective belief that extreme metal is counter-culture and elite to other popular music genres.

The current routinization of the extreme in popular culture has involved the appropriation of the musical sounds and visual markers of extreme metal. This turn to extremity has seen the marketing of the extreme as something beyond the ordinary and offering excitement as an end in itself. Extreme culture can be seen in the popularity of extreme leisure and aesthetically in the depiction of interiorized and spectacularized bodies. What seems particular about the metal genres is the combination of a valuing of virtuosity with spectacle and transgression. While the extreme appears to be a significant trait of extreme metal music, my respondents placed extreme metal in the realms of 'high' culture via their connoisseur values. In so doing, they legitimated and separated extreme metal and its extremity from the wider cultural democratization of extremity. This indicates that a counterculture has to continually reinvent itself as wider culture changes around it.

My respondent's connoisseurship also reveals particular features of individual and collective identities and forms of solidarity in late-modern societies. One can consider that in late-modernity people continue to follow the modern project of self-identity, and participate in various attempts to reflexively construct the 'self'. The position of the connoisseur (a subspecies of the flâneur) represents the figure of modernity holding on to the importance of permanence, identification and status. This is in opposition to the postmodern and post-subcultural shift to hyper-individualism, fluidity and fragmentation. Unlike the connoisseur and flâneur, however, the extreme metal fan is active. S/he participates in the DIY culture of the scene. Moreover, extreme metal identity is managed as the fan tries to conceal the bodily, emotional and political elements of the extreme metal experience. Connoisseurship, therefore, has several functions for the extreme metal fan. It is a form of distinction work within the scene, a defence of policing authorities outside the scene, a form of identity-work in late-modern times, and a strategy that is ever-more significant in the current turn to the extreme.

Notes

1. The Columbine high school massacre (20 April 1999) involved two students killing 12 students and a teacher and wounding 23 others before committing suicide.
2. Blast-beats involve rapid alternating strokes primarily on the bass and snare drum.
3. Double-bass pedal is a method of beating the bass drum on the drum kit with a double kick pedal that enables one to hit the drum faster creating fast bass rhythm.
4. The magazines that the group considered were issues of UK magazines *Terrorizer*, *Zero Tolerance* and one issue of the fanzine *Morbid Tales*.
5. 'Bloodstock '06' in *Terrorizer* (2006).

6. The readers' poll requests readers' choices for particular categories such as 'best band' or 'best vocalist'; the most popular choices are then published in the annual article.

7. The 'anti-mosh' stance involves audience members' refusal to move. The term originated from the black metal scene. The phrase 'anti-mosh' appeared on the CD codes of Deathlike Silence Productions, an independent record label founded in the late 1980s in Oslo, Norway by Aarseth (aka Euronymous of black metal band Mayhem).

Bibliography

Beckwith, Karl. 2002. 'Black Metal is for White People'. *M/C: A Journal of Media and Culture* 5(3). http://journal.media-culture.org.au/0207/blackmetal.php

Berger, Harris M. 2004. 'Horizons of Melody and the Problem of Self'. In *Identity in Everyday Life: Essays in the Study of Folklore, Music and Popular Culture*, ed. Harris M. Berger and Giovanna P. DelNegro, 43–87. Middletown, CT: Wesleyan University Press.

Boothroyd, Dave. 2006. 'Cultural Studies and the Extreme'. In *New Cultural Studies: Adventures in Theory*, ed. Gary Hall and Clare Birchall, 274–92. Edinburgh: Edinburgh University Press.

Bourdieu, Pierre. 1991. 'Sport and Social Class'. In *Rethinking Popular Culture: Contemporary Perspectives in Cultural Studies*, ed. Chandra Mukerji and Michael Schudson, 357–73. Berkeley: University of California Press.

Epstein, Debbie, and Deborah Lynn Steinberg. 2003. 'Life in the Bleep Cycle: Inventing Id-TV on the Jerry Springer Show'. *Discourse* 25(3): 90–114. http://dx.doi.org/10.1353/dis.2005.0002

—2007. 'The Face of Ruin: Evidentiary Spectacle and the Trial of Michael Jackson'. *Social Semiotics* 17(4): 441–58. http://dx.doi.org/10.1080/10350330701637049

Fiske, John. 1992. 'The Cultural Economy of Fandom'. In *The Adoring Audience: Fan Culture and Popular Media*, ed. Lisa A. Lewis, 30–49. London: Routledge.

Frank, Thomas, and Matt Weiland. 1997. *Commodify Your Dissent: The Business of Culture in the New Guilded Age*. New York: W. W. Norton.

Goodrick-Clarke, Nicholas. 2003. *Black Sun: Aryan Cults, Esoteric Nazism and the Politics of Identity*. New York: New York University Press.

Halnon, Karren Bettez. 2005. 'Alienation Incorporated: "F*** the Mainstream Music" in the Mainstream'. *Current Sociology* 301(3): 743–79.

Hebdige, Dick. 1979. *Subculture: The Meaning of Style*. London: Routledge. http://dx.doi.org/10.4324/9780203139943

Hills, Matt. 2005. *The Pleasures of Horror*. London: Continuum.

Jancovich, Mark. 2002. 'Cult Fictions: Cult Movies, Subcultural Capital and the Production of Cultural Distinctions'. *Cultural Studies* 16(2): 306–322. http://dx.doi.org/10.1080/09502380110107607

Jenson, Joli. 1992. 'Fandom as Pathology: The Consequences of Characterization'. In *The Adoring Audience: Fan Culture and Popular Media*, ed. Lisa A. Lewis, 9–29. London: Routledge.

Kahn-Harris, Keith. 2004. 'The "Failure" of Youth Culture: Reflexivity, Music and Politics in the Black Metal Scene'. *European Journal of Cultural Studies* 7(1): 95–111. http://dx.doi.org/10.1177/1367549404039862

—2007. *Extreme Metal: Music and Culture on the Edge.* Oxford: Berg.

Kosut, Mary. 2010. 'Extreme Bodies/Extreme Culture'. In *The Body Reader: Essential Social and Cultural Readings*, ed. Lisa Jean Moore and Mary Kosut, 184–200. New York: New York University Press.

McNair, Brian. 2002. *Striptease Culture: Sex, Media and the Democratisation of Desire.* London: Routledge. http://dx.doi.org/10.4324/9780203469378

Moore, Ryan M. 2009. 'The Unmaking of the English Working Class: Deindustrialisation, Reification and the Origins of Heavy Metal'. In *Heavy Metal Music in Britain*, ed. Gerd Bayer, 111–60. Surrey: Ashgate.

Moynihan, Michael, and Didrik Søderlind. 1998. *Lords of Chaos: The Bloody Rise of the Satanic Metal Underground.* Venice, CA: Feral House.

Mudrian, Albert. 2004. *Choosing Death: The Improbable History of Death Metal and Grindcore.* Los Angeles, CA: Feral House.

Nead, Lynda. 1996. 'Troubled Bodies: Art, Obscenity and the Connoisseur'. *Women: A Cultural Review* 7(3): 229–39. http://dx.doi.org/10.1080/09574049608578279

Nilsson, Magnus. 2009. 'No Class? Class and Class Politics in British Heavy Metal'. In *Heavy Metal Music in Britain*, ed. Gerd Bayer, 161–79. Surrey: Ashgate.

Purcell, Natalie J. 2003. *Death Metal Music: The Passion and Politics of a Subculture.* North Carolina: McFarland.

Redhead, Steve. 1997. *Subcultures to Clubcultures: An Introduction to Popular Cultural Studies.* Oxford: Blackwell.

Sandvoss, Cornel. 2005. *Fans: The Mirror of Consumption.* Cambridge: Polity Press.

Straw, Will. 1997. 'Sizing Up Record Collections: Gender and Connoisseurship in Rock Music Culture'. In *Sexing the Groove*, ed. Sheila Whiteley, 3-16. London: Routledge.

Terrorizer. 2006. 'Bloodstock '06'. December, issue 151. London: Dark Arts Limited: 84-85.

Tester, Keith. 1994. *The Flâneur.* Oxon: Routledge.

Thornton, Sarah. 1995. *Club Cultures: Music Media and Subcultural Capital.* Cambridge: Polity Press.

Walser, Robert. 1993. *Running with the Devil: Power, Gender and Madness in Heavy Metal Music.* London: Wesleyan University Press.

Wright, Robert. 2000. '"I'd Sell you Suicide": Pop Music and Moral Panic in the Age of Marilyn Manson'. *Popular Music* 19(3): 365–85. http://dx.doi.org/10.1017/S0261143000000222

Black metal soul music

Stone Vengeance and the aesthetics of race in heavy metal

Kevin Fellezs

Columbia University, USA

> 'Some people refer to us as a Christian metal band! Christian! You know, I told the guy, that's not what we are. I can understand, they hear the Bible references—but that's the blues! That's from the blues. I'm just carrying on [the black musical] tradition in rock'n'roll. It's a code, you know, and a part of who I am'.
>
> —Mike Coffey, leader of Stone Vengeance[1]

Near the beginning of his incisive study of heavy metal, Robert Walser asserts,

> A heavy metal genealogy ought to trace the music back to African-American blues, but this is seldom done. Just as histories of North America begin with the European invasion, the histories of musical genres such as rock and heavy metal commonly begin at the point of white dominance. But to emphasize Black Sabbath's contribution of occult concerns to rock is to forget Robert Johnson's struggles with the Devil and Howlin' Wolf's meditations on the problem of evil (1993: 8).

African-American guitarist and Stone Vengeance founder, Mike Coffey, does not hesitate to trace rock music and by extension, heavy metal, from the blues:

> I listen to stuff from the '20s. Charley Patton, Blind Lemon Jefferson, Blind Blake, Robert Johnson from the '30s. Lonnie Johnson, who's just as good, probably a little better than Robert Johnson. Robert Johnson just got popular because Eric Clapton put his stamp [of approval] on him. But you ask BB King and all those guys, [they'll tell you that] Lonnie Johnson's bad as hell, man. Skip James. That's what happens when you put the drums and the bass behind the guitar, it's rockin' now! *You can't get heavy metal—if you don't have that guitar, it'll be something else.* You can have a loud bass and drums but without that guitar, it's another music. *The guitar is primary because of the blues.*

While Walser allows the blues to shimmer behind the remainder of his book without further comment, I want to note the ways in which black (African-American) heavy metal musicians confront the reality that, as Walser and other heavy metal scholars such as Deena Weinstein readily acknowledge, heavy metal is a genre with an audience that is 'mostly young, white, male, and working class' (Walser 1993: 3).

Moreover, black heavy metal musicians must also confront the practices of a music industry that bases its decisions about marketing, artist development and genre configuration on that reality. These assumptions cum practices inadvertently silence black rock musicians by reinforcing tautological links between genre and race that ensure audiences, critics and music industry personnel identify certain musical sounds and gestures with particular types of bodies. While the global reach of contemporary metal complicates Walser and Weinstein's assertions about the core constituency for heavy metal, the overarching racialization of rock as a 'white' genre remains, particularly in the United States, black African metal bands notwithstanding.[2]

Stone Vengeance (l-r: Mike Coffey, Darren Tompkins, Anthony Starks) ©1998 Paul Trapini

Stone Vengeance is a heavy metal band whose members are all African American and, while enjoying a primarily white male audience, formed their aesthetic in recognition, even celebration, of their blackness. Initially formed in 1978, Stone Vengeance have remained a cult favorite for a small if dedicated core audience who can be found 'on every continent but Antarctica', as Coffey boasts. Their fans have named them the Lords of Heavy Metal Soul, a moniker, while clearly meant to praise, that speaks to Stone Vengeance's racialized positioning outside the inner sanctum of metaldom, pointing as it does to a long history of primitivist tropes concerning black Americans' 'soul', a nonintellectual, body-oriented essence that opposes the figuration of thrash metal as a complex musical form. As John Sheinbaum warns rock scholars, while rock's increasingly canonical historical narrative presents white rock musicians as artists and black soul musicians as craftspeople, 'race-based constructions of difference we may hear should not lead us, unthinkingly, to assert that [music produced by white or black musicians] somehow possesses different levels of value' (2002: 127). Sheinbaum's point—that an unspoken and therefore often unacknowledged idea lurking behind critical judgment holds that exemplary black musicians are unschooled 'soulful performers' while ideal white musicians are highly trained 'skillful artists'—reveals the predetermined ways in which black cultural production enters critical discourse in an already subordinate position.

My interest in Stone Vengeance lies in this very predicament: the relationship between race and value as experienced by musicians who challenge conventional genre boundaries through an embodied difference to assumed genre expectations.[3] In fact, my initial interest was in studying the 1980s San Francisco thrash metal scene that had served as Metallica's formative ground. However, as I began researching, I became increasingly interested in Stone Vengeance because of their longevity—most of the other bands from the original scene have long since disappeared.[4] More importantly, as the sole representatives of African-American musicians in the scene, Stone Vengeance provides a uniquely productive vehicle for reflecting on the relationships among processes of racialization, critical appraisals of aesthetic and historical value and music industry assessments of commercial interest precisely because Stone Vengeance makes visible the underlying tenets for recognition by other metal musicians, critics, fans, and music industry personnel—all of whom begin their appraisal of bands and musicians on presumptive notions of genre, including the bodies deemed appropriate for a particular genre. As Fabian Holt argues in his insightful study of popular music genre, a '*genre can be viewed as a culture* with the characteristics of a system or systemic functions ...[and] are identified not only with music, but also *with certain cultural values, rituals, practices, territories, traditions, and groups of people*' (Holt 2007: 23, 19, added emphasis). It is reasonable to assume that the 'cultural values, rituals, practices, territories, traditions and groups of people' associated with thrash metal do not normally call to mind African-American musicians or black musical traditions. Yet, as Stone Vengeance effectively posits, despite working within a genre discursively constructed as a space for the expression of white masculinity, thrash metal can be thought of as part of a black American musical tradition.

Before allowing Coffey's narrative to center my discussion, I want to be explicit about not taking his comments at face value. However, throughout all my work (and not exclusively for this book), I aim to highlight musicians' voices in order that we might gain knowledge from their perspective. Too often musicians' voices are muted or muffled by scholars, critics and fans with a real loss in the ways in which historical narratives, aesthetic choices and music industry practices are framed. By giving ample space to Coffey, I hope to serve as an interested interlocutor of Stone Vengeance's working aesthetic in heavy metal as an articulation of a black aesthetic. In this way, I mean to foreground Coffey's role as musician—both agentive and reactive, both expressive and constitutive—in negotiating musical discourse, audience desire and critical hermeneutics.

For example, at one point in a conversation with Coffey and drummer/vocalist Darren Tompkins, I referred to Jimi Hendrix and his role in shaping psychedelic hard rock and, consequently, heavy metal through his technical mastery of the blues combined with the sonic assault of hard rock and his creative use of distortion.[5] But the mention of Hendrix elicited a heated reply from Coffey. After quickly assuring me that he loves Hendrix's music, Coffey became decidedly less appreciative of the aims to which Hendrix's representation has been mobilized by rock critics and fans, particularly after his death. I quote Coffey's response at length:

> I always think about it. People act like they really love Hendrix. But, you know what? If that is the case, it wouldn't be so hard for black people to get *in* to this music. So I feel like, well, Hendrix is gone and he's no longer an obstacle or a threat or something—so it's easy, [he's] safe to like. That's what I feel about Hendrix because people like me, and you...we're children of Hendrix through the discipline of rock'n'roll.

> But there's no apparatus to help us *at all*. So, I think it's bullshit. I think it's a fake love affair with Hendrix. It's just he's gone, and money can be made off of him, you know what I mean?

> Think about it. He didn't make it here in the States. We have to *look* at that. He was *struggling* in the States, just like us. Just like Living Colour wouldn't have made it if it wasn't for Mick Jagger, you know what I mean? So it's bullshit, dude.[6]

Noting how a fetishized Hendrixian presence allows white rock fans to proclaim their admiration for a dead black musician while disenfranchising living black rock musicians, Coffey insists that despite the adulation Hendrix receives within rock culture, the real status of black rock musicians is evident in the racialized conditions that remain within the music industry and within rock discourse writ large that keep black musicians from full participation within rock—even, as Coffey points out, for an artist as revered as Hendrix.[7] Coffey's view that the figure of Hendrix has allowed an obscuring of the lack of apparatus—lack of structure, of legitimation, of support, of authority—for other black rock musicians in the commercial music market provides the chance to briefly address the underlying issue of musicking, in thrash metal or otherwise, as labor.

Something else

Stone Vengeance was not successful in turning home court to their advantage in the burgeoning San Francisco Bay Area metal scene of the 1980s. Despite moderately large sales of a homemade cassette recording at the Record Vault, an important heavy metal music store in San Francisco at the time, Stone Vengeance remained a club band unable to secure a recording contract with heavy metal labels such as Megaforce, Roadrunner or Combat or touring opportunities as opening acts for better known bands.[8]

The musicians of Stone Vengeance provide a perspective that is important *precisely because of* their positions as working-class black musicians whose professional music careers confront the intertwining pinschers of race and class as articulated in musical discourse, including practices and norms within the music industry. Born and raised in the black working-class neighborhood of the Bayview-Hunter's Point area of San Francisco, California, Coffey, Tompkins and Starks see their creative efforts as both art and commerce.

Indeed, the fact that Stone Vengeance performances are self-conscious acts of labor formed a large part of our discussions. Coffey and Tompkins recognize that their musical labor is harnessed to racialized conceptions of professional musicking that are reinforced structurally through music business organization norms and practices (not to mention institutes of music education). Coffey points to racialist thinking as impacting his professional efforts: '[Record] labels are set up for white groups. I learned that a long time ago. I didn't go into this with my eyes closed. I knew we were black and I knew about racism. But I just didn't think it would be this hard. I really didn't. *I was willing to work hard and prove myself and put in the work'* (emphasis added).

Similar to Coffey's reminder about the way in which Robert Johnson was legitimated through Clapton's imprimatur, Maureen Mahon notes the troubled entry of another African-American rock band, Living Colour, into the mainstream rock market: 'Whether one reads Living Colour's alliance with [Mick] Jagger as the calling in of a debt, the ultimate sellout, or a savvy manipulation of resources, it exemplifies the race and power dynamics of the music industry. Most disturbing for Black Rock Coalition members was the fact that a white star had to validate a black band before it could gain recognition' (2004: 156). While race is not the only element in play, it is difficult to deny that racialized conceptions of musical genre form a significant part of the larger context in assessing a particular band's perceived mainstream marketability. Further, these assessments usually carry negative repercussions for black musicians engaged in genres not typically identified as 'black music' genres (e.g., rhythm and blues, rap).

In defending his choice to pursue an interest in heavy metal, Coffey maintains that black American music has always dealt with the themes identified with heavy metal: individualism, anti-authoritarianism, anti-bourgeois sentiments connected to working-class alienation and a morbid fascination with death and apocalyptic imagery that is often drawn from anti- or, perhaps more accurately, pre- or non-Christian beliefs. Stone Vengeance treats these themes *as a fundamentally black aesthetic* thereby presenting thrash metal as part of a larger black music tradition.[9]

Stone Vengeance articulates their heavy metal-ness in explicit dialog with ideas about, for instance, black masculinity. But their performances repudiate popular culture stereotypes of blackness. Coffey describes the band's outlier position in heavy metal by recalling a scene in the film, *Blade*, in which the black 'half-vampire daywalker' played by Wesley Snipes is helped by a black woman, who asks him, 'You're one of them [a vampire], aren't you?' Blade replies, 'No, I'm something else'.[10]

Coffey continues,

> That's what we are. We're not what the white guys are [i.e., conventional rock groups]. We're not what the black guys are [i.e., conventional funk or hip hop groups]. So, to manage a band like us, you have to think about that because we don't fit. Because there are no record labels looking for black rock bands. You have some [black rock bands] that are out there [now] but we were the first black *heavy metal* band. Stone Vengeance is notable for being the first black *thrash heavy metal* band. More and more people now are starting to see that.[11]

The continued silence around Stone Vengeance in the increasing catalog of heavy metal texts, however, belies Coffey's assertion.[12] What might Stone Vengeance's invisibility reveal?

Black thrash roots

Coffey is adamant that rock is based on the blues. While he admires guitarists such as Randy Rhoads, Ulrich Roth, Ritchie Blackmore and Yngwie Malmsteen for their efforts to combine elements of European art music with hard rock, he insists,

> If you don't like the blues, I guarantee you, your heroes like the blues [he is specifically discussing Rhoads *et al.*]. Black Sabbath, you know they were called Earth at first, a blues band. Van Halen was into [Eric] Clapton. AC/DC—they *crazy* about the blues. KISS—listen to Ace Frehley, that's the blues. *All* of those guys who established heavy metal were into the blues.

Coffey points out that the relationship between the blues and rock extends beyond the 'merely musical', noting,

> You can't take the blues out of it. People ask, why do you sing about Satan? That's the same thing in the blues, it was the devil's music. It's the same shit today. We sing about god, the devil, sex—it's the same thing. You can't really get away from it. They can only pull that on people who don't know the history of the music.

> But I studied the music. When I got into it, I would go to the library and read the history of [rock music]. So, I know where it came from—it came from what they called 'race music' or 'that nigger bop' music. It was [initially perceived as a] strictly black [music] and then it became rock'n'roll, which was [a] strictly white [music]. I remember some guy tried to come with some bullshit, trying to say that Elvis Presley had his rockabilly, his country style—trying to take away from the black influence. But that's not what [Sam Phillips] said. He said, 'If I can find a white man that sings like a black man, I'll make a million dollars'. *He wasn't looking at Elvis's country roots, he was looking for Elvis to sound like a black man.*

This is no small point for Coffey. Phillips, whose Sun label had primarily recorded African-American rhythm and blues musicians, was looking for a white singer who could sing with an authentic black feeling in order to leave the secondary race record market and move into the mainstream popular music market. While Elvis Presley might have given Phillips what he wanted, the singer's career with Sun Records was brief (1953–1956). By 1960 Elvis was charting with ballads such as 'Are You Lonesome Tonight?' and 'It's Now or Never' for RCA rather than reproducing the energetic rock'n'roll sound of his earlier Sun recordings 'Hound Dog' or 'Baby, Let's Play House'. As Elvis's recordings indicated, the rapid transformation of rhythm and blues into rock and roll in the late 1950s eventually advanced rock to the center of American popular music culture in a process captured by Reebee Garofalo's apt description as a movement from 'black roots to white fruits' (2002).[13]

However, Coffey's early music listening experiences pierced through rock's whitewashed veneer. His involvement with heavy metal was a natural outcome of being exposed to a wide variety of music despite growing up in a working-class African-American neighborhood. Coffey: 'I was exposed to a lot of music [through] the radio. And I remember hearing "A Day in the Life" on the radio. That was one of the songs, The Beatles' "A Day in the Life", that *stuck* with me. I was like, there's something about that music—just *magical*'. Coffey is unequivocal about The Beatles as source and inspiration for making music central in his life, displaying his continuing reverence for the band by The Beatles posters that hang in his band's rehearsal space and his frequent references to them in interviews.

In fact, *The Beatles at the Hollywood Bowl* (Capitol 1977), a live recording compiled primarily from two performances at the Hollywood Bowl in 1964 and 1965, was the first recording Coffey purchased. While his claims to having listened to the record over one thousand times may be hyperbolic, it indicates the central place the recording occupies in his musical development. He was initially disappointed as the sounds of a noisy, screaming audience first greeted him. However, his buyer's remorse soon turned to appreciation as his room filled with the sound of electric guitars. He recalls, 'They start off with "Twist and Shout". And, dude, it was the *sound* of it. So, [the reason] I got into wanting to play music [was through a] fascination with the electronic side of it. The sound of *amplified* blues, man. *The sound of the equipment*. The *power* of just a few instruments on a stage being amplified and the *power* rolling off that stage'. Like many rock fans, Coffey was attracted to two elements in rock that partially define its aesthetic: loud volume and complexity in the service of expressing power.

Coffey's attraction to rock's volume as an instantiation of power indicates the resistive, even rebellious, potential rock music holds out for him. Coffey's immersion in the forceful 'sound of amplified blues' allows him to wield power through rock's volume and use of distortion against unspoken 'genre rules', a term I borrow from Simon Frith to describe the formal and (mostly) informal set of evolving rules—prohibitions, restrictions, qualifications—that determine the ordering of sounds, and the bodies who produce them, into specific genres.[14]

Returning to Coffey's musical roots, he points to the influence of the free-form FM radio of the late 1960s and '70s, whose DJs introduced him to classical music by Igor Stravinsky, jazz by Sun Ra and, most importantly, the metal of the New Wave of British Heavy Metal (NWOBHM). As noted, Coffey idealized the music of The Beatles but it was the wide spectrum of music that was played on San Francisco Bay Area stations during the 1970s that freed him from the music of his neighborhood. As he put it, 'I felt so liberated' by the radio.[15]

Two isolated instances in 1977 constitute Coffey's entire formal instruction on guitar. He had learned 'Day Tripper' by ear. However, he still hadn't learned how to tune a guitar in standard tuning and would 'de-tune' guitars at music stores to sound like the one he had at home. One day, perhaps intrigued by his detuning, an employee at Angelo's House of Music asked Coffey to perform a song. After performing 'Day Tripper' with a single finger, the employee informed him that he was playing incorrectly and taught him not only how to perform 'Day Tripper' more easily but taught him standard tuning as well. Around the same time, Joseph Smiel, a German-American music teacher at Woodrow Wilson High School, gave Coffey a single lesson, which consisted of showing the beginning guitarist some basic skills such as proper hand positioning and giving him a ripped-out chord chart from a Mel Bay guitar instruction book.

Music stores also provided a way to learn about developments in hard rock and heavy metal. Coffey remembers, 'I'd see a white guy [who] looked like he rocked and ask him, "Which band do you like?" because I wanted to find out about new bands. Now, I knew about the big bands like Judas Priest and Iron Maiden'. Tellingly, Coffey searched for 'white guys' rather than black musicians for recommendations about rock bands. While Judas Priest and Iron Maiden formed the foundation for his music, Coffey also began taking cues from the punk scene:

> When I heard Iron Maiden, that band really made me feel pretty good about what we were doing because I liked their music so much that it let me know that we were on the right track. I mean, we were already playing hard shit then but bands like them inspired me further. We were just like Metallica and others. We were taking our influences from the New Wave of British Heavy Metal and the hardcore punk. *That's* what made thrash—it was a mixture of those two. The speed and aggression of the hardcore punk mixed with the NWOBHM. Man, we just made a hybrid of it.

Keeping in mind that Coffey was captivated by 'A Day in the Life' because of its compositional intricacies, his attraction to thrash metal exemplifies Glenn Pillsbury's assertion that thrash metal's musical complexity serves to promote masculinist values such as musical virtuosity that are deeply embedded within Eurocentric models and taste hierarchies. In accepting Pillsbury's contention that Metallica's 'production of identity through complexity' (2006: 60) rests on ideas about whiteness and masculinity, however, I mean to point out that Stone Vengeance's articulation of musical complexity in thrash metal rests on *opposing* stereotypes about blackness and masculinity in which black masculinity is equated entirely with the body rather than the mind. Importantly, Stone Vengeance uses thrash metal's musical complexity to demonstrate their musical abilities *beyond* those normally equated with black musicians, namely rhythmic complexity and emotional expression, *without abandoning* them as anyone familiar with thrash's speed and visceral appeal can appreciate.

Coffey continues,

> Motörhead—you gotta give them credit, too. Songs like 'Iron Fist' and some of that early stuff—that was an influence. Even Loudness from Japan—we listened to all that shit. Venom was one of my favorites, Iron Maiden. Judas Priest before all of them 'cause I was into the Priest, all their '70s stuff. The early stuff like 'Sad Wings of Destiny' and 'Sin After Sin' and 'Stained Class', all of that. Great shit. That's where we got our scream from—Rob Halford was the man. Raven, John Gallagher. Those were the two guys, we started going [screams]. Also, a small part, Robert Plant.

Coffey and his band mates drew from the same pool of artists as their white counterparts despite their relative isolation in a working- class black neighborhood. In an ironic reversal of white teens who accessed black R&B and early rock and roll through radio broadcasts in the 1950s, the members of Stone Vengeance gained entrance into the hard rock world of the 1970s through the countercultural mediation provided by predominantly white DJs on independent FM radio stations. The ironies would not end there.

Black thrash routes

Similar to burgeoning teen-aged rock guitarists everywhere, Coffey decided to start a band, recalling, 'It was a rock band from the beginning. I wanted to *rock*. Boston [and Ted] Nugent were already in my head'. However, as a largely self-taught guitarist who was attending a predominantly African-American high school, Coffey had little of the conventional connections to other heavy metal musicians that white suburban schools in the United States offered to most heavy metal fans. Instead, Coffey tried to meet likely band members through music stores. Coffey recalls,

> [Bassist] Anthony [Starks] and I were hanging out at Guitar Center,[16] trying to get another guitar player. We'd meet different white guys because [by the mid-1970s], I [had given] up on meeting another brother [African American] who wanted to [perform rock music]. So, I'd try to meet these white guys. They'd talk good but they wouldn't show up to rehearsal, they wouldn't even call back.

Still, a white musician briefly held the drum chair in Stone Vengeance: 'Arthur would hang with us at the house and at school. He was kind of a loner because there weren't that many white people at Woodrow Wilson [high school] at that time'. But soon, Arthur quit, telling Coffey, 'I just can't see a black rock band making it'.[17] Eventually giving up on finding another guitarist, Coffey began to envision a guitar-based power trio.

Coffey initially named his band the Dreamers but, after about a year, he wanted a more appropriate name for a heavy metal group. He recalls it was in 1978 when:

> It took me a couple of weeks to come up with [Stone Vengeance] because I knew a name meant everything. There was a spiritual base of what I wanted to say but not [as] a 'religious' band. It's not that. I just know that people use religion to control people in certain ways so I'm not into following [any religion] under [those conditions].

> So, the 'stone' is from the Bible. The stone that the builders rejected—that's us. That stone is a people, an ancient people. The builders are the 'civilized' nations of the world. Black people are rejected.

> That's what the stone represented to me—the despised, the rejected, the hated. The builders—those that build civilizations—scorned [us], looked down upon us. That has been our experience in this music.

> You see the star and all that in our [band logo] and [people] don't know what that means. But it's heavy symbolism. You have six points, each one is sixty degrees, 6 times 60 equals 360 degrees, that's a circle, a circle of knowledge with 6 points of light. You have the skull, which everyone knows represents death. So, it's a balance. Knowledge is power, knowledge is life—if you have knowledge, you can survive.

Stone Vengeance logo ©1987 Stone Vengeance

As Walser cogently argues, 'Heavy metal's fascination with the dark side of life gives evidence of both *dissatisfaction with dominant identities and institutions and an intense yearning for reconciliation with something more credible*' (1993: xvi–xvii, emphasis added). Clearly, Coffey sees Stone Vengeance as part of a long history of enduring African-American cultural resistance, embodying the 'rejected' legacy and rhetorically prevailing over death. Stone Vengeance's preoccupation with heavy metal iconography and a shared ideological resonance with its dark themes are derived from a legacy of black American biblical 'readings against the grain', echoes from the spirituals of black slaves as well as the secular and often sacrilegious concerns of the blues—musical anchors distinct from, for example, the Norse mythology ascribed by Norwegian black metal groups.

In addition to Pillsbury's description that thrash emerged from 'reworkings of British metal groups such as Diamond Head, Iron Maiden and Motörhead' (2006: 3), Coffey includes the blues as a means to recognize heavy metal as a black American musical practice. Moreover, Stone Vengeance's rebuffs by the music industry echo the marginalized position from which Coffey announces an African-American thrash metal band named to invoke the long history of black repudiation of 'the builders of civilization'. Coffey is unambiguous on this point:

> Stone Vengeance has existed and survived by my iron will. I would not give up. I knew Stone Vengeance was a square peg but I have enough pride as a black man that I wasn't going to force myself into a round hole. I was never going to do that. We're nice guys and people will tell you that we're one of the easiest bands to work

with in the business. But we're not what you would call Uncle Toms. And that is part of the reason that freezes a lot of people, because in this country, the black man is made to look a certain way and if you can't be used or ridiculed—some people just don't like that. They feel more comfortable if you're in a position where you're not taken seriously. So you can be a joke, know what I mean?

Black outlaws

Coffey identifies Stone Vengeance as a San Francisco thrash band that emerged from the same early 1980s scene in which Metallica and Exodus cut their teeth:

> Back then, when [the] heavy metal [scene] was starting [to form in San Francisco], the bands that were playing sounded like either [Judas] Priest, Iron Maiden or they were more commercial sounding. But there [weren't] that many bands. There was us, Metallica coming up [from Los Angeles], Slayer, Exodus. And from what I remember, honestly, we were probably the first to come out of San Francisco. Because Metallica was not from here. Slayer wasn't from here. Exodus was from the East Bay somewhere.

Yet, even in an underground metal scene in which they were literal 'home boys', Stone Vengeance remained external to much of the social aspects of a scene through which musicians interact in competitive as well as collaborative ways. Coffey admits,

> We were already [blending NWOBHM and punk influences] and I didn't even know we had any peers. *Because I didn't really hang with rockers.* I found out about Metallica through the Record Vault [a well-known San Francisco metal music store in the 1980s]. They said, 'You gotta check these guys out'. This was when Dave Mustaine was still in the band. And Kirk [Hammett] was with Exodus. When I first saw those bands, I was like, 'Oh! This is where *we* belong!' Because, to me, the only people that were doing what I was diggin' was Iron Maiden, Venom, Raven and all those [type of] bands.

Coffey disclosed that while Stone Vengeance never hung out with many other rock bands except when playing shows together, a number of them were fans:

> You know, you talk to 'em, you meet 'em [backstage]. [Deceased Metallica bassist] Cliff Burton liked our music a lot. The guys in Lääz Rockit, they liked us. Suicidal Tendencies, they liked us. So many people. [Charged] GBH was *crazy* about us! All the guys in Metallica

> were cool with us, hanging out with us backstage at the Stone [a San Francisco rock club] when we were playing with Trouble and Slayer. This was when [Metallica] had just gotten signed with Elektra.

Yet, despite well-intentioned music industry insiders who offered to manage the band, they all eventually came 'up against forces that they didn't anticipate'. When asked to describe those forces, Coffey was straightforward:

> Well, just the racism. For instance, when we tried to book ourselves into certain clubs. People tell me that it's a shame that Stone Vengeance hasn't been in the Fillmore, hasn't been at the Warfield. There were just a few clubs [that would book us]. We never had a shot like [the other San Francisco] bands. I would see bands in a club like at Ruthie's Inn in '84, and they're getting signed a year later. And I'm hearing some of our influence on them. But we're just getting left in the underground. Exodus got signed, all of those bands were on major labels. Testament, Exodus, Heathen—all these bands benefited from a scene that we helped build. They came along later and we got the least out of it.

Additionally, when asked whether he endured any provocation from African-American neighbors, Coffey admitted that he faced 'all kind of insults. Yeah, I remember the insults, man. The pressure of that made me more determined'. It is not only white audiences who, tacitly or explicitly, exclude black participation in rock music. Black audiences have been 'taught' to uphold musical segregation, as well. Indeed, Coffey admits that while 'there were always some black people in the 'hood that could dig [our music], but of course we didn't fit in, we were outcasts, man. Definitely Stone Vengeance is outlaws' (Joseffer 2010: 165).

Under those circumstances, Coffey went about setting up his own DIY (do it yourself) network, recalling,

> You know how it was in those days. The network was the tape, the cassette tape. I would always take a cassette, put it in an envelope and send it to fans, whoever wanted it. All over the world, man. I was sending shit behind the Iron Curtain when it was still the Soviet Union. So we had fans there, then. So you can imagine what was happening when a person would get his hands [on it] because it was illegal. And I would get these letters from all over the world. Sometimes I would get money. It would've cost more [to change into US currency] but I would send it to them anyway. And that's how I did it, man.

In 1985, Coffey used his contacts with the Record Vault to promote Stone Vengeance in a similar DIY fashion:

> I'd take a cassette tape—it wasn't even a demo! I took a boom-box, set it in the studio, rehearsed with the guys. So I took it to the Record Vault, they listened to it and they asked me, 'Can we sell this?' [Laughs] 'Yeah, if you think so'. And, apparently, man, they *knew* so. So they gave a copy to Ron Quintana and he played it on KUSF, which is good for us because that was exposure.[18]

Besides being a radio disc jockey, Quintana was an avid heavy metal collector who produced the fanzine, *Metal Mania*, and whose influence would be crucial in the development of the San Francisco metal scene. But Coffey's attempts to grow beyond contacts with individual fans or the market of a local, if influential, heavy metal retail store were disheartening and revealed the ways in which the world of independent label thrash metal reproduced the larger music industry's racialized sensibilities. Steve Waksman's important study of the cross-genre impact of punk and heavy metal includes a chapter on the role of the independent, or indie, label in developing the heavy metal scene in the 1980s. Focusing on SST, Metal Blade and Sub Pop, Waksman notes how each label 'did not forsake genre as a tool to achieve their ends'. Importantly, however, 'Once these labels were established, they did not merely reproduce the already defined aesthetics of the genres with which they were associated [but] updated and redefined in line with changing local conditions and the importation of new sounds from afar' (2009: 255).

Yet Coffey, in describing his own interactions with indie labels, reveals the limits 'updating and redefining already defined genre aesthetics' held in Stone Vengeance's particular case:

> I remember we would get record companies back in those early days that would be interested. So nobody can tell me, 'No, it's not racism'. OK, in the '80s—this happened numerous times—I would get a letter from a record label and they would be interested in signing the band. A record company doesn't write you unless they're already familiar with your music and they're interested.
>
> But they didn't know what we looked like. They would just hear the music—'Oh, I'm interested'. [They knew we were an] American metal band. They'd ask me for a press kit, wanting to see what we looked like. Then I would send them a picture and they would just back up. Or, this is what they would say—and it's a trip because initially they would be totally enthusiastic—'we're totally interested, send us a bio, send us a picture'. Then all of a sudden, they freeze: 'You don't have the right look'.

> It happened so much that when I would get interest [later], I wouldn't send them shit. I'd go make a Xerox copy of [our photo] because I didn't want to waste the time or the postage sending them my music for nothing. I'd rather keep my music and give it to a fan instead of sending it to them when they aren't going to do anything with it. So, I started to just send them a picture and that would end that.

A final example: Stone Vengeance was remastering their first compact disc recording, *To Kill Evil*, and the mixing engineer, Jeff Risdon, knew a casting director who was looking for a heavy metal group for a movie that was being shot in the San Francisco Bay Area. But Coffey told Risdon, 'Look, man, I appreciate what you're saying but when they say they're looking for heavy metal, they're not looking for us'. But Risdon insisted and, as a favor to him, Coffey called the casting director, telling her that Stone Vengeance was an African-American heavy metal band. After talking with the producers, the casting director informed Coffey that the producers felt that having a black metal group in the film would be 'presenting a whole other type of statement'.

Conclusion

Coffey notes:

> See, when I tell people this stuff, I'm talking from what white people said, not from what *I'm* saying. *We never intended to make a statement. We just wanted to rock.* But to white people, [Stone Vengeance is] 'another statement'. I don't know what kind of statement exactly—I can *guess*—but think about it, a black band trying to play [heavy metal]. We just happen to be black but we have to be making a statement now. *We can't just rock. So, it shows that we are perceived [through race].*

My central interest has been to trace the roots and routes Stone Vengeance mobilizes in order to tease out the band's claims for thrash metal authenticity and authority based on foundational black American blues traditions. But as the quote above suggests, while Coffey foregrounds Stone Vengeance's interpretation of rock as a black musical expression, he also desires to be known simply as a 'thrash metal musician' rather than as a 'black thrash metal musician'. Yet Coffey's positionality—embedded in a narrative of aural trespassing and sonic acculturation that complicates the links between phenotype and audiotype by seeking to redefine the look and sound of embodied difference in thrash metal—is caught within the complications such desires entail. On one hand, regardless of how Stone Vengeance may simply 'want to rock',

Coffey is unable to dislodge the racialized terms of engagement set in motion by the band's performances and recordings.

On the other hand, Stone Vengeance makes a strong case for considering thrash metal as a black musical tradition by remembering the links between the blues and rock. The argument not only legitimizes the band's position within rock but also forces a reconsideration of commonplace notions of the links between musical genres and performing bodies. The band's professional experiences underscore the ubiquity of these ideas and highlight the difficulties black musicians face in their attempts to expand conceptions of heavy metal from a space of white working-class masculinity into a more inclusive genre.

Stone Vengeance may be finally receiving overdue recognition. Remarkably, after over thirty years, there is a renewed interest globally for Stone Vengeance's recordings and live performances. Access to worldwide audiences through new media outlets such as YouTube and Myspace has opened up fresh possibilities for the band. Continuing festival appearances and favorable critical reviews speak to Coffey's disciplined work ethic and steadfast determination to keep Stone Vengeance relevant. In fact, Stone Vengeance has been re-invited to the Metal Assault Festival in Würzburg, Germany, along with an offer to tour South America in 2011.

In a largely instrumental Black Sabbath-inspired song, 'Wrath Cometh', Coffey sings a single line, 'And in the end, we are justified by revenge'. The stone, in other words, will someday prevail over the forces that reject and despise it. Indeed, Stone Vengeance's music persists as a vital testament to metal's core principle of individual empowerment rallied against larger structural and discursive forces while allowing the band to demonstrate that thrash metal's roots run deep within the enduring legacy of black American blues traditions.

Notes

1. Interview with author, 10 December 2009. All Coffey quotes are from author interview unless otherwise credited.
2. Indeed, the articles that deal with African metal carry titles such as '"White Music" in the Black Continent?' (from http://newschoolthoughtsonafrica.wordpress.com/2010/10/05/white-music-in-the-black-continent/, no longer available). While many African heavy metal bands are composed of white Africans, the hypermasculinist orientation of heavy metal remains wherever it has taken root, as a quick investigation of the Myspace pages for black African heavy metal bands such as Crackdust or Wrust attests.
3. In fact, this chapter is part of a longer project in which I will investigate various non-white heavy metal bands including the Filipino American thrash band, Death Angel, and others.

4. For a view of the rise of a resurgent thrash metal scene in the San Francisco Bay Area, including a brief mention of Stone Vengeance, see Richardson 2010. However, out of the many bands that came out of the 1980s San Francisco Bay Area metal scene—such as Exodus and Heathen—it is only Metallica that enjoys a truly international audience, in terms of critical value, musical influence and commercial presence.

5. See Weinstein 2000 in which she traces the link between psychedelic rock and heavy metal, beginning with Hendrix; see, in particular, pages 16–18. See also Waksman 2009 for a broader look at the various ways in which heavy metal was influenced by psychedelic, or acid, rock.

6. In an expanded version of this chapter, I spend some time thinking about Coffey's comment that 'people like me and you...we're children of Hendrix through the discipline of rock'n'roll'. He is discussing people of color here ('people like me and you') and the notion of being a 'child of Hendrix' evokes a shared sense of alterity to cultural norms. His ideas about the constituent elements for a 'discipline of rock'n'roll' provide interesting avenues for thinking through his workingman's ethos dedicated to a regular schedule of individual practice sessions and band rehearsals.

7. See Dettmar (2010: B13–B14) for a lucid account of Dettmar's personal interaction with the discourse around Hendrix and the racial implications of that interaction. Coffey also notes that the critical reception for Band of Gypsys—Hendrix's band with drummer Buddy Miles and bassist Billy Cox—was cool at best, suggesting that race played a part in the ways the Hendrix Experience and Band of Gypsys were evaluated.

8. The importance of music stores in the development of the heavy metal scene of the 1980s is an understudied phenomenon. However, Steve Waksman mentions Johnny and Marsha Zazula's record store, Rock'N'Roll Heaven, as a major source of underground metal recordings as well as being '*the* place to hang out for specialist Heavy Metal music on the East Coast' (2009: 235, original emphasis) and emphasizes the role music stores played in shaping local heavy metal scenes throughout the US.

9. As detailed later in the text, Coffey renamed his rock band, the Dreamers, to Stone Vengeance in San Francisco in 1978. The Black Rock Coalition formed in New York City in 1985. Stone Vengeance was isolated for the most part from other black rock fans and musicians. Unaware of the Black Rock Coalition (BRC) until Living Colour's success gave BRC national exposure, Stone Vengeance has remained outside the BRC orbit to this day due in large part to Stone Vengeance's genesis prior to the formation of the BRC as well as the band's thrash metal orientation.

10. Coincidentally, a Stone Vengeance composition, 'I Vampyre', almost made it onto the *Blade* soundtrack.

11. There were a handful of other African-American heavy metal groups in the 1980s who formed in the wake of Stone Vengeance, most notably Znowhite, Black Death, Sound Barrier, and Death.

12. The lack of an African-American presence in the following books (not meant to be exhaustive but merely indicative of a larger trend) illustrate my point about Stone Vengeance's literal silencing in an increasingly 'official narrative' of heavy metal historiography and scholarship: Jeffrey Jensen Arnett, *Metalheads: Heavy Metal Music*

and Adolescent Alienation (Boulder, CO: Westview, 1996); Ian Christie, *Sound of the Beast: The Complete Headbanging History of Heavy Metal* (New York: It-Harper Collins, 2004); and Natalie J. Purcell, *Death Metal Music: The Passion and Politics of a Subculture* (Jefferson, NC: McFarland, 2003). To be fair to Coffey, he may be referring to the growing acknowledgement of Stone Vengeance in fan discourse.

13. Additionally, similar to Coffey's complicated view of Hendrix, while he is clearly critical of some of the uses Presley has served within rock discourse, he was also frank about his admiration for Presley's music.
14. See the chapter 'Genre Rules' in Frith 1996.
15. For more on the underground FM phenomenon of the 1970s, see Neer 2001.
16. A national United States retail music instrument chain store.
17. Coffey only recalls the drummer's first name, Arthur.
18. The 'Wrath Cometh' Rehearsal Demo, as it was later titled, included the songs, 'Stone Vengeance', 'Time is at Hand', 'The Great Controversy', and 'The Persecution'.

Bibliography

Dettmar, Kevin J. H. 2010. 'Racism, Experienced: Listening to Jimi Hendrix—Then and Now'. *Chronicle of Higher Education*, 2 April.

Frith, Simon. 1996. *Performing Rites: On the Value of Popular Music*. Cambridge, MA: Harvard University Press.

Garofalo, Reebee. 2002. 'Crossing Over: From Black Rhythm and Blues to White Rock'n'Roll'. In *Rhythm and Business: The Political Economy of Black Music*, ed. Norman Kelley. New York: Akashic.

Holt, Fabian. 2007. *Genre in Popular Music*. Chicago: University of Chicago Press.

Joseffer, Jordan. 2010. 'Stone Vengeance'. *Thrasher* (March).

Mahon, Maureen. 2004. *Right to Rock: The Black Rock Coalition and the Cultural Politics of Race*. Durham, NC: Duke University Press.

Neer, Richard. 2001. *FM: The Rise and Fall of Rock Radio*. New York: Random House.

Pillsbury, Glenn T. 2006. *Damage Incorporated: Metallica and the Production of Musical Identity*. New York and London: Routledge.

Richardson, Ben. 2010. 'Headbanging History'. *SF Bay Guardian*, 14 December. http://www.sfbg.com/2010/12/14/headbanging-history.

Sheinbaum, John. 2002. '"Think about What You're Trying to Do to Me": Rock Historiography and the Construction of a Race-based Dialectic'. In *Rock Over the Edge: Transformations in Popular Music Cultures*, ed. Roger Beebe *et al.* Durham, NC and London: Duke University Press.

Waksman, Steve. 2009. *This Ain't the Summer of Love: Conflict and Crossover in Heavy Metal and Punk*. Berkeley: University of California Press.

Walser, Robert. 1993. *Running with the Devil: Power, Gender, and Madness in Heavy Metal Music*. Hanover, NH and London: Wesleyan University Press.

Weinstein, Deena. 2000. *Heavy Metal: Its Music and its Culture*. New York: Da Capo.

'[I] hate girls and emo[tion]s'

Negotiating masculinity in grindcore music

Rosemary Overell

University of Melbourne, Australia

Grindcore is more than representational music. That is, grindcore scenic participation is less about how many lyrics you know, or t-shirts you own, than it is about an ability to enact an affective sensibility. Affect describes an embodied intensity, which is impossible to pinpoint through representative forms, such as writing (Massumi 2002: 77). Nevertheless, Lorimer (2008: 552) uses writing to define affect thus:

> [A]ffect [is] properties, competencies, modalities, energies, attunements, arrangements and intensities of differing texture, temporality, velocity and spatiality that act on bodies, are produced through bodies, and transmitted by bodies.

I call the affective sensibility grindcore scene members experience 'feeling brutal' after the ubiquitous catchcry of 'brutal' heard at at gigs. This utterance goes some way towards articulating the affective experience grindcore generates.

In this chapter, I use feeling brutal as an entry point for a discussion on how affect relates to, and troubles, metal masculinity. There is a recurrent assumption in metal studies that Western metal is sexist, masculinist, and even misogynist (Arnett 1996; Kahn-Harris 2007; Walser 1993; Weinstein 2000). I ask whether grindcore participants really do, following a song title from band Blood Duster, 'Hate Girls and Emotions'.[1] I concur that metal imagery, particularly in death metal and gore-grindcore, regularly represents women as sexualized objects at best and objects for rape, torture and murder at worst. Metal signifiers, often literally, scream masculinity. In such a masculine discourse, it is rare for metal songs to articulate emotions, which are, in Western culture, feminized. Instead, the male protagonist is busy 'doing'—battles, riding motorcycles or, in the case of death metal, killing. As Massumi (2002: 27) emphasizes, affect is not synonymous with 'emotion'. Nevertheless, the difficulty in articulating affect means that representations of its intensities depend heavily on the language of emotions. Grindcore scene members regularly experience affect as feeling brutal. However, they also avoid articulated affect, that is, emotions, because they are categorized 'feminine' in Western culture.

A focus on affect yields a more complex understanding of metallers' relation to gender. In particular, feeling brutal veers from the masculinist cognitive response to music of critical distance. Affect allows for a sense of belonging that is not entirely bound to representations of scenic status. It speaks to the intense and inarticulable experience of being at a grindcore gig.

In this chapter, I draw out the relation between feeling brutal and gender through a case study of grindcore music in Melbourne, Australia. In the first section, I outline how grindcore is more than representational. That is, affective. In this section, I also unpack brutal in relation to gender. In layperson's terms, brutal connotes masculinized violence. However, brutal also implies the scenic experience of affective belonging. Affect, I suggest, is coded feminine and troubles the masculine connotations of brutal. Brutal in Melbourne grindcore encompasses both meanings, and thus gestures towards masculinity and femininity.

In the second section, I offer the interview as a demonstration of masculinized brutal sociality that builds scenic belonging on a representational level. Interviews, of course, differ, depending on context. I compare my ethnographic interviews, foregrounding my position as a woman, with grindcore media interviews. Both forms of interview build belonging. Yet, my ethnographic interview—mediated by my femininity—allows more room for the articulation of affect, than the by men/for men standard of grindcore media interviews.

Finally, in the third section, I present a close analysis of grindcore's relation to articulated affect (emotions). Through a case study of one Melbourne band's response to the pop-punk-rock genre emo, I highlight the tensions between the experience of affect (brutal and masculine) and the articulation of affect (emotional and feminine).

Methods

Thrift's (2008) work on 'non-representational theory' (NRT) informs this chapter. NRT advocates a shift from reading sociality as a set of static signifiers. Instead, Thrift calls for accounts of the myriad, lively, and often contradictory, sensations experienced by people through social processes. Thrift (2004) also concedes the clunkiness of the NRT moniker. He emphasizes that the privileging of affect, which NRT requires, does not assume exclusivity from representational elements. Instead, he calls for understandings of sociality as more than simply representational.

I attempt to access this more-than-ness through an ethnography of grindcore music in Melbourne. I draw on interviews conducted with 25 scene members and participant-observation at grindcore events between 2004 and 2009. Having been a member of the scene since 2003 in a fan capacity, I drew on personal contacts and employed a snowball methodology to broaden my sample. The interviews were primarily in person, with two exceptions, conducted via email. I also conducted follow-up questions over email. While the verbal medium of interviews remains representational, scene members regularly highlighted the difficulty of linguistically representing affective experiences.

Fuck...I'm dead: brutal belonging and the evacuation of 'self'

Brutal—meaning and context
Melbourne grindcore scene members constitute belonging by generating an affective intensity, which I label feeling brutal. Brutal is also a linguistic representation. In Melbourne's scene, and globally, it is the ultimate commendation. To yell 'brutal!' at the end of a set validates the performers as authentic grindcore scene members. The speed and intensity of play, particularly, measures authenticity:

> [B]rutal means any music that sounds either harsh to the ears, very heavy, or sounds aggressive/physically taxing/intense to play... 'Brutal' has ended up being bastardized into a general term of approval among people into that stuff [grindcore] (Carsten, via email).

As Carsten points out, brutal is also a 'term of approval'. In venues, on fan forums and Myspaces, brutal is a welcoming salutation. The aesthetics of grindcore also incorporate intertextual understandings of brutality. That is, brutal represents the masculine aggression and violence present in media accounts of brutal crimes, which generally focus on crimes by men, against women. Brutality, then, indicates grindcore's violent aesthetics, as well as the broader masculine significance of such actions:

> Brutal: Punishingly hard or violent. (Mick, via email)

> [Brutal] can be a...a bad thing...a brutal bashing. (Jim)

In fact, Melbourne lyricists cited media representations of crime as a significant influence:

> I read about it in some... I don't know, I found it pretty disturbing where...two sixteen year olds...held up a service station with a diseased blood syringe... And I go 'fuck—that's so fucked up'... So I have to write about it. (Will)

> [T]here's one song recently that I...got the idea from *Crime Investigations Australia*. About this guy who was called 'The Mornington Monster'... And he killed...his wife and kids with a bloody...spear gun. (Tommo)

Only the last example demonstrates a brutal crime where a man was the perpetrator. However, Will and Tommo's other examples regard deviant female subjects. That is, 'junkie mother[s]' and 'fucked up...young girls' who do not fit the normative parameters of femininity. Notably, these deviant females are categorized as working class. This is evident when Tommo discusses his inspiration for the song 'Barefoot and Shitfaced'. He explained how he was inspired by an article in daily Melbourne tabloid *Herald Sun* which quoted a 'junkie woman' (Tommo's words) describing a fellow resident from the Housing Commission as 'barefoot and shitfaced'. In Australia, the Housing Commission was the name of the department, established in the 1960s, charged with building public housing for low-income citizens.

Brutality—the uncontainable self and collective belonging
However, brutality is also an affective intensity:

> Firstly, to me it means something intense or uncontrolled. (Jim)

> Brutal means heavy, short, fast [music]...blows you away. (Anita)

Scene members experience this intensity subjectively.[2] However, it is also externalized onto other scene members and scenic spaces. This process builds belonging in the scene—the scene member experiences the sense of sharing their affective intensity with other people and things. Anita's articulation that it 'blows you away' indicates something of the subjective bodily sensations experienced by scene members when feeling brutal. That is, Anita alludes to the sense that a cognitized sense of coherent self, and bounded body, evaporates when experiencing grindcore. This echoes Massumi's (2002) understanding of affect and belonging as the 'openness of bodies to each other and to what they are not—the incorporeality of the event' (76).

The Melbourne gore-grind band name 'Fuck... I'm Dead' unintentionally encapsulates this evacuation of the self, through the implication that the 'I' is, in fact, 'dead' when experiencing grindcore. This 'blowing away' of the self constitutes the process of externalization. Scene members immerse themselves in scenic events—experienced as brutal affective intensities. This builds a sense of belonging with other scene members.

The process of being, and becoming, brutal demonstrates that identity is processual, rather than fixed, and more about the projection and reception of diverse intensities of selfhood, than a solid self. This is evident in Carsten's description of his favourite gig:

> Every band fucking killed. Every band played the best they've ever done...just about the best thing I've ever seen and I—couldn't contain yourself. (Carsten)

His sense of self was uncontainable; indeed it became an Other—'you(r)'— during the gig. This highlights the process of brutal externalization. While 'I' may be 'dead', the self's transgression of the bodily borders which 'contain' it allows for an intense sense of belonging with others to a particular space and music. This echoes Thrift's (2008) suggestions that bodily proximity is more conducive to affective encounters than mediated contact.[3] At a gig, scene members experience brutality collectively:

> It's like the audience is one big living creature. (Jim)

jagodzinski (2005: 48), in his Lacanian analysis of pop music, contends that the experience of listening to a singing voice prompts an experience of *jouissance* similar to affect. He suggests that in the moment of listening, the listener can potentially experience an exhilarating sense of disembodiment. The audience and the performer(s) become 'all voice' (56). This experience, he suggests, grants the listeners a sense of belonging with their fellow listeners, as well as performers, in the moment of listening. Notably, jagodzinski emphasizes that such an experience is 'best felt "live"' (ibid.)—a notion to which Jim appears to agree.

Feeling brutal, nevertheless, stems from an individual sense of brutal-ness. It is partly a disposition, which allows the self to immerse in external subjectivities and events. However, it is through the externalizing of this disposition, transmitted via affect, that belonging in grindcore is constituted. Without feeling brutal, one cannot authentically claim scenic belonging.

How does brutal affect impact grindcore sociality?

Massumi (1998: 59) suggests that affect suffuses 'the chaotic co-functioning' of the political, economic and cultural spheres, which he broadly dubs 'the social' (59). Thrift (2008: 207) concurs. Certainly, representation influences sociality. However, as Thrift (2008: 207) points out, sociality also uses a 'massively extended affective palette'. This manifests in what he dubs 'interactional intelligence' (207). Such intelligence depends on affective intuitions of social encounters. It is a shared and mutual expectancy of a situation or, as Thrift (2008: 208) puts it, '[a]ffect...act[s] as the corporeal sense of the communicative act'.[4] One scene member's account of how he feels during gigs indicates this, evident in his difficulty in describing affect as a vague 'something':

> You just like look around you and go 'hey everyone! Yeeaaaah!' You know? It's, it's—I don't know, maybe it's—I don't know...*something*, I don't know... It's just—you share the love of the music. And I, I, I, I always find myself standing at gigs [*laughing*] with this huge, stupid grin plastered across my face, 'cause I just love it. And, ssssss—yeah— you've got, sort of these characters hidden in the crowd who sort of get everyone else feeling relaxed and that kind of thing. (Will, my emphasis)

Will's enthusiasm depends on sociality fostered through bodily proximity. In fact, for Will, the 'something' he describes is sociality—the act of 'shar[ing] the...music' with other scene members. Will's experience is more than simply the exclamation of 'hey everyone!' His grin derives from the inarticulable 'something' and 'sssss' generated through affect. Such vagaries demonstrate Thrift's suggestion that the retrospective, (re)cognized description of affective experience is beyond words. It is beyond the representative structures of language.[5] As jagodzinski (2005: 49), again following from Lacan, points out, language 'devitalis[es] the body' through the exteriorization of affective experiences. Like Will, other scene members highlighted the difficulty of linguistically representing affective experiences:

> It [going to gigs] is sort of a [*sic*] unspoken thing as well. Like, you can't really explain the way you feel. (Hayley)

> It's really hard to describe... It's an energy rush. It's...nerve racking and highly exciting. (Jim)

> It [singing] is just an expression...of that shit [*laughs*]. You know what I mean? (Graham)

For Hayley, Jim and Graham, grindcore's intensity is inarticulable. It is 'unspoken', 'hard to describe' or an expletive.

In fact, participants' descriptions of grindcore sociality lacked explicit reference to grindcore as an object for discussion or representation. Rather, they recounted an ambience where grindcore brutality is embodied in how people feel:

> Oh—[I] feel pretty, what's the word? [*pause*] Can't think of the word. Comfortable! Comfortable...it's just, I don't know...there was just a lot of...good people. (Tommo)

[P]laying live I feel like I—something different comes over me when we play...or something like that...it just feels intense and the vocals are really [*hits a fist into his other hand twice*] bang, bang... Something does sort of—you can feel something sort of come over you like 'ooorgh eurgghh' and, it is sort of kind of cool and it's just [*claps hands*]—lovin' it—you know? [*laughs*] (Will)[6]

These affective experiences could be understood, following from jagodzinski, as encounters with the Lacanian Real (2005: 39). That is, in the non-sense space prior to the subject's incorporation into the symbolic order as articulable language. An understanding of the brutal experience as pre-symbolic also accounts for the pleasure Tommo and Will describe ('comfortable!'; 'lovin' it—you know?') when at a gig. In the moment of brutality, when 'something different comes over' them, scene members can experience the affective *jouissance* of the pre-symbolic.

Affect and gender

Brutal as masculine and more-than masculine
I have demonstrated how brutality enables belonging in the Melbourne scene. The sense of belonging experienced by scene members depends on the subjective ability to *be affected*, and, in the external movement, be affective. Interviewees generally glossed this as a 'good' feeling shared between performers and audience. However, affect is not necessarily an uplifting intensity. Power relations mediate affect. Gender identity, in particular, potentially enables or restrains scene members' ability to be 'blown away' by brutality.

The connotations of brutal are gendered masculine—in lay and grindcore parlance. In media representations, brutal murderers are usually men, while victims of brutality are generally women.[7] Further, instances of extreme-metal taking the blame for male sexual violence against women are so common they are almost banal (Dunn, McFadyen and Wise, dir. 2005; Weinstein 2000).[8] Melbourne grindcore scene members rarely enact brutality as physical violence.[9] However, through its brutal sensibility, Melbourne grindcore becomes a masculine scene. This consideration of Melbourne grindcore is neat. Indeed, in terms of representation, brutal masculinity blasts from every t-shirt, lyric and line of on-stage patter. Yet, understanding brutality as also highly affective, opens the seemingly bounded 'masculine' grindcore scene to a more complex reading of gender relations.

The brutal voice. In grindcore, brutality is most present at live gigs. It is the affective sensations experienced by the audience and performers. However, brutality is also present, more specifically, in the voice of grindcore singers.

The guttural, often pitch-shifted vocals of grindcore music distinguishes the genre from other forms of metal, particularly heavy and thrash metal. Further, non-fans often single out grindcore vocals as the key point for their dislike of the genre. During my research, I have regularly heard statements like 'oh you're writing about that roargh roargh roargh stuff? That's not music!' Grindcore's vocals push the genre from music into noise. It is here that brutal affect originates. The noise of grindcore vocals makes linguistic representation impossible. In the global grindcore scene, bands often compensate for the lack of lyrical enunciation with extensive liner notes, which include lyrics. However, in Melbourne, it is rare for bands to have printed lyrics, or lyrics at all. Tommo explains:

> Well, I don't really have...lyrics—really. I cheat a bit—yeah. That song [Slowly Raped with a Chainsaw]...doesn't have any real lyrics... Yeah. Like Captain Cleanoff—he doesn't have one lyric... *He's just all noises.* (Tommo, emphasis added)

For Tommo, and the singer from Adelaide band Captain Cleanoff, the vocals are 'all noises'. Tommo's phrase 'all noises' is illuminating. It recalls jagodzinski's (2005) notion of 'all voice'—that is, in the moment of becoming 'all noise', the vocalist experiences something more than the bounded masculine body. The vocals (d)evolve into Lacanian *lalangue* the pre-symbolic and pre-gendered babbling of the infant. This is the affective moment of becoming brutal. As jagodzinski points out, noise is often considered 'ugly' (206), because of its deviance from normative ideas of melodic and harmonic music. Melbourne grindcore practitioners, following global grindcore trends, constitute an ugly aesthetic. This is demonstrated in song titles and artwork. The brutal grindcore voice is also ugly, not simply because of its difference from more popular types of music, but also because of its refusal to be anchored in a gendered body. The noise of the grindcore voice is disembodied—it is not sung—and it is produced by a subject who is 'all noise' and no corporeality. The brutality of the grindcore voice challenges the stability of the symbolic order; it affronts the common-sense reading of grindcore as inherently masculine and patriarchal.

Grindcore vocals are also growled and screamed. This obviously contributes to the overarching experience of the vocals as 'all noise'. However, growling and screaming can also elucidate the relation between brutality and gender. Screaming in music is often associated with men, particularly with rock and heavy metal (Apolloni 2008; Walser 1993). However, screaming is also feminized in dominant Western culture. The horror movies, which sometimes screen alongside grindcore bands performing in Melbourne, regularly feature a cowering, screaming young woman.[10] Pornography, too, often includes women screaming (Jensen 2007). Men's screaming is considered feminine. In his study of non-heterosexual men and house music, Amico (2002) quoted one informant as explicitly associating screaming with women. He said: 'in our society men just don't go around screaming' (368). Further, as jagodzinski (2005) points out, high-pitched screaming is associated with *castrati*, who were literally de-masculinized men, and latterly so-called 'boy bands'. Thus, screaming in music connotes both masculinity and femininity. In Melbourne's grindcore scene, I suggest, screaming constitutes the noise of brutal affect. Graham, the vocalist for Melbourne band Shagnum, explains his approach to performance:

> **Rosemary:** So do you have lyrics?
>
> **Graham:** Um [pause] no—a lot of the stuff I do there—there will be set sections where I sing set lyrics, and then stuff in between, generally just comes out, ah... I just scream, 'cause I just feel like screaming... I don't wanna, I mean, I find with some lyrics that it's really trying to intellectualise yourself and make yourself—people'll think 'oh wow—there's—'... [T]here's some people that really—that is their calling, to write lyrics and have songs, like, songwriters basically. I'm not one of them—I just enjoy having a yell and getting the shit out of me, basically.

He concurs that Shagnum does have lyrics—though they are inaudible—which come from a cerebral, 'intellectual' place. Cerebrality and intellectualism are, of course, masculine traits. However, what Graham really enjoys is 'just screaming...having a yell'. His account of the pleasure of screaming is notable in that he positions it as the 'stuff in between' representation (the lyrics). That is, for Graham, screaming is outside the symbolic order. It is noise. The noise in between representation, and its affective potential, has been explored by other cultural studies of music (jagodzinski 2005; Smith 2000). However, these have focused on popular and classical music. Further, particularly in Smith's study, focus is placed on the near-absence of sound in between music. To follow Graham's understanding, however, of the in-between of grindcore vocals as screaming noise yields an excess of sound. This excess is feminine. In dominant, Western culture, excessive noise—chattering, nagging and, indeed, screaming—is feminized. Screaming, in particular, is associated with 'hysterical' women (Dolar 2006: 69). Graham's embrace of the in between moments of screaming, then, temporarily challenge his masculine identity. The space of the scream is beyond 'intellectual[ism]' where Graham can take pleasure in transgressing the bounds of masculinity to revel in the excess of screaming.

Melbourne bands The Kill, Super Fun Happy Slide, Vaginal Carnage and Roskopp use pitch-shifted vocals. Common in global gore-grind, pitch-shifters down-tune vocal screams to sound like a growl or gurgle. When growling, the masculine body is further displaced, the voice separates from the human body in a moment that jagodzinski (2005: 205) describes as 'becoming-animal'. This concept refers to the sound of the scream, 'stuck' (205) in the throat of the screamer. Growling is neither part of the symbolic order of speech, nor is it the affective *jouissance* of screaming. Like screaming, it is un-gendered and disembodied. However, when asked to describe the experience of performing, vocalists never mentioned growling or gurgling. Instead, they focused on screaming or making noise as the key moment of pleasure. This was even the case for vocalists who alternated between pitch-shifted and screamed vocals. Zak, the vocalist for Roskopp, described how it took practice to make pitch-shifted vocals feel 'natural':

> I've, I've always just sort of done it and sort of experiments at prac-tice with the pitch-shifter, though so, it feels really natural. (Zak)

Here, Zak acknowledges a sense that the technology of the pitch-shifter medi-ates the brutally affective experience (the Real) of screaming. Onstage, the brutal voice is expressed through noise and screaming. In the next section, I discuss what happens when scene members were asked to articulate the experience of brutality, and how this relates to masculinity, in the ethno-graphic interview.

Brutal responses in the ethnographic interview

Articulated affect is feminized as 'emotion' or 'feelings'. My requests to artic-ulate 'feelings' regarding live grindcore performances were often met with awkwardness:

> **Tommo:** [T]his'll sound a bit funny—it [watching a band] gives me a warm feeling! [*laughs*]

> **Rosemary:** So, how do you feel, like, say in [Melbourne band] Shagnum, when you're 'in the moment'—performing?

> **Graham:** Um, [pause] pretty, yeah, pretty—I don't know... Um, it's—is—I actually haven't been asked that before! [*laughs*]

Tommo distances himself from the 'warm feeling'—affect—which live perfor-mances prompt through the acknowledgement that it 'sound[s]...funny' for a man to articulate affect. Both respondents use laughter to distance them-selves from their affective responses.

The male aversion to articulation of feelings is, of course, culturally constructed and much discussed by feminists (Jensen 2007; Plumwood 1994) and even metal scholars (Walser 1993).[11] Affect is often erroneously elided with 'emotions', coded as female. However, as Massumi points out, affect is a 'pre-personal intensity corresponding to...an augmentation or diminution in that body's capacity to act...an encounter between the affected body and a second, affecting, body' (in Deleuze and Guattari 1987: xvi). This differs from emotion, which is the outward display of feelings, based on one's subjective history.

Elaborating on Massumi, I consider 'feelings' an articulation of affect. They are informed by history and culture in the sense that the shift from affect (something more than representational) to feeling (signified as emotion) is cognitive. The forced articulation of affect in the ethnographic interview troubles brutal's masculine connotations. To articulate feeling is to acknowledge the 'blowing away' of the (masculine) self in the affective moment. Popular rock music is male-dominated. Yet, pop-rock performers are expected to express emotion on cue to fulfil their status as authentic artists and appeal to a wide audience. Extreme metal, including grindcore, is just as masculinist. However, the marginality of extreme-metal, and its proponents' aversion to rock aesthetics, means that verbally articulated affect is incongruous. Chart success is unlikely, and rarely a goal for extreme-metallers (Kahn-Harris 2007). Instead, they appeal to listeners, partly through blunt representations of masculinity, who share their brutal disposition. Indeed, the affective, uncontainability of the self in grindcore contexts is referenced, but also recuperated in the 'Fuck... I'm Dead' moniker. The swearword 'fuck' aligns the band with the supposed coarseness of male culture. The taboo of swearing also draws attention away from the notion of the self becoming 'dead'. The controversial use of 'fuck' becomes the focus.[12]

My respondents' awkwardness partly reflects my diversion from the standard interview and interviewer. As Graham notes above, it is rare for metallers to be asked about feelings in interviews. Firstly, my position, as a woman, was unusual. A look at contributors to global extreme metal magazine, *Terrorizer*, shows that the reporters are mainly men, though the editor is a woman (Terrorizer, n.d.). My gender, I believe, contributed to repeated questions about why I was studying grindcore and whether I 'really' liked it. When I revealed that my partner was a band member, interviewees generally took this as the only acceptable explanation for my presence in the scene and my academic interest. This matches the popular assumption that women generally form the periphery of rock scenes—as fans, groupies and 'girlfriends' (Apolloni 2008; cf. Garber and McRobbie [1975] 1976).

Case study: Blood Duster

Apart from the gender of most interviewers of grindcore musicians, the interview structure fosters a masculine perspective.[13] 'Feminine' areas such as emotions are rarely discussed. Keeping it brutal means keeping it manly. Melbourne group Blood Duster is Australia's most successful grindcore band. A brief analysis of their media interviews demonstrates the normative masculine tone. I located four interviews with the band, in local and foreign press. This may seem a small number. However, relative to other Melburnian bands, this is significant, particularly because they are interviewed in *Terrorizer* (Christ 2009) and mainstream Australian rock press *Beat* (Wang 2007), as well as fanzines (Goreripper 2007; Ward, n.d.).

Firstly, it is noteworthy that all the interviewers used pseudonyms or nicknames. This suggests a fluid gender identity, for instance the handle 'Goreripper', or indeed any of the names, could be appropriated by either sex. However, the specific reference to the penis in two of the pseudonyms suggests that, even if one is a woman, it is better to identify as a man when interviewing grindcore musicians. The first is 'Nutso' Ward (n.d.), who interviewed Blood Duster for Sydney punk/metal zine *Unbelievably Bad*. Second is 'Bobus Wang' (2007), who interviewed the band for *Beat*. Here, I will focus on Ward's interview.

The *Unbelievably Bad* interview begins with a standard dialogue about the band's upcoming tour (Ward n.d.: 46). However, the interview becomes (brutally) masculine when discussion turns to the band's DVD *The Shape of Death to Come* (Blood Duster, 2005). Interviewee, Jason P. C.,[14] provides information that the disc features multiple 'tittie [and]...cunt shots' (Ward n.d.: 47). For Jason, this fits into the band's image as tasteless. He notes, 'we know...we can show a vagina as long as there's no penetration' (Ward n.d.: 46), conceding that the pornography on the DVD is an attempt to push legal parameters. Ward rises to Jason's introduction of pornographic subject matter by adopting the tone of a 'mate', swapping stories about female conquests:

> I remember seeing you at Caringbah nearly a year ago and before the show the whole band was watching...while Tony ['Tonebone' Forde—vocalist] tried to pick up some chick. Apparently you needed one final shot to complete the DVD (Ward n.d.: 46).

Jason responds in a similarly matey way—imparting details of Tony's dalliances and describing how they incorporated footage of them into the DVD:

> We got some...cool shots of him fucking this chick in Perth somewhere. He had her doing all kinds of shit and we thought it was hilarious—we all watched it the next day... [H]e's doing like full porno talk (Ward n.d.: 46).

Ward and Jason's conversation depends on understanding that women are sexual objects to be 'fuck[ed]', watched, re-watched and described by men. Importantly, the interviewer's identification as a masculine mate of Jason's allowed Jason to move from being a band-member recounting details of musical conquests, to a mate recounting sexual conquests. Further, the matieness that surrounds the consumption of pornography normalizes, via complicity, the objectification and degradation of women that most pornography expresses (Jensen 2007).[15]

The rest of the interview follows this masculinist structure. Jason recounts a tale of an 'uptight' American grind band who took offence at his repeated reference to his partner as a 'cunt' (Ward n.d.: 46). Ward heartily agrees with Jason that this is outrageous; though still, apparently, an amusing—'classic'— anecdote (Ward n.d.: 46).[16]

The process of objectification allows the subject, doing the objectifying, to experience wholeness, in the face of the amputated partiality of the object. However, Jensen (2007) notes an interesting paradox within the objectifying process of pornography consumption. He suggests that male pornography consumers use pornography to objectify themselves (113–14). That is, pornography produces an 'emotional numbness' (113) which avoids facing sex as 'always *more than a physical act*' (114, my emphasis). For Jensen, this process maintains dominant masculinity, which represses female-coded emotions (26).

The avoidance of emotions is evident in the Blood Duster interviews I studied. They work in a cerebral, cognitive mode. That is, both Jason (he is the only band member to participate in interviews) and the interviewer appear to have calculated, clever responses, which always shy away from articulating affect. However, in such discussions masculinity depends on a relation to arguably the most affective of human experiences: sexual intercourse. The feminine Other is not simply the physical female—or in Wang's (2007) words, a 'gooey vagoo' (n.p.)—it is affect. Thus, it is necessary for both interviewer and interviewee to maintain distance from sex's affective elements. Sex, like the women and feminized emotions it prompts, becomes an object. It is something to be watched, categorized into bests, and discussed with detachment.

Thus, in my interviews, it was common for male interviewees to assert their masculinity through crass descriptions of sex and gender. Such responses evaded the necessity of speaking feminized feelings when articulating affect. In response to a question about affect and performance, Leon asserted his masculinity through the literal invocation of the phallus:

Rosemary: ...So how does it feel when you're up there [onstage]?

Leon: A group of friends who are just being dicks.

Thus, for Leon, being brutal is synonymous with being male—represented by the phallic slang 'dick'.

Feeling brutal/feeling ambiguous
Blood Duster's misogynistic 'brutality' is not indicative of the entire Melbourne grindcore scene, nor does it mean that a brutal disposition excludes affect. On the contrary, brutality as something not articulable through speech or representation, that is, 'feeling brutal', suffuses the grindcore scene. However, the moment of articulation—necessary to the ethnographic interview—requires recognition of brutality's affectiveness and a compartmentalization of such intensities into speech. Speech's inadequacies locate affect in the emotional and, thus, a feminine, register. For some respondents, my identity as a woman perhaps allowed a greater exploration of affective experience. Tommo, despite feeling 'funny', still conceded to experiencing the intensity of a gig affectively. Zak also described the affective experience in detail:

> [G]enerally it's...sort of excitement. That kind of music, I think, um... sort of really strikes me more than, anything else does. I don't get the same kind of feeling from anything else. And, generally, no other music really sort of holds my attention, sort of, yeah, has the lasting, or strong sort of presence, as that. But, um, yeah, it's sort of, um, an excitement. And I find when I'm watching bands as well, it's—it's a funny thing... (Zak)

Further, discussions of the reactionary politics of black metal as well as gore-grindcore prompted a certain amount of reflexivity regarding misogyny in the scene. Many interviewees acknowledged grindcore's own reactionary elements and were emphatic that grindcore's apparent misogyny is, or *should* be, expressed from a critical distance:

> [W]ith gore-grind for instance, in America, there was a lot of...really shitty bands that were like really, ...misogynistic, and, um, like just those sort of one-man bedroom bands that—when you look at it— you know, okay, this is obviously some sort of frustrated redneck guy who's seen all these bands with porn on the covers and shit. And thought 'oh cool! This is a good way to fucking write songs about... women who I hate' (Carsten)

Carsten's critique employs typical elements of distinction. Carsten is 'obviously', being a true grind fan, able to recognize 'shitty' gore-grind as being the work of a (lower-class) 'redneck guy' unable to distance himself from the implied irony of pornography on gore-grind album covers. While scene members were generally assertive in their outrage at neo-Nazi black metal, their encounters with reactionary politics, in particular misogyny, in grindcore were more ambiguous:

> I'm not singing about stuff like a lot of the gore-grind bands sing about... I find that, I mean, I can have a chuckle with all of them about—you know—some funny stuff they say or whatever—but I'm not into—into the violence and kind of, um, I guess the porn side of it as well, I'm not into that at all, either. (Graham)

Graham asserts he is 'not into [gore-grind] at all'. Yet, he admits that he does take an interest in the genre as humorous. That is, Graham feels he is able to assume the distance needed to find gore-grind's misogyny amusing while also claiming to be 'not into...the violence and...the porn' represented in the genre's lyrics and artwork.

Burning emos—disavowing articulated emotions in grindcore

Emo, femininity and grindcore

Grindcore scene members' ambiguous relation to distanced/affective engagement with grindcore music is even more apparent concerning 'emo' music. Emo is a type of punk music characterized by its lyrical depictions of emotions (hence the 'emo' moniker). Musically, emo has heavy, punk riffs, interspersed with melodic, quieter parts. Vocalists wail, or scream lyrics during the heavy parts and sing during the quieter sections. Emo's chart success, particularly in the 2000s, led to a visible emo youth culture. Emo fans were identified in the media, particularly after a series of emo panics related to self-harm and suicide (ABC4 2007; CBS 47 2007; Fox 11 2007; TCN 7 2007; TCN 9 2007; WDAZ 2007). The media created a folk devil out of emos. They emphasized their androgynous 'uniform' of dark make-up, 'girls' jeans' and long fringes, as well as emos' supposed ascription to 'depressed' attitudes (ABC4 2007).

As Thornton (1996) points out, music cultures require an Other to maintain a sense of coherent scenic identity. Such Others are more likely to be from inter-dependent or related scenes. The relative musical similarities between the heavy parts of emo songs and grindcore make emo a proximate target of Othering by grindcore scene members. Scene members constitute emo's Otherness along gender lines. They position themselves as brutally masculine. Emo, on the other hand, is feminized. One online 'Grindcore Lifestyle' group declares it is 'anti-emo' (esclavodelgrind 2008) and has this to say to 'emo scen[e] fags': 'go fuck yourself [*sic*]!!!!' (esclavodelgrind 2008). Emo's association with femininity makes it emphatically, as one online grindcore fan put it, 'Not Brutal At ALL'[17] (Aric-Anti-Emo-RickrollKing! 2008).[18]

Emo's femininity is not solely associated with surface signifiers of female-ness—women's clothing and make-up. The emotional nature of emo music cements its position as feminine. From a musicological perspective, emo regularly employs minor chords. In Western culture, such chords connote sadness and tragedy, due chiefly to their association with apparently sad classical music and their later use in pop-ballads from the 1960s onwards (Krims 2007). Minor chords are unusual in rock and metal music, which follow a major chord structure. Minor chords' association with feminized music genres position emo as generically female.

Emo's lyrical themes also constitute emo as feminine, because emo focuses on the culturally feminized realm of feelings.[19] Further and unlike metal, or even most rock music, emo presents a passive lyrical perspective. Emo and rock both focus on human relationships for lyrical material. However, emo lyrics position the masculine narrator (emo bands being almost entirely male) as a passive victim within such, heterosexual, relations. This differs from both rock and metal music.

Emo men have plenty to articulate, but not much to do. The lyrics to a Hawthorne Heights' (2004) song, 'Ohio is for Lovers', are illustrative. This song focuses on a female partner being unfaithful. However, rather than deferring an articulated response onto a plea to another 'girl' to be 'his', the male lyricist / singer wails 'I can't make it on my own'. He goes on to outline how he will surely die without his female partner: 'fall[ing] asleep...until my final breath is gone'. The male protagonist is passive. Instead, the woman is, sadistically, active:

> You kill me
> ...
> You kill me well
> You like it too (ibid.).

Blood Duster and emo

All Melbourne interviewees professed a dislike of emo. However, Blood Duster's response, again, illustrates grindcore's complex relation to affect and masculinity.

In 2007, Blood Duster released the album *Lyden Na*. It featured the song, 'THE NIGHT THEY BURNED OLD EMO DOWN' (TNTBOED), which regards 'the joys of burning down a venue full of emo kids' (Raw Nerve Promotions, 2007). This song's lyrics appropriate emo lyrical aesthetics of death and fire, and refer to emo fashion, as a way of expressing their hatred for the genre:

The studio now becomes a grave

...

Licking flames they kiss the sky
The scene is swallowed in a cloud of dirty smoke

....

Fire engulfs the back packs
Singes fringes and burns tattoos (*Lyden Na* 2007)

More significant, though, is Blood Duster's musical shift in TNTBOED. The song bears no grindcore signifiers, apart from its Othering of emo. Instead, it is an acoustic slide-guitar piece, with a guest vocalist[20] crooning the lyrics in a country style. This is a joke song, and has been described as such in interviews with band members (Goreripper 2007). However, the lack of musical brutality is telling. Instead, brutality is shifted into the realm of critical distance—the ability to 'take the piss'—as well as the more blunt violence of the lyrics. Blood Duster rejects the atypical helplessness—feminized passivity—of emo, despite the emo style of their lyrics. Of course, Blood Duster is holding the 'box of matches' which burns the emo venue to the ground. Through parodic appropriation, Blood Duster re-affirm their position as patriarchs—capable with tools (matches) and in control of those identities coded as feminine.

The easy appropriation of emo lyrical aesthetics dovetails with the wider rhetoric surrounding *Lyden Na*, which emphasized the supposed pretentiousness of emo culture. In interviews, band members position emo as shallow, manufactured pop music:

I don't really understand emo. To me it sounds like Florida death metal. It's Morbid Angel with a clothing endorsement (Goreripper 2007).

Another band member, Leon, confirmed this attitude in my interview:

[I]t's [emo is] extreme music that's made to be not extreme...like Kmart metal... The whole 'scene' thing has just changed so much. Like, it used to be you started a band—you had a concept or an idea for everything—and then you'd get at more like an art thing. Now, it more comes from a commerce thing...everyone affiliates themselves with all the companies and stuff, and makes a fortune in a couple of years—'cause there's a consumer base readymade for it. Where, we're still going—rocking up to a place going 'we should've fucking printed some t-shirts'... It's just a whole different mindset.

Leon suggests that emo is incorporated into popular music's political economy. It is 'Kmart metal'—mass-produced and motivated by 'a commerce thing'. Leon presents emo's presumed commercialism as Other to the 'mind-set' of Blood Duster. Emo musicians are market-savvy while Blood Duster are naïve—thinking more about playing music than 'print[ing] some t-shirts'. Leon goes on to say:

> ...we try and do everything completely in-house. You know, besides manufacture...all artwork's done by us... All recordings, you know, eventually up to the point where no-one touches anything.

Here, Leon aligns Blood Duster with grindcore's often mythologized (Mudrian 2004) relation to DIY punk, where multi-skilled band-members undertake all elements of production (O'Hara 1999). As Kahn-Harris (2007) points out, an association with the 'right' metal moments, ideals and figures is essential for maintaining extreme-metal subcultural capital. Blood Duster reiterates this in media interviews:

> **Goreripper:** You've always had that punk ethic.
>
> **Jason P.C.:** Yeah. Well I think some bands do well by not having fucking managers and by not having fucking mixers and shit, and be forced to fucking do something off their own bat (Goreripper 2007).

Of course, such acknowledgement of grindcore's, and Blood Duster's, punk roots depends on a synchronous establishment of an Other who do not 'do... thing[s] off their own bat'. The Other here is emo, which Jason P.C. had been discussing in the previous question.

Piss takes and pissing
The sense that emo is a mass-produced cultural commodity is elaborated in *Lyden Na*'s promotional image. Here, the band are dressed up as emos (see Figure on p. 219), further demonstrating the assumption, that, unlike grindcore, other forms of music are shallowly bound to mass produced 'image':

> There's some emo photos...we're using for advertising for the album. We've put neck tatts on ourselves, and fringes and eye-make-up (ibid.).

By simply 'put[ting]...on' emo style, Blood Duster imply that emo is superficial. It is something feigned,[21] presumably unlike grindcore brutality, which is something more than an affectation.

Blood Duster 'dress up' as emos to promote *Lyden Na* (2007), 'taking the piss' out of the style of emo bands (photo by Jason Fuller)

Emo's femininity is tied partly to lyrical content, which foregrounds representations of emotions. As noted above, grindcore scene members, keen to demonstrate masculine brutality, disavow articulated emotion, except from the distance of parody. Emo's lyrical form is also significant. In grindcore, song structure is based primarily around the heaviness of the music. Sung verses and chorus are non-existent. In emo, however, the traditional sung verse/chorus/bridge structure is used. Further, emo songs generally have a narrative, such as 'Ohio is for Lovers', which regarded a memory of a break-up and a description of the singer's current state of mind. The emphasis on narrative builds emo's emotional register. The singer offers an apparently deep account of his feelings. This re-affirms connotations of femininity, through an association with so-called women's cultures of confessional television, agony aunt columns and self-help magazines.

Blood Duster provide an example of grindcore's rejection of deep narrative and thus also of the femininity it connotes. Their songs lyrics are sound-bytes of taboo, generally misogynist, imagery.[22] For example, these lyrics from 'Simultaneous Pleasure Pinch':

> Up the date
> And up the cunt
> With my fingers
> I will hunt (*Yeest*, Blood Duster 1996)

Further, unlike emo songs, which often stretch to 4 minutes or more, many of Blood Duster's songs are less than a minute. The shortest is the lyric-less, but no less misogynist, 'Bitch' (*Yeest* 1996) at 7 seconds.

Blood Duster also refuses deep narrative at gigs. That is, unlike rock and emo, grindcore bands are more likely to heckle audience members than thank them for coming along. This is, of course, considered a joke. So Blood Duster's regular lines, such as 'fuck you cunts', are yet another deferral of affect—the aggression and energy generated by performance—onto piss takes. Emo musicians, on the other hand, are effusive at live shows. Artists often entertain the audience with lengthy personal anecdotes between songs (Simon and Kelley 2007). Blood Duster's response to this story-telling rejects the feminized genre of confessional narrative. They affirm their brutal masculinity through a stifling of meaningful banter. Leon explains:

> We've...been going through a thing lately...where we've been...telling stories that lead nowhere. You know, like, you, you tell a story that's really monotonous and they think it's going to lead somewhere and you tell it like 'and then the door just shut!'

This approach is intended to induce an affective response in the audience. Importantly, though, it is not intended to stimulate adoration from fans, but shame at having let themselves be mesmerised by the band. Blood Duster's repartee reminds audience members that the truly brutal remain detached from their emotions. Leon continues:

> You know, we played in Adelaide...and um, after we played the last song, we acted like we were going to do an encore—*that there was a special moment*—so we convinced the whole crowd that they had to move back, like, ten or fifteen steps and it took a little while for everyone to do it, but we managed to get the whole venue back a few steps. And then we just said 'seeya' and walked off. And it was just like a big, collective 'ohhh', you know? Because they'd been letdown. Just letting down the crowd's, like, actually become heaps of fun (emphasis added).

Nevertheless, other members of Blood Duster still experience grindcore brutality through affect. Jules, like others, has trouble articulating affect, describing it as a 'buzz' and 'spin[ning]' out' from himself:

[I]f you play in front of, say, like a packed Hi-Fi Bar. That's always a buzz...or whatever, so it's, um, yeah, it's good... Sometimes you spin out, sometimes you don't. You couldn't give a shit.

Like other scene members, Jules' attempt to speak about affective brutality demonstrates the loss of self experienced during performance. The sense of 'spin[ning] out' is described in the third person. This alludes to Jules' feeling that 'I' recedes and affect takes over. This is not a troubling experience ('*You* [the self separate from 'I'] couldn't give a shit'), because it avoids any association with articulated emotions.

Blood Duster's concern with distancing themselves from the Other/emo betrays a fear of identification with the Other. The Other manifests as emo culture. However, emo, of course, stands in for (feminized) emotions. Recently, emo has occasionally been literally proximate to grindcore in the form of mixed-bills. In Blood Duster's case, this proximity prompted a display of extreme masculinity in order to fend off any association with their bill-mates. In an interview, Jason P. C. firstly emphasizes that the bill was, of course, a joke:

Someone thought it would be funny to put all these emo bands on with Blood Duster and someone else, [Brisbane band] Fort I think it was (Ward n.d.: 47).

Nevertheless, the prospect of playing in front of emo fans, and with emo bands, required an assurance that emo remained a feminine Other and Blood Duster/grindcore was constituted as brutally masculine. Jason P. C. achieved this through a blunt display of masculinity: the exposure of his penis.

The emo kids [were there]...had their backpacks on and shit, so I'm standing onstage, pissed [drunk] as hell, and I could see them out there with their arms crossed, so I just pissed [urinated] on [guitar-player] Matt Collins' leg. It was just like, 'Yeah, fuck you, I'm drunk, I'm pissing on the stage, I don't give a fuck (Ward n.d.: 47).

Jason P. C. reveals his anxiety—over the invasion of emo culture into his brutal space of the grindcore gig ('I could see them out there'). He appears perturbed by the refusal of the emos to move ('their arms crossed'). Jason P. C.'s act of urination may simply have disgusted emo audience members. However, its purpose, I believe, was largely to alleviate his own anxiety that the division between Blood Duster and emo was effacing. Thus, his 'pissing'—again, offered as a piss-take/joke—reassures Jason P. C. of his own masculinity and his distance from 'you', the Other. His identity, from his perspective, is bound to his ability to piss—'fuck *you... I'm* pissing'. Notably, this differs from Jules' affective experience of '*you*' referring to the self's immersion in the feminized Other of affect. Jason P. C. resists the 'spin out' (Jules) of the self into affect through his emphasis on the *I*/self bound to his masculine body.

Conclusion

In this chapter, I contended that grindcore is a more than representational music culture. Using the concept of feeling brutal, I established grindcore music as prompting an affective intensity, which grants grindcore scene participants a sense of belonging. Through an ethnographic case study of Melbourne's grindcore music scene, I proposed that feeling brutal potentially makes room for a feminized grindcore subject. This subject contradicts understandings of metal, in particular extreme metal, such as grindcore, as inherently masculine.

However, I also showed how 'brutal's masculinist connotations, associated with representations of brutal male criminals in the media, also suffuse Melbourne's scene. An analysis of Blood Duster's media interviews showed that being brutal sometimes also means articulating a misogynist rhetoric. Nevertheless, this rhetoric was also openly contradicted or at least rendered ambivalent in the ethnographic interview context. This was potentially because, unlike most grindcore media interviewers, I am a woman.

Finally, I presented a case study of grindcore's response to emo music as a means for teasing out scene members' complex responses to affect and articulated affect (emotions). Again, a case study of Blood Duster provided a fruitful example. I suggested that the brutally masculinist responses of the band to emo masked an acknowledgement of the affective experience of 'feeling brutal'. I proposed that this experience troubled some scene members enough for them to effect a masculine-coded response, often shrouded in the phallicly inspired notions of 'piss-takes' and literal 'pissing'.

Notes

1. This is a quotation from the title of a song by Melbourne grindcore band, Blood Duster, 'Hate Girls and Crusty Punx', which is on *Str8 Outta Northcote* (1998).
2. Jim makes this explicit: 'brutal...is quite a subjective term'.
3. He also, rightly, acknowledges Brennan's (2004) findings on affective intermingling (221–22).
4. Brennan's work (2004) is largely about this same intuition. See particularly her 'Introduction' (1–23), where she writes: 'The origin of affects is social in that these affects do not only arise within a particular person but also come from without' (3). She also emphasizes the biological and physiological factors present in the 'transmission' of affect (1–23 *passim*).
5. See also Wood and Smith's (2004) work on the 'soundworld'. Here, music fans and

musicians display a similar difficulty in expressing affect. Their participants say, 'you can just go jjjjjjjjjjj' (537). Massumi also discusses the impossibility of containing affect in discursive structures (2002: 1–21 *passim*).

6. Will's sense of affect's pre-cognitive and external ('something comes over you') position supports Brennan's (2004) work on the 'transmission' of affect between people, spaces and things. She offers compelling scientific evidence that such intensities are, in part, biological and move between subjects and objects through olfaction (Brennan 2004: 51–74).

7. See Seltzer's (1998) work on serial killers, which looks particularly at the gendering of serial sexual violence. He writes that such crimes are 'nearly consisten[ly] gender[ed]...a male violence that is anti-female and anti-homosexual or more exactly a male violence that is directed at the anti-male or "*un*male"' (67). Recent examples in Melbourne media to use the phrase 'brutal' when describing crime perpetrated by a man against a woman include: the murder of Tracey Greenbury by Leigh Robinson (ninemsn 2008); Peter Caruso's murder of his wife, Rosa (Oakes and Arup 2008); and Peter Dupas' alleged killings of multiple women (Norrie 2011).

8. Perhaps the most famous example is the serial slayings conducted by Richard Ramirez in the 1980s. He claimed the song 'Night Prowler' by AC/DC was an influence on his violence. The media ran with this idea, dubbing him, incorrectly, the 'Night Stalker'.

9. The only exception being, during my fieldwork, an incident when a group of 'right-wing...Nazi' (Carsten) black metal fans attended a grindcore gig. The black-metallers picked a fight with a male scene member who was wearing a dress and a brawl ensued. The venue where it occurred is now widely black-listed as a 'Nazi pub' (Boycott the Birmingham 2007) and no longer attended by grindcore scene members.

10. The most telling example was Tasmanian band Intense Hammer Rage's tour of Melbourne in 2003. During their show at the Green Room, *Texas Chainsaw Massacre* (Hooper 1974) played on multiple screens. See my article on grindcore spaces in Melbourne, for a more indepth discussion of the homology between horror movies and Melbourne grindcore (Overell 2010).

11. However, despite an awareness of the problematics of coding feeling, and thus affect, 'feminine', a large proportion of affect studies remain in 'Women's Studies' faculties (Clough 2007).

12. One acquaintance, not a scene member, on hearing my research was on the Arthouse, said 'oh I just love the band names they put up on the blackboard at the front—Fuck... I'm Dead—hilarious'.

13. The masculinist bias of media interviews is not peculiar to grindcore, or even extreme-metal. As Connell (2000: 81) demonstrates in his ethnography of masculinity and sports, 'media talk' reinforces dominant conceptions of masculinity.

14. His name being a joke on 'politically correct'—he and his band deliberate try to be politically *incorrect*.

15. Jensen (2007) describes pornography's 'whisper' (33) to men as the voice of a friend who validates the male subject's masculinity by approving of pornography consumption: 'It's okay, you really are a man, you really can be a man...if you come

into my world' (ibid.). He also notes that, in Western culture, most men are introduced to pornography as teens, through their male peer-group (38–40).

16. Other Blood Duster interviews follow a similar matey and sexist tone. *Terrorizer* asks: 'Which European country does the best porn?' (Christ 2009). *Beat's* Bobus Wang (2007) enquires: 'Which Suicide Girl would you most enjoy throwing one up? Personally I'd rev the guts out of that Ciara chick'. These interviews depend on the construction of a feminine Other to the interviewers', and interviewee's, brutal masculinity. The female figure is objectified in the bluntest manner: she becomes 'guts' (Wang 2007: n.p.); 'tits' (Christ 2009) and the ubiquitous 'cunt' (Christ 2009; Wang 2007; Ward n.d.) to be 'rev[ved]' (Wang 2007); 'pick[ed] up' and 'fucked' (Ward n.d.).

17. The full quote reads thus: 'the USED[a popular emo band]?!?!? Thats [*sic*] Not Brutal At ALL!!!! Im [*sic*] Mean BRUTAL!!!!... NOT EMO CUT YOUR THROTE [*sic*]****!!!!!!!!!!!' (Aric-Anti-Emo-RickrollKing! 2008). It was a reply to a post with the topic 'Brutal Song Names?' The homophobic response to emo echoes heavy metal's response to glam metal in the 1980s. Walser (1993) discusses heavy-metallers' obsession with denouncing glam as inauthentically 'feminine' in heavy metal fan media. He cites one fanzine that offered thrash metalheads a sticker declaring 'No Glam Fags! All Metal! No Make-up!' (Walser 1993: 130).

18. Mainstream heavy musicians also categorize emo as pejoratively female. Maynard James Keenan of hard rock band Tool describes male emo performers and fans as 'pussy-ass, makeup-wearing...mama's boys' (Draiman 2006: 67). Clearly, Keenan is a man concerned with emphasising his masculinity. The band's name means, in his words, 'exactly what it sounds like: It's a big dick. It's a wrench...we are...your tool; use us as a catalyst in your process of finding out whatever it is you need to find out, or whatever it is you're trying to achieve' (Zappa 1994: 15).

19. As Aklaksen (2006) points out, such lyrics are also, contradictorily, misogynist—regarding fantasized acts of violence against women who have wronged them. See also Greenwald (2003) and Simon and Kelley (2007) for journalistic discussions on emo and misogyny.

20. The vocalist was Craig Westwood, the lead singer of seminal Melbourne stoner/grindcore band Christbait.

21. Blood Duster's caption for the Figure 2 photograph on the music website 'Reverb Nation' is 'emo grind is the new black' (Blood Duster 2010). This is an obvious linking between the fast turnover of styles in the fashion industry and emo music.

22. Further, they are generally 'intro-ed' by soundbytes from horror or pornographic movies.

Bibliography

ABC4. 2007. 'Emo Culture'. *Close to Home*. Utah, 27 May.

Amico, S. 2002. '"I Want Muscles": House Music, Homosexuality and Masculine Signification'. *Popular Music* 20(3): 359–78.

Apolloni, A. 2008. 'Rebel Grrls in the Classroom: Vocality, Empowerment and Feminist Pedagogy at Rock and Roll School for Girls'. *Thinking Gender Papers*. http://escholarship.org/uc/item/0b18q8fb#page-1

Aric-Anti-Emo-RickrollKing! 2008. *Brutal Song Names?* Yahoo Answers: http://answers.yahoo.com/question/index?qid=20080602013529AA4J2d9.

Arnett, J. J. 1996. *Metalheads: Heavy Metal Music and Adolescent Alienation.* Boulder, CO: Westview Press.

Blood Duster. 2010. *Blood Duster: Photos,* March 10. Reverb Nation: http://www.reverbnation.com/bloodduster#/page_object/page_object_photos/artist_698631?sel_photo_id=2021110.

Boycott The Birmingham. 2007. *Boycott the Birmingham: Campaign to Boycott The Birmy, a Neo-Nazi Venue in Melbourne, Australia,* 17 February. http://birmyboycott.wordpress.com/.

Brennan, T. 2004. *The Transmission of Affect.* Ithaca, NY: Cornell University Press.

CBS 47. 2007. 'Emo'. *Investigators,* 11 July.

Christ, J. 2009. 'Blood Duster on New Album and Obscene Extreme'. *Terrorizer,* 11 May. http://www.terrorizer.com/content/blood-duster-new-album-and-obscene-extreme (accessed 1 August 2009).

Clough, P. T. 2007. 'Introduction'. In *The Affective Turn: Theorising the Social,* ed. P. T. Clough and J. Halley, 1–33. Durham, NC: Duke University Press.

Connell, R. W. 2000. *The Men and the Boys.* Berkeley: University of California Press.

Deleuze, G., and F. Guattari. 1987. *A Thousand Plateaus,* ed. B. Massumi. Minneapolis: University of Minnesota Press.

Dolar, M. 2006. *A Voice and Nothing More.* Cambridge, MA: MIT Press.

Draiman, D. 2006. 'Who Hates Emo the Most?' *Rolling Stone* (October): 67.

esclavodelgrind. 2008. *GRINDCORE LIFESTYLE (anti-emo group),* 20 May. last.fm: http://www.last.fm/group/GRINDCORE+LIFESTYLE+(anti-emo+group).

Fox 11. 2007. 'Emo'. *Fox 11 News,* May 10. California.

Garber, J., and A. McRobbie [1975] 1976. 'Girls and Subcultures'. In *Resistance Through Rituals,* ed. Stuart Hall and Tony Jefferson. London: Hutchinson.

Goreripper. 2007. *The Sporadic Gazette: Blood Duster,* 7 May. PyroMusic.net: http://www.pyromusic.net/index.php?p=interviews_interview&id=44 (accessed March 2009, no longer available).

Greenwald, A. 2003. *Nothing Feels Good: Punk Rock, Teenagers and Emo.* New York: St Martin's Griffin.

jagodzinski, j. 2005. *Music in Youth Culture: A Lacanian Approach.* New York: Palgrave Macmillan.

Jensen, R. 2007. *Getting Off: Pornography and the End of Masculinity.* Cambridge, MA: South End Press.

Kahn-Harris, K. 2007. *Extreme Metal: Music and Culture on the Edge.* Oxford: Berg.

Krims, A. 2007. *Music and Urban Geography.* New York: Routledge.

Lorimer, H. 2008. 'Cultural Geography: Non-representational Conditions and Concerns'. *Progress in Human Geography* 32(4): 551–59. http://dx.doi.org/10.1177/0309132507086882

Massumi, B. 1998. 'Requiem for Our Prospective Dead (Toward a Participatory Critique of Capitalist Power)'. In *Deleuze and Guattari: New Mappings in Politics, Philosophy, and Culture,* ed. E. Kaufman and K. J. Heller, 40–64. Minneapolis: University of Minnesota Press.

—2002. *Parables for the Virtual: Movement, Affect, Sensation*. Durham, NC: Duke University Press.

Mudrian, A. 2004. *Choosing Death: The Improbable History of Death Metal and Grindcore*. Los Angeles: Feral House.

ninemsn. 2008. 'Mum's Brutal Murder: Suspect Named'. ninemsn, 29 April. http://news.ninemsn.com.au/article.aspx?id=453779.

Oakes, D., and T. Arup. 2008. 'Murder Charge over Wife's Fatal Bashing'. theage.com.au. 3 July. http://www.theage.com.au/national/murder-charge-over-wifes-fatal-bashing-20080702-306m.html.

O'Hara, C. 1999. *The Philosophy of Punk: More Than Noise!* London: AK Press.

Overell, R. 2010. 'Brutal Belonging in Melbourne's Grindcore Scene'. *Studies in Symbolic Interaction* 35: 79–99. http://dx.doi.org/10.1108/S0163-2396(2010)0000035009

Plumwood, V. 1994. *Feminism and the Mastery of Nature*. London: Routledge.

Raw Nerve Promotions. 2007. 'Blood Duster—new album coming on Obscene Productions'. Raw Nerve Forums, 27 June. http://rawnervepromotions.co.uk/forum/viewtopic.php?f=66&t=32120 (accessed 25 July 2009, no longer available).

Ross, Norrie. 2011. 'Serial killer Peter Dupas given leave to appeal conviction over Mersina Halvagis murder'. News.com.au, 14 December 2011. http://www.news.com.au/breaking-news/dupas-given-leave-to-appeal-conviction-over-mersina-halvagis-murder/story-e6frfku0-1226221943983.

Seltzer, M. 1998. *Serial Killers: Death and Life in America's Wound Culture*. New York: Routledge.

Simon, L., and T. Kelley. 2007. *Everybody Hurts: An Essential Guide to Emo Culture*. New York: HarperCollins.

Smith, S. J. 2000. 'Music (2)'. In *City A-Z*, ed. S. Pile and N. Thrift, 156–58. London: Routledge.

TCN 7. 2007. 'Death Pact'. *Today Tonight*, 23 April. Melbourne.

TCN 9. 2007. 'Web of Darkness'. *60 Minutes*, 20 May. Melbourne.

Terrorizer. n.d. 'Terrorizer: Extreme Music No Boundaries'. http://www.terrorizer.com (accessed 30 July 2009).

Thornton, S. 1996. *Club Cultures: Music, Media and Subcultural Capital*. Hanover, CT: Wesleyan University Press.

Thrift, N. 2004. 'Summoning Life'. In *Envisioning Human Geographies*, ed. P. Cloke, P. Crang and M. Goodwin, 81–103. Oxford: Oxford University Press.

—2008. *Non-Representational Theory: Space | Politics | Affect*. Oxon: Routledge.

Walser, R. 1993. *Running with the Devil: Power, Gender, and Madness in Heavy Metal Music*. Hanover, CT: Wesleyan University Press.

Wang, B. 2007. 'Blood Duster'. *Beat: Melbourne's Biggest Streetpaper*, 4 April.

Ward, N. n.d. 'Bloody Crackheads'. *Unbelievably Bad #1*, 46–49.

WDAZ. 2007. 'Emo'. *WDAZ News at 10*, 23 February. Grand Forks.

Weinstein, D. 2000. *Heavy Metal: The Music and its Culture*. New York: Da Capo Press.

Wood, N., and S. J. Smith. 2004. 'Instrumental Routes to Emotional Geographies'. *Social & Cultural Geography* 5(4): 533–48. http://dx.doi.org/10.1080/1464936042000317686

Zappa, M. U. 1994. 'Tool Rules'. *Ray Gun* (April): 15.

Discography
Blood Duster. 1996. *Yeest*. Dr. Jim's.
—1998. *Str8 Outta Northcote*. Dr. Jim's.
—2007. *Lyden Na*. Shock.
Hawthorne Heights. 2004. 'Ohio is for Lovers' [single]. Victory Records.

Filmography
Dunn, S., S. McFadyen and J. Wise (dir.). 2005. *Metal: A Headbanger's Journey*.
Fuller, Jason (dir.). 2005. *Blood Duster: The Shape of Death to Come*.
Hooper, T. (dir.). 1974. *The Texas Chainsaw Massacre*.

Heavy metal and the deafening threat of the apolitical

Niall Scott

University of Central Lancashire, UK

First thoughts on heavy metal and the subject of politics may well lead to the assumption that they make strange bedfellows. Indeed this is borne out in many conversations and discussions I have had with fans, musicians and those outside the scene. A disdain for politics is further encountered in interviews strewn throughout the music press. Heavy metal is frequently referred to as being apolitical; this is a phrase used by critics, fans and musicians alike. Often this is a veiled rejection of politics understood as meaning governmental party politics or state organized political processes.

Yet at the same time the heavy metal movement embraces a community, expresses tribal identities and is proud in voicing its connections to historical facts and myths of its working-class heritage. It is a movement with a definitional breadth that is analogous to a spectrum personality disorder. As a result, the term 'heavy metal' has both general applications as well as specific understandings and concerns that attach themselves to only a few heavy metal subgenres. Thus, sometimes the term will be used to make general claims about the genre, and in other places heavy metal is qualified in terms of those subgenres and examples provided. As a spectrum movement, bands will be discussed that provide illustrations, but these may well be on the fringes of heavy metal or even thinly associated with it through, for example, their sound or for historical reasons. It is important too for my argument to note that heavy metal is not merely a commercial product, as recognized by Deena Weinstein:

> Perhaps the audience is a sheer creation of the genre and its commercial mediators. Although that is what some disparaging critics think that the audience is a sheer creation of the genre and its commercial mediators, it is not true. Music is the master emblem of Heavy Metal subculture, but not its meaning. Indeed, from the aspect of the audience, the music is a function of the lifestyles and mythologies of a youth group, and must be consistent with those lifestyles and mythologies in order to be appropriated by the group (Weinstein 2000: 99).

At the time of writing, heavy metal now spans a 40-year history, so it is no longer accurate to confine its definition to youth. Regarding politics and the apolitical, heavy metal has elements involved in local and global pursuits of social justice, expressions of individual and national identities as well as being a music entertainment medium. Thus, the subject matter of politics is not only on the lips of many metal scene members; one can find artists who are politically engaged, through their work in expressing particular views or being politically active. So is the view that heavy metal has nothing to do with politics a justifiable one? First we will need to look at what is meant by politics, and what it might mean in this context.

The claim that heavy metal is an apolitical movement is an interesting one and we will investigate what it could mean for metal to be apolitical, whether this is a sustainable position to hold, and what alternatives might be available. This question will take us into a critique of heavy metal culture and its relation to mass culture and a serious challenge presented by Herbert Marcuse's notion of repressive desublimation. Heavy metal can, I think, be successfully defended against this. Deena Weinstein, one of the first metal scholars, importantly supports the idea that heavy metal is not a movement that is created and sustained by entrepreneurial forces, of the kind that Marcuse and other theorists of mass culture are so critical of. However, we shall see that is not a straightforward case to argue.

There are important distinctions to identify when regarding something as vast as the heavy metal scene, where one finds a diverse range of positions and outlooks under a political heading. So we would want to recognize that there are specific expressions of political, apolitical and anti-political stances, and under the political heading again, a range of incompatible values are to be found in heavy metal culture, from left-wing ideologies through to the extreme right. Heavy metal in this sense holds a spectrum of identities and values. One would want to distinguish between the orientations of fans as scene members and expressions held by the protagonists of the music and images and ideas presented in the music press. These are going to be further complicated by motivating factors such as the commodification of the music and its position in entertainment culture as a product: a political or politicized perspective may be presented as a marketing opportunity, but may not actually represent the views of those presenting it. But in these complexities we may find the seeds that undermine the very apolitical autonomy that heavy metal culture claims for itself.

The apolitical presentation of metal can be found in countless examples from the scene. Ryan Moore, in his analysis of the origins of British heavy metal and its relationship to the working class, notes that because of heavy metal's lack of political engagement and its low cultural status in its early days, it received little critical attention from scholars (Moore 2009). The Birmingham-based band Bolt Thrower in a *Terrorizer* magazine interview with Jimmy Christ, referred to their compositions as apolitical:

> Bolt Thrower's birth as the heavier, groovier offspring of the more metallic end of the anarchopunk underground, the first generation of British death metallers, if not necessarily in style, then certainly in terms of sepulchural atmosphere and apolitical themes, saw them siblings in a sprawling clan, one that included the likes of Carcass, Cancer, Benediction and Napalm Death (Christ 2010).

The mention of Napalm Death as part of the 'clan' is interesting because Napalm Death are above all known for strong politicized statements, most notably their anti-fascist stance (see for example their unequivocal cover of the Dead Kennedy's song 'Nazi Punks Fuck Off!' on their same titled 1993 EP), and their left-wing and green politics.

There are extremes and oppositions in the heavy metal movement that span the political and apolitical spectrum. So from within the scene, political statements distancing one section of the movement from another can be seen in Watain's response to a question concerning their possible relations to National Socialist Black Metal (NSBM):

> NSBM is a joke, a despaired approach of people who're incapable to comprehend the perversion and the insanity of Black Metal. They're trying to appear extreme and limit their selves in their conception to that kind of society, which describes something that we wouldn't care less about. Fuck the world! Black Metal doesn't have anything to do with the world as you know it[1] (Endres 2007).

Further evidence of individual incidents of political action in the broad spectrum of heavy metal culture involve some fairly high-profile events. Recently the music industry saw fans support Rage Against the Machine's *Killing in the Name Of* climb to a number one spot in the UK charts through downloading the single prompted by a Facebook campaign, started by part-time DJ John Morter, to prevent Simon Cowell's *X-Factor* competition winner from reaching the Christmas number one position (Pidd 2009). It was a demonstration against mainstream and mass pop media, it would seem, though I will turn to criticize this story later. Another example of the politicized face of heavy metal can be seen in its campaign for scene participants to put heavy metal down as their religion in the UK census. Initiated as a fun satirical activity, Alex Milas, editor of *Metal Hammer*, notes it as more serious criticism of the categorization of a population according to certain religious identities and not others, mirroring the previous campaign to try and have 'Jedi' recognized as a religion. Milas stated in *The Independent on Sunday* that

> ...this campaign makes a serious point in critiquing the whole notion of a census. We were asking what defines faith? Because if you take the criteria that are generally used, there's absolutely nothing that excludes Heavy Metal—many of the practices are the same. If anything, you probably have a more faithful flock than most actual religions do (Tuckey 2010).

Further examples of explicit political action can be seen in the Taiwanese symphonic black metal band Chthonic's activism, drawing attention to the cause of Tibetan independence, yet at the same time denying any political content in their music. Vocalist Freddy Lim declares: 'I never put any political ideals in my music. If there's something in our music, it's happened naturally. Outside of music I try to fight for the ideals I believe in' (Lim 2009). Yet another openly political metal band is System of a Down, who collected petition signatures to push the US Congress to convene a review of the Armenian genocide question. Their efforts were brought together on film looking into the issue of genocide and political intransigence, in the documentary *Screamers* (Garapedian 2008).

Defining politics and the apolitical

It is difficult to isolate a meaning for the term 'politics' that does not carry implications for any argument that proceeds from it. D. D. Raphael, in his introduction to *Problems of Political Philosophy* (1990), seeks to distinguish the political from the social and restricts the meaning of the term to affairs that concern government and the state. When heavy metal asserts itself against politics, it often does so against this kind of politics. However, a broader understanding of politics allows it to be a component of the social that extends beyond government and the state, and is a description of certain kinds of human behaviour in the context of institutions. The question of what sort of political institutions there ought to be is one of the central concerns of political philosophy. If heavy metal is conceived of as a music movement in the entertainment industry, it would be disinterested in the idea of a political institution because it is simply not that kind of thing. However, heavy metal as a cultural movement is much more complex than merely an offshoot of the music entertainment industry. As we proceed, we shall see that it may well have something to say in its stance as to what kinds of political values ought to be promoted, and one of those stances is that of the apolitical. In addition to this, heavy metal often expresses certain values that are socially and politically interesting. For example, a vibrant gender politics can be read from the scene, noted by bands, fans and critics alike. It is a movement that is identified by a fierce expression of autonomy and individuality and, to a degree, tolerance of others, although in the broad spectrum of the heavy metal movement, issues of racism, sexism and homophobia can be encountered in bands and fans alike. It also can be associated with a pursuit of authenticity, honesty and integrity, as is clear from Dom Lawson's introduction to an article on the band Grand Magus:

> If heavy metal is about anything, it is about passion and belief. If the tragic loss of Ronnie James Dio has taught us anything, it must be that metal fans are a devout and emotional breed and that the most important thing that any of us look for in the music we listen to is a sense of integrity and honesty... When Heavy Metal is at its best, you can hear and feel truth and honesty and belief in the riffs, melodies and the soul stirring clangour of that proud bombastic whole, regardless of whether the lyrics are about real life or the stuff of fantasy (Lawson 2010b).

This demand for honesty is precisely what lies at the heart of the rejection of governmental politics and the image of politics in terms of the state. In this sense heavy metal is indeed apolitical. But as we have seen, heavy metal does engage in broader conceptions of politics, where members of the scene are politically active or present certain values that have a broader social impact.

The apolitical can be understood in a range of ways, all of which need to be made sense of in the context of human social being. It can mean that one stands outside the political, but that is dependent on defining the political in a particular way. It can mean that one is apathetic towards politics; that one does not accept it as a binding feature of human relations, denying the power of the term over oneself and as a description of certain kinds of human relations, when the apolitical becomes a sort of political stance itself. It can also mean that one has an unbiased view towards political matters, political organizations and political descriptions. This is well captured by James Hetfield's introductory call and answer chant a few songs into the concert recorded in 1997 on the DVD *Cunning Stunts*, in Austin Texas, where he and the audience repeat 'we don't give a shit'. In fact this captures both a sense of apathy, a complete, but knowing lack of concern and an unbiased view of the world; a blanket, uncritical criticism that is knowingly disengaging. This apolitical stance in heavy metal is beautifully captured by Keith Kahn-Harris' study on extreme metal where he introduces the notion of 'reflexive anti-reflexivity'.

He comes back with a more sophisticated analysis of the all too easy criticism directed at the extreme metal scene's members being 'wilfully ignorant, lacking in self awareness and politically naïve' (Kahn-Harris 2007: 144). This insight came from his analysis of interviews with members of the extreme metal scene who apparently expressed racist statements, or used fascist symbolism, but then denying that these had any significance. He described this as 'knowing better, but deciding not to know'. That is, members of the extreme metal community are capable of reflective political engagement, but choose not to.

However, the reflexive capacity and political capacity are seen in both the extreme scene as well as in other subgenres of heavy metal, most notably in the critical sense of self-awareness displayed through the use of humour and self-parody. So, despite the recognition of serious issues such as racism, Kahn-Harris holds that reflexive anti-reflexivity 'allows scene members tactically to marginalize that which they don't want to know' (Kahn-Harris 2007: 151). In a playful use of such material—be it racist, homophobic or sexist—scene members may well distance themselves from the meaning of offensive discourses that they participate in, but these can still cause offence and harm. This distancing from the direct harmful effects of such discourses is, I think, a feature of the attempt to maintain an apolitical stance under the banner of heavy metal. More important than this expression of heavy metal as apolitical, however, is its subversive rejection of mass culture that arguably has the most profound impact.

Given these attempts at definition, the question that challenges us is: can there be such a thing as the apolitical in heavy metal? Does it deny the very integrity and honesty it promotes as a value by referring to itself as apolitical? Heavy metal like other music forms links to its own culture and subcultures through symbolic presentation. As such, it exerts a universalizing effect that removes itself from the political, in the same way that music expressed in notation and in symbols is apolitical in becoming universally accessible across cultures and history (Bohlman 1993: 420–21). On this point, again Keith Kahn-Harris has observed that virtually nothing in the extreme heavy metal scene is political, where members of the metal scene see their music as 'ideally removed from social forces' (Kahn-Harris 2007: 154). But as we shall see later, on the whole this meets a considerable problem when we treat heavy metal as subject to technology and the market in mass culture. Contrary to this view is the position that the arts in general provide a way of understanding the political life in a unique way (Negash 2004). One can even find the stronger view that politics emerges from the arts: 'art is the fountainhead from which political discourse, beliefs about politics and consequent actions ultimately spring' (Edelman 1995), Edelman further holding that new meanings emerge through art that shape political ideas. This echoes the exploration of the relationship between the arts and national socialism in Peter Viereck's 1941 assessment of Wagner's influence on the thought of Bismarck and of and Hitler and recognizes that this relationship between politics and the arts has a long history: 'That evil can overlap with a tyrant's sincere love of art should have been obvious ever since Nero's "quails artifex pereo"' (Viereck 2004: xxii). The Medici period in florentine Italy saw artists acting out their own dirty deeds done dirt cheap, representing the forbidden through painting under the guise of something else. This was manifest in the relationship between patron and artist and the institution of the church; specifically this could involve showing off one's own magnificence and power by being presented as royalty when one was nothing of the sort, as is evident in the Medici brothers appearing as royalty, even the three kings in the art work *Adoration of the Magi*:

> It permitted a manner of ostentation that was inadmissible in normal life. In their confraternity, under the sanction of traditional forms of devotion, the brothers—including the Medici—might do no less than pose as lords. And in the *Festa* they carried that pose before the people. Although just play, the game was ominous (Hatfield 1970: 143).

Parallels can be drawn here in the political statement of the ostentatious posing of the metal musician as having divine status—the 'rock god'—and the parody of the rock god displaying positions of importance and magnificence often as a statement lampooning the notions of status and power. Thus, not only are there examples of overt political expressions in heavy metal music and culture, but also subversive political statements from within the movement directed back at itself.

Metal shoots itself in the foot: Metal and mass culture

A challenge that apolitical heavy metal presents is a rejection of 'mass culture', understood as an offshoot of popular culture that 'levels and standardizes all values' (Gross 1980). Gross goes on to hold that mass culture does not emerge as an autochtonous expression of popular attitudes, but is imposed, decomposing elite and folk culture into, as he puts it, a 'slushy compost'. What typifies mass culture is consumption *of it* rather than participating *in it* in a manner that shares intersubjective meanings (Gross 1980). On the one hand heavy metal is a movement that expresses a vigorous rejection of the status quo, and rejects integration of other forms of mass culture into it, by maintaining a strong conservative link to its histories. Yet paradoxically, on the other hand, it is continuously creative and stretching its self-imposed definitional boundaries. Members of the metal scene participate in and appreciate its more fringe areas expressed musically through other traditions, the most important of these being heavy metal's relationship to the blues and folk traditions, as well as recent explorations into rap funk and industrial music forms, commonly exemplified by bands such as the Red Hot Chilli Peppers, Cypress Hill, Nine Inch Nails and Rammstein, to name but a few. Heavy metal in this way is an incredibly fluid and slippery movement engaged in internal discourse that reflects on its own nature.

To complement heavy metal's authentic apolitical stance, it can be argued to be apolitical in the sense that the values and norms generated and maintained in the movement develop independent of externally imposed norms of mass culture. Above all it rejects conformism to mass culture and other popular cultures and allows its own internal sources of values to inform a perspective on the external world. Yet, at the same time, heavy metal uses and expresses itself through mass media and is commodified, taking advantage of human behaviour and participation in the market for the distribution of its product in music, fashion and lifestyle. This is apparent in the various recognizable uniforms of the band t-shirts, denim and black and studded apparel, pierced and tattooed bodies, and so on. To the cynic, metal's claim to being opposed to conformity and somehow separate and different from mass culture is downright contradictory. Rather than being apolitical, subversive and culturally dangerous, heavy metal shoots itself in the foot. Let us look at how this criticism can be damning to heavy metal's posturing, when considering Herbert Marcuse's perspective on the power of the market in destroying autonomy in the arts as well as Horkheimer and Adorno's famous criticism of mass culture.

Heavy metal, I will go on to argue later, escapes the indictment of Marcuse's criticism of damage done by the market and the mass reproduction of culture and art. Heavy metal rejects both high and low art as a distinction in its assertion that it is 'simply what it is'. This may seem a naïve and simplistic position to take, and critics may disagree, but when one is embedded in the metal scene, or takes the time to observe it in detail, this straightforward attitude that metal has can be understood. However, let us consider the criticism levelled above in more detail. Herbert Marcuse, in his broadly political project, held that higher order culture and its alienating capacity and the other dimension of reality that lower order culture operates in, are dissolved by incorporation into the established order. This is done through utilization of mass reproduction, making the artistic output available for consumption by the masses. Capitalist market forces make this reproduction and availability possible so that items that are politically and ideologically incompatible can be acquired and ingested uncritically by the individual. In this way, communication allows the blending of, as Marcuse holds, 'art, politics, religion and philosophy through the common denominator—the commodity form' (Marcuse 1991: 57). This, then, could be a damning indictment for heavy metal's claims to supporting autonomy, authenticity and difference from the world. It would allow one to scoff at the vocalizations of deeply held integrity and honesty in the movement, as expressed above in Lawson's interview with Grand Magus. This criticism levelled by Marcuse's position is echoed in Horkheimer and Adorno's claim directed specifically at cinema, but with broader implications for mass culture in general:

> The culture industry does not sublimate: it suppresses. By constantly exhibiting the object of desire, the breasts beneath the sweater, the naked torso of the sporting hero, it merely goads the unsublimated anticipation of pleasure, which through the habit of denial has long since been mutilated as masochism (Horkheimer and Adorno 2002: 111).

Thus, any of the myriad of values supposedly presented in the various articulations of heavy metal music and its culture feed into its commodfication—replicating and packaging Satanism, rebellion, the repetition of images of violence and horror in the metal music video or raging against the system all to be theatrically played out in the safety of metal's symbols, gestures and the mosh pit. This critique can be used to illustrate the pluralism of values and political perspectives presented above—from Napalm Death's anti-fascism through Mötley Crüe's hair metal hedonism to Graveland's fascism as precisely the features that are both ideologically incompatible and reproduced as commodities for the metal market to consume. A note of caution must be given, though, echoing the diversity in metal culture as pointed out in the outset of this essay. The spectrum of positions presented in heavy metal's culture needs to be recognized in anticipating the rescue of heavy metal in the face of this criticism. There are some features of the movement which fall head over heels into Adorno, Horkheimer and Marcuse's trap, while others importantly are able to escape it. The way in which 'hair metal' is generated and commodified is arguably rather different from the way in which Napalm Death and grindcore music are produced and accessed. The black metal scene, arguably the least commercial of the subgenres of metal, is again even less commodified (however there are clear exceptions where black metal has succumbed to more popular commercial success, in bands such as Dimmu Borgir, Satyricon and Cradle of Filth). Hair metal and similar commercialized forms of the heavy metal spectrum fall foul precisely of Adorno and Horkheimer's comments on style. The generation of hair metal hand in hand with the emergence of marketing power of MTV and its consumable catchy pop-metal-booze-and-sleaze musical product exemplifies Horkheimer and Adorno's claim that style emerging from within the culture industry 'springs from the same apparatus as the jargon into which it is absorbed' (Horkheimer and Adorno 2002: 103). Perhaps style in hair metal is an attempt at recapturing and replicating a retro-spective fantasy of New York Doll's punk, Hanoi Rocks, or something of a nod to a previous gender experimenting decadence. Hair metal both is a product of what it mocks and mocks what it has produced.

Is heavy metal then utterly deluded about its independence? Its active participation in the market, the commodification of its products, and the dependence on these to manufacture and sell an image of its values to the members of the movement mean it is no different from other technologized forms of mass culture. Most notably concerning the plurality of values and perspectives—both social and political—that I have promoted as being spe-cial to the movement, heavy metal fails catastrophically. The 'Fuck the World' logo on a back patch emblem has been sold and bought, the countless slogans that repeat sentiments in song lyrics are paraded on t-shirts that attribute authenticity to the scene: 'Pure Fuckin' Metal' shows that in fact any notion of a pursuit of 'true metal' is mistaken. Heavy metal has gone the same way as punk, a music and protest culture that was generated as a commodity from the outset contradicting the very anti-capitalist values it professed to repre-sent. Marcuse continues, regarding this process as leading to repressive des-ublimation: 'In the realm of culture, the new totalitarianism manifests itself precisely in a harmonising pluralism where the most contradictory works and truths peacefully coexist in indifference' (Marcuse 1991: 61). Assimilated into and entirely dependent on the behaviours of mass culture, heavy metal's apo-litical stance as well as its sustaining of a range of contradictory values, hap-pily held under the banner of heavy metal, do exactly what Marcuse holds to be the case in the historical assimilation of high culture into mass culture. Heavy metal simply serves the goals of the politics of the market, and is guilty of betraying its followers who think otherwise. Heavy metal presents us with, as Marcuse would state: '...no longer images of another way of life, but rather freaks or types of the same life, serving an affirmation, rather than negation of the established order' (Marcuse 1991: 59). For example, we could then see the campaign to get Rage Against the Machine's *Killing in the Name Of* to number one for Christmas in 2009—in opposition to Simon Cowell's stranglehold on pop and music chart culture (Pidd 2009)—as a stunt that demonstrates heavy metal and the broader rock fan base as being participants in the market forces that they aim to criticize. Instead of demonstrating a rejection of the commerce of pop, the campaign only succeeded in supporting the mechanism and technologies that enable this mass culture to operate. Interestingly, a *Guardian* article notes that both Rage Against the Machine and the other *X-Factor* song in this race were linked to Simon Cowell through Sony BMG. Purchasing of the single and supporting the Facebook campaign set up by Jon Morter leads to an illusion of the practice of liberty, yet at the same time intensifies the dominating power of market forces in music culture.

Indeed, this is example is laden with irony, as the lyrical content of the song and Rage Against the Machine's politics are known to be left-anarchist. Although not a metal band as such, RATM's history emerging during the commercial phase of the grunge movement in the early 1990s and performances with Suicidal Tendencies and House of Pain arguably gives them their own place on a branch of the heavy metal tree. So it would seem that if we follow Marcuse's criticism of the influence of technology and the market expanding into art and culture, heavy metal is assimilated into mass culture and fails in its apolitical stance, its anti society-at-large otherness, its belief in nonconformism and so on. Marcuse laments this passing in the arts in general, referring to a pre-technological and romantic culture: 'The rhythm and content of a universe in which valleys and forests, villages and inns, nobles and villains, salons and courts were part of the experienced reality' (Marcuse 1991: 59). Tom Franks provides a further support for such a criticism:

> Regardless of the tastes of republican leaders, rebel youth culture remains the cultural mode of the corporate movement, used to promote not only specific products but the general idea of life in the cyber-revolution. Commercial fantasies of rebellion, liberation and outright 'revolution' against the stultifying demands of mass society are commonplace almost to the point of invisibility in advertising, movies and television programming (Franks 1997: 6).

Franks thus shows that apparent resistance strengthens the corporate and marketing control over a movement, even if the conservative moral critics of counterculture miss what might be going on.

Deafening A-politics: heavy metal's great refusal

I think, though, that some movements in heavy metal can be rescued from Marcuse's criticism. Heavy metal culture is ideally placed to show that such culture and art can be reborn in a post- technological culture. Given the clear interest and orientation towards a romantic culture of the kind that Marcuse mentions—found and exemplified in folk, fantasy, and Viking metal (Heesch 2010)—certain subgenres of heavy metal, despite this destructive criticism above, are in a position to resist, and even transcend, this negative impact of repressive desublimation. Heavy metal in general retains its relationship to romantic art and is counter to the assimilating forces expressed above. Alienated from and aesthetically incompatible with mass culture, it retains its abject separation from the masses. Perhaps the 'Rage Against the Machine to number 1 at Christmas' was simply a glimpse of the politically apolitical threatening potential that heavy metal could display if the scene was mobilized. Heavy metal retains its subversive force and destructive content, even being deeply aware of the Marcusian threat hanging over it. This is illustrated by, for example, the underground features of the black metal community's celebration of misanthropy and obsession with self-loathing, misery, and the void, where an altogether different kind of subversive discourse from the RATM campaign is on display. Stephen Shakespeare (2010) in his 'Black Notes', quotes an interview with Wolves in the Throne Room (WITTR):

> Why are we sad and miserable? Because our culture has failed, we are all failures. The world around us has failed to sustain our humanity, our spirituality. The deep woe inside Black Metal is about fear that we can never return to the mythic, pastoral world that we crave on a deep subconscious level. Black Metal is also about self loathing, for modernity has transformed us, our minds, bodies and spirit, into an alien life form; one not suited to life on earth without the mediating forces of technology (Smith 2006).

WITTR identify the disastrous impact that technology has had on humanity as Marcuse did, but articulate this through their art so that their take complements Marcuse's invitation to escape from the impact of repressive desublimation by metal revealing a dimension of man and nature which is repressed and repelled in reality (Marcuse 1991). Slayer's work also focuses on such repelled human attributes, more evident than ever in the hatred and misanthropy expressed on the album *God Hates Us All* (2001). Nonetheless it would be naïve to not recognize the liberating contribution of technology, especially the necessary component of volume in heavy metal's distorted deafening expression. This is especially evident in the liberation that DIY music (re)production provided in the very origin and sound of Burzum in the first wave of Norwegian black metal and in the origins of the UK's Birmingham and Black Country grindcore scene.

It can be deeply insulting to the notion of authenticity in the metal community when on its fringes a piece of music is subsumed into household culture. This is inevitable, however, given the way in which the music industry and market operate. Heavy metal distances itself from these shifts and retains its role as 'The Great Refusal', to use Marcuse's term. In turn, mainstream mass culture often refuses to engage with it, save the occasional, often cynical and mocking media interest. To see an articulation of this refusal coming from mass culture, simply turn to Deena Weinstein's (2000) introduction to her book where she articulates all manner of hostile criticisms of heavy metal culture. Heavy metal rejects most forms of incorporation; it offers the Great Refusal to both politics and domination from external forces other than that which it generates from within. Above all, the subgenre of black metal threatens, as it exemplifies break in communication with the world outside itself. The audible but utterly indiscernible lyrics carried on the wall of sound express a deliberate disruption in language and comprehensibility, presenting and distorting the very tools of speech and audible clarity that make political communication possible. Black metal rejects the meaningfully clear. It thus initially cuts off immediate political engagement, exterminating communication and reason in favour of the viscerality of the auditory experience, a feature held in common with many metal performances, but to a much greater degree in black metal.

However, at the same time for those who are challenged by this dark art within and without the heavy metal scene, it is an invitation to draw near, engage with and question, research and enquire as to what is being declared. Mass culture that does not heed and rejects the Great Refusal of heavy metal, bathes in its own laziness at its peril. By being apolitical heavy metal loudly communicates the negative, thus reasserting the alienating and sublime power of art. In sum, heavy metal opposes repressive sublimation. It is liberating, but in a manner that peculiarly and playfully accepts the market forces that support the dissemination of its product among the metal community. It manages, in tension, to also fiercely defend autonomy and the freedom of choice for the individual.

To recognize that there is something 'true' in the heavy metal community that is apolitical in the sense of being outside of state and governmental politics and opposed to mass culture, yet participates in elements of it, can analogously be seen as a multiple personality disorder that the metal community is quite comfortable with and prepared to flaunt, with no need of therapeutic intervention. It is precisely this contentedness in living with paradoxes that make it a movement capable of presenting a challenge to the mainstream. The key to the capacity of metal to so transcend its apparent contradictions is this: where Lowenthal (Gross 1980) recognizes that mass culture is produced for people and not by them, heavy metal, like its blues and rock roots, is sustained and generated by people in subterranean movements from the underground up. Market and media forces document and respond to this and collaborate with the material produced, but metal in its stability over the past 40 years of its existence is also wedded to remaining true to its origins. The heavy metal movement in all its guises works both as a barometer of social change and as a consumer of its own product. It is thus a movement that can simultaneously provide, as an art form, a critical insight into contemporary culture, and as a counterculture a looming threat to a social and political realm trapped by the domination of mass culture.

Where Theodor Adorno and Lowenthal saw the power of market and entrepreneurial forces as capable of destroying autonomy, heavy metal prides itself in maintaining autonomy: 'Life is ours we live it our way' as Metallica express in the track 'Nothing Else Matters' (*Metallica* 1992). A foray into the heavy metal underground, especially the black metal, doom and drone scenes, is where one encounters how deep this sentiment is carried. A reflective understanding of the scene's commitment to such a value is evident also in its self-lampooning as mentioned above. Steel Panther's song 'Death to All but Metal' (2009) targets among several subjects pop musicians, MTV, record companies, and anything that is not 'true' metal in a parody of eighties poodle hair metal that is subject to the same criticisms. The kinds of paradoxes that are generated support this distancing from political motivation, but are arguably also quite political. For example, Shagrath from the Black Metal duo Ov Hell, discussing their new album *The Underworld Regime*, asserts: 'For the lyrics I ended up digging into my archives and using a lot of lyrics that I had written a long time ago, even as far back as 1992! This has a total satanic anti-christian state of mind thing going on, and I like that a lot'. This is followed by his band member King ov Hell asserting: 'I'm not thinking about Satan when I'm writing and I'm not thinking about politics or religion. It's about atmosphere' (Lawson 2010a).

Conclusion

Heavy metal shuns politics in the governmental sense of the term, but also in the sense of avoiding conflict that can do damage to the unity of what it means to be metal—a being that transcends political perspectives and identities. Heavy metal coalesces around an art form that is sustained and often at its foundations generated by its audience, from which eventually the more common names grow, such as those identified as the 'Big Four': Anthrax, Megadeth, Metallica and Slayer. The transcendence of metal and its attachments to a purity that is continuously under debate and being re-evaluated suggests that it connects to an art form in the music that also goes beyond its audience, but without any sense of pretention to snobbery. The apolitical politics of metal is then controversially not dissimilar to Adorno's modernist approach to Schönberg (Adorno 1978). In Schönberg's vein heavy metal presents us not only with an apolitical politics, but a political atonality. It avoids resolution of any particular position on the scale points of is diversity. It is destined to not resolve itself in the direction of a definitional grasp.

Marcuse is supportive of the political potential of art that is empty of political intent. In heavy metal we encounter a liberated environment where there is a coincidence of advanced technology and aesthetic vision. In being apolitical, however, heavy metal functions as an embracing term of an art form and culture that holds together a diverse community of practices, perspectives and beliefs. It engages in all the apparent features of a social-political realm in dialogue, reflection, association and community. This is precisely where heavy metal succeeds and this is the apolitical political threat it poses in its achievement: its deafening sonic aesthetic paired with the scene's tolerant pluralism mediated through advanced technology. The politics of the apolitical is both heavy metal's *Weltanschaungung* and its auditory threat.

Note

1. The original interview in German reads: 'Was hälst du von NSBM und sollte Black Metal überhaupt einer politischen Ideologie folgen bzw. diese beinhalten? NSBM ist ein Witz, ein verzweifelter Versuch von Leuten, welche unfähig sind, die Perversion und den Wahnsinn des Black Metals zu ergründen. Sie wollen extrem erscheinen und limitieren sich in ihrer Konzeption an diese Art von Gesellschaft, was etwas darstellt, was uns nicht noch weniger interessieren könnte. Fuck the world! Black Metal hat nichts mit der Welt zu tun, wie ihr sie kennt.'

Bibliography

Adorno, Theodor. 1978. 'On the Social Situation of Music'. *Telos* 35: 129–65.

Bohlman, Philip. 1993. 'Musicology as a Political Act'. *Journal of Musicology* 11(4): 411–36. http://dx.doi.org/10.1525/jm.1993.11.4.03a00010

Christ, Jimmy. 2010. 'The Dawn of War: Bolt Thrower and the Birth of British Death Metal'. *Terrorizer.* http://trucultheavymetal.com/blog1.php/2010/05/06/interview-dawn-of-war-bolt-thrower-and-the-birth-of-british-death-metal.

Edelman, Murray. 1995. *From Art to Politics: How Artistic Creations Shape Political Perceptions.* Chicago: Chicago University Press.

Endres, Markus. 2007. 'Watain Interview'. http://www.metal.de/stories.php4?was=story&id=897.

Franks, Thomas. 1997. *The Conquest of Cool: Business Culture, Counterculture and the Rise of Hip Consumerism.* Chicago: University of Chicago Press.

Garapedian, Carla. 2008. *Screamers.* http://www.screamersmovie.com/story.html.

Gross, David. 1980. 'Lowenthal, Adorno and Barthes: Three Perspectives on Popular Culture'. *Telos* 45: 122–39.

Hatfield, Rab. 1970. 'The Compania de' Magi'. *Journal of the Warburg and Courtauld Institutes* 33: 107–161. http://dx.doi.org/10.2307/750893

Heesch, Florian. 2010. 'Metal for Nordic Men? Amon Amarth's Representations of Vikings'. In *The Metal Void*, ed. Niall Scott and Imke Von Helden. Oxford: Inter-disciplinary Press.

Horkheimer, Max, and Theodor Adorno. 2002. *The Dialectic of Enlightenment*. Palo Alto, CA: Stanford University Press.

Kahn Harris, Keith. 2007. *Extreme Metal, Music and Culture on the Edge*. London: Berg.

Lawson, Dom. 2010a. 'The Flame Game'. *Metal Hammer, Subterranea* 202 (March): 125–26.

—2010b. 'Warrior Souls'. *Metal Hammer* 207 (July): 68–69.

Lim, Freddy. 2009. 'Chthonic'. *Terrorizer* 187 (Summer): 24–28.

Marcuse, Herbert. 1991. *One-Dimensional Man*. London: Routledge.

Moore, Ryan M. 2009. 'The Unmaking of the English Working Class: Deindustrialisation, Reification and the Origins of Heavy Metal'. In *Heavy Metal Music in Britain*, ed. Gerd Bayer. Farnham: Ashgate.

Negash, Girma. 2004. 'Art Invoked: A Mode of Understanding and Shaping the Political'. *International Political Science Review* 25(2): 185–201. http://dx.doi.org/10.1177/019 2512104041284

Pidd, Helen. 2009. 'Rage Against the Machine Beats X-Factor's Joe to Christmas No 1'. *The Guardian*, 20 December. http://www.guardian.co.uk/music/2009/dec/20/rage-against-machine-christmas-number-1.

Rage Against the Machine biography at: http://www.ratm.com.

Raphael, D. D. 1990. *The Problems of Political Philosophy*. London: Macmillan.

Shakespeare, Stephen. 2010. 'Black Notes'. In *Hideous Gnosis, Black Metal Theory Symposium 1*, ed. Nicola Masciandaro. New York: Open Access Publication.

Smith, Bradley. 2006. 'Interview with Wolves in the Throne Room'. http://www.nocturnal-cult.com/newcontents.htm.

Tuckey, Bill. 2010. 'God Gave Rock and Roll to You'. *Independent on Sunday*, 1 August.

Viereck, Peter. 2004 [1941]. *Metapolitics: From Wagner and the German Romantics to Hitler*. New Jersey: Transaction Publishers.

Weinstein, Deena. 2000. *Heavy Metal: The Music and its Culture*. Cambridge, MA: Da Capo Press.

Discography
Metallica. 1992. 'Nothing Else Matters'. *Metallica ('The Black Album')*. Electra records.

—1998. *Cunning Stunts*. DVD. Universal.

Slayer. 2001. *God Hates us All*. American Recordings.

Steel Panther. 2009. 'Death to All But Metal'. *Feel the Steel*. Universal Republic.

Index